MW00749467

Dear Uncle Shiro
Let us build a better
country together!
Aly J.L
May 19th/10

With best wishes
Ronald Grey

UNDERSTANDING
TERROR

UNIVERSITY OF
CALGARY
PRESS

UNDERSTANDING

TERROR perspectives
for canadians

Editor: Karim-Aly S. Kassam

University of Calgary Press
2500 University Drive NW
Calgary, Alberta
Canada T2N 1N4
www.uofcpress.com

LIBRARY AND ARCHIVES CANADA CATALOGUING IN PUBLICATION

Understanding terror : perspectives for Canadians / editor: Karim-Aly S. Kassam.

Includes bibliographical references and index.
ISBN 978-1-55238-272-1

     1. Terrorism. 2. Terrorism–Canada.
I. Kassam, Karim-Aly S., 1964-

HV6431.U54 2010   303.6'25   C2009-907188-6

The University of Calgary Press acknowledges the support of the Alberta Foundation for the Arts for our publications. We acknowledge the financial support of the Government of Canada through the Book Publishing Industry Development Program (BPIDP) for our publishing activities. We acknowledge the financial support of the Canada Council for the Arts for our publishing program.

Canada Council   Conseil des Arts
for the Arts   du Canada

Printed and bound in Canada by Marquis
∞ This book is printed on FSC Silva paper

Cover design by Melina Cusano
Page design and typesetting by Melina Cusano

For Rafia, Sinan, and safer homelands for all children

Contents

ACKNOWLEDGMENTS

The idea for this collected work emerged on a sunny summer's day on July 7, 2005. The day was punctuated by shocking news of the suicide bombings in the public transport system in London by four men who were Muslim. As a result of these bombings, fifty-six civilians were killed, seven hundred people were injured, the four bombers also died, and an innocent twenty-seven-year-old Brazilian commuter was killed by the British police. On that tragic afternoon, the then Dean of the Faculty of Communication and Culture at the University of Calgary, Dr. Kathleen Scherf, asked me to explain why such things happen. I could not. But we both knew that her question arose because I was a Muslim. Is every atheist, Buddhist, Christian, Jew, or Hindu responsible for the actions of those that share a similar religious, cultural, or intellectual heritage? The answer, of course, is emphatically: No!

However, since September 11, 2001, many thoughtful voices have been drowned out by a cacophony of pronouncements on terror which have a polarizing effect on societies across the western world. Tenured academics have the intellectual space and the ethical responsibility to examine and comment on issues of relevance to society that are within the ambit of their expertise. Therefore, I took up the challenge to gather individuals who could examine the issue of terror from a variety of lenses hitherto not considered. Dr. Scherf's encouragement was invaluable, even though the task was both time-consuming and challenging. But most useful activities tend to be demanding in that way. Since my move to Cornell University, the Department of Natural Resources and the American Indian Program in the College of Agricultural and Life Sciences has continued to provide the intellectual space and encouragement that has resulted in this publication.

The challenges to this collection were, first, to find the best possible contributors who were willing to participate in an unconventional but meaningful examination of terror; and, second, to get it published in an academic press having undergone the test of peer-review. I turned to Haroon Siddiqui, editor emeritus of the *Toronto Star*; David Taras, Director of the Alberta Global Forum; Lorry Felske, Coordinator of the Canadian Studies Program; and Michael Keren, Canada Research Chair, for advice on whom to invite to participate.

As I developed the vision for the book, some declined to participate due to time commitments, but others shared my vision and developed it further. I am deeply indebted to Brent Beardsley, Gwynne Dyer, Stuart Farson, Doug Firby, Ronald Glasberg, Jim Lassoie, George Melnyk, and Reg Whitaker as contributors for their insights in the form of the essays that make up this collection, their invaluable suggestions along the process, and patience for its publication.

It has taken long to get this work published. I am grateful for the commitment of the Editorial Board and the Director, Donna Livingstone, of the University of Calgary Press in upholding the commitment to rigorous scholarship as well as remaining true to the objectives of the Press, namely: "making a difference" and "making you think." I would also like to thank the four reviewers for taking the time to read and report on this manuscript. Scholarly critique is the cornerstone of academic rigour, and it is especially challenging to review a manuscript of collected essays. Furthermore, it is difficult to assess a work on terror because this issue has been highly politicized, is intimately connected to ideological perspectives and vested interests, and, therefore, is more difficult to assess.

Jeffrey Halvorsen, my research assistant, who has since graduated and even started a family, has invested precious time with me in helping put this collection together.

Yasmin, Tahera-Rafia, and Sinan-Saleh, my family, are an unending source of support and encouragement in all my ventures. Their gentle smiles make all the hard work worthwhile.

Notes on Contributors

BRENT BEARDSLEY – Major Brent Beardsley is a Staff Officer in the Leadership Lessons Learned Section of the Canadian Forces Leadership Institute of the Canadian Defence Academy at the Royal Military College of Canada. He has been with the institute since 2002. He holds a pre-arts diploma from Sir George Williams University, a bachelor of arts degree in History from Concordia University, a post-graduate diploma in Education from McGill University and a master's degree in Applied Science in Management from the Royal Military College of Canada (RMC). He is currently completing his second master's degree in war studies at RMC, where the focus of his studies is on genocide and humanitarian intervention in the current and future security environment. Major Beardsley is an Infantry Officer with the Royal Canadian Regiment. He has served four tours of Regimental Duty with all three battalions of his regiment. On extra-regimental employment, he has served as a course officer at the Canadian Forces Officer Candidate School, a staff officer on the Army Doctrine and Training Staff and as Chief Instructor of the Canadian Forces Peace Support Training Centre. Major Beardsley has served on NATO and UN tours in Norway, Germany, Cyprus, UN Headquarters New York, and Rwanda. He was the personal staff officer to General (ret'd) Romeo Dallaire before and during the genocide in Rwanda in 1993–94. Subsequently he co-authored the award-winning book *Shake Hands with the Devil: The Failure of Humanity in Rwanda*, has collaborated in the production of several documentaries, and speaks across North America to audiences on a wide range of topics related to the Rwandan Genocide.

GWYNNE DYER – Gwynne Dyer has worked as a freelance journalist, columnist, broadcaster, and lecturer on international affairs for more than twenty years, but he was originally trained as a military historian. Born in Newfoundland, he received degrees from Canadian, American, and British universities and has taught at the Canadian Forces College and the Royal Military Academy Sandhurst. He writes a twice-weekly column on international affairs, which is published by over 175 papers in some 45 countries. His first television series was the 1983 documentary "War," one episode of which was nominated for an

Academy Award. His more recent works include the 1994 series "The Human Race," and "Protection Force," a three-part series on peacekeepers in Bosnia, both of which won Gemini awards. His award-winning radio documentaries include "The Gorbachev Revolution," a seven-part series based on his experiences in Eastern Europe and the former Soviet Union in 1987–90. Books by Dyer that are still in print include *War, Future: Tense, Climate Wars,* and *The Mess They Made* (published in the United States and the UK as *After Iraq*).

STUART FARSON – Stuart Farson has taught political science since 1991 at Simon Fraser University, where he is currently an adjunct professor in the Department of Political Science and a Research Associate of the Institute for Governance Studies. He has also been a research consultant engaged in projects concerning strategic planning, communications research, public policy analysis, and various matters to do with the national security. Between 1989 and 1990, he served as Director of Research for the Special Committee of the House of Commons on the Review of the CSIS Act and the Security Offences Act. He has worked with academic research institutes in Europe, North America, and the Pacific Rim and has testified before numerous parliamentary committees, as well as provided advice to Canadian government and NATO task forces and workshops. Recently, he was involved in developing resiliency systems to further the sustainability of cities of the future as part of Canada's award-winning CitiesPlus Project. He has been an expert witness for both the Arar Commission and in recent national security litigation involving port workers and the Marine Transportation Security Clearance Program.

Farson is the author of numerous articles and book chapters on security, intelligence, policing, and political violence. He was co-editor of *Security and Intelligence in a Changing World: New Perspectives for the 1990s* (Frank Cass, 1991) and *Intelligence Analysis and Assessment* (London: Frank Cass, 1996). He was also co-editor of the two-volume work *PSI Handbook of Global Security and Intelligence: National Approaches* (Westport, CT: Praeger Security International, 2008). His most recent article, "Rethinking the North American Frontier after 9/11," was published in a special issue of the *Journal of Borderlands Studies*.

DOUG FIRBY – Doug Firby works as a communications consultant and nationally syndicated columnist with Troy Media Corporation. He worked in Canadian commercial newspapers for thirty-one years, including six years as Editorial Pages Editor of the *Calgary Herald*, from November 2001 to June 2008. Before that, he was Managing Editor of the *St. Catharines Standard* in St. Catharines, Ontario. A graduate of the journalism program at the University of Western Ontario, in London, Ontario, he has also worked at newspapers in Winnipeg, London, and Windsor, Ontario. In addition to guest lectures, he has taught journalism and communications courses at Calgary's Mount Royal College, the University of Windsor, and several community colleges in Ontario. In addition to his award-winning editorial writing, he is a frequent contributor to the *Herald*'s Books pages.

RONALD GLASBERG – Ronald Glasberg obtained his doctorate in French intellectual history at the University of Toronto. He taught at Mount Saint Vincent, Trent, and the University of Western Ontario before assuming his current position at the University of Calgary (1989), where he teaches courses on the evolution of ideas in the history of Western Civilization. His basic research interest lies in the area of knowledge unification strategies. Dr. Glasberg has received a dozen Student Union Teaching Excellence Awards for his courses in the history of ideas.

KARIM-ALY KASSAM – Karim-Aly Kassam is International Associate Professor of Environmental and Indigenous Studies at Cornell University. He has a doctorate in Natural Resource Policy from Cornell University, a master of science in Social Policy and Planning from the London School of Economics, and a master of philosophy in Islamic studies from Cambridge University. Karim-Aly Kassam is an internationally recognized scholar in the area of applied participatory research in the service of communities. His work covers interdisciplinary areas such as Development Studies, Indigenous Ways of Knowing, Human Ecology, Arctic Social Science, Natural Resource Policy, Social Policy, and Socio-cultural History of Muslim Societies. Specific areas of applied research include: relationship between biological and cultural diversity, climate change, indigenous land and marine use, gender analysis, and women's empowerment. He undertakes research work in strategic regions of the world as the Alaskan, Canadian, and Russian Arctic and sub-Arctic, the rainforest in the south of India and mountainous regions of Afghanistan and Tajikistan. Among his many publications, Kassam has co-edited *Canada and September 11: Impact and Response* and authored *Biocultural Diversity and Indigenous Ways of Knowing: Human Ecology in the Arctic.*

JAMES LASSOIE – James P. Lassoie is a Professor of Natural Resources in the Department of Natural Resources, Cornell University, and a College of Agriculture and Life Sciences Professor of International Conservation. Originally trained as a forest ecologist, Lassoie's professional interests have evolved greatly over his almost thirty years at Cornell. Two general questions now motivate his professional interests. First, what are the key ecological and social variables underpinning the decision-making process related to natural resource and environmental management? And second, how can local communities become more effectively involved in such decision-making processes? He is particularly interested in agroforestry, social forestry, integrated resource conservation and management, ecotourism, and parks and protected area management and has worked extensively in Africa, Asia, and Latin America, as well as Canada and the United States.

GEORGE MELNYK – George Melnyk is an Associate Professor of Canadian Studies and Film Studies in the Faculty of Communication and Culture, University of Calgary. He is a founding member of the Consortium for Peace Studies at the University of Calgary and served as its co-chair from 2004 to 2008. He is also the General Series Editor for the Global Peace Studies Series at Athabasca University Press. Author or editor of twenty books on Canadian culture and society, Melnyk is a cultural historian who values the deconstruction of political rhetoric.

REG WHITAKER – Reg Whitaker is Distinguished Research Professor Emeritus at York University, and Adjunct Professor of Political Science at the University of Victoria. He is the author of many books on Canadian history and politics, security and intelligence, and the politics of information, including recently *The End of Privacy* and *Canada and the Cold War* (with Steve Hewitt). He has recently served in a number of advisory capacities to the Government of Canada on issues of national security and accountability.

Introduction: Why Try to Understand Terror?

KARIM-ALY KASSAM
Cornell University

Terror is experienced in a variety of ways and it is felt among all members of civil society. While much has been said on "the global war on terror," it remains cunningly elusive and yet pervasive. The very act of critical reflection renders a concept or idea approachable. The aim of this collection of essays is to *understand* terror and not to *describe* it. It is on these grounds that this work differs from other works on the subject. Its originality arises not from new material on the subject of terrorism, but from viewing terror from a diversity of perspectives, hitherto not considered when discussing terror.[1] We feel the imminent threat of terror through its metaphorical power in our daily dosage of news (Melnyk's essay; chap. 4), from the environmental crisis (Lassoie's essay; chap. 7), and its impact on food security, or as experienced by Canadian peacekeeping troops during the Rwandan genocide, which claimed nearly a million lives (Beardsley's essay; chap. 8) or from the continuing loss of life suffered by Canadian soldiers in Afghanistan. Just a few years ago, in Calgary, we feared for the polarization in our social fabric resulting from the reprinting of the Danish cartoons of the Muslim Prophet Muhammad (Firby's essay; chap. 5). As I am writing this introduction, the swine flu pandemic is receiving media attention. At the height of global fears over the swine flu pandemic, while I was queued to get coffee at Cornell University, a Mexican graduate student, having noticed me, walked over to shake my hand. When I returned his gesture of greeting, he suddenly became apologetic and alarmed, insisting that he had washed his hands. I explained to him that I did not understand what he was talking about. The hysteria caused by the media (possibly justified) had effectively made him deeply sensitive to how he would be perceived as a Mexican national. Even simple but essential things to our social fabric such as manners and courteous interactions were affected by the fear surrounding the swine flu (H1N1) virus. Subsequently, as I travelled to Afghanistan, China, Tajikistan, and Turkey to undertake research, I was viewed with suspicion for possibly carrying the virus that may infect others. Now, I was the one who was viewed with anxiety. The reasons for my travel were irrelevant, the lowest common denominator, the fact that I was a North American was sufficient to warrant concern. I, like other travellers, had to follow different procedures and rules devised by each of these countries to satisfy their legitimate concerns for the safety of their citizens. While in China, ironically, an American colleague wittily asked: "Does a person with a Muslim background catch swine flu?" Like Jews, Muslims do not eat pork (although you cannot get the virus from eating pork). The *double entendre* was clear. I was both Muslim and North American – two reasons for 'concern.' Even in barbed jest there is room for thought, so I could not help but reflect on the relevance of Glasberg's essay (chap. 9) that explores how terror and suspicion pervades our civilization. The world is made up of complex-connectivity and it demands answers to questions we may not have considered before. The uniqueness of this collection arises from the integration of essays, which are a combination of narratives in the first person with grounded explanations and analysis of historical events as provided by Dyer (chap. 1), Whitaker (chap. 2), and Farson (chap. 3).

Terror is multi-causal and cannot be reduced to single principles. This work urges the reader to reflect on its diverse contexts and expressions, and confront terror's pervasiveness in today's society. This collection does not presume to give answers but juxtaposes events and analysis that are normally not considered part of terror. While some may consider them to be tangential, we (the contributors) believe they are central to an understanding of terror. *Understanding Terror*, as a collection, views "the global war on terror" from a different lens. It defines the boundaries of terror, examines its construction in the media, and explores its relationship to the "other." *Understanding Terror* takes a historical approach to consideration of terror through specific examples and its presence in the media, in North American society, in general, and Canada, in particular. It offers insights from those who have viewed and experienced terror. The aim is to engender questioning and discourse.

This work is primarily situated in a pluralistic orientation typical of Canadian pragmatism. Terror is multi-causal. Understanding it requires an interdisciplinary perspective informed by values of pluralism, which are distinctly Canadian. This work is uniquely Canadian because it is not easily found or taught in university classes that address terrorism. Canadian characteristics of this work do not merely arise from our own experiences of terror, such as the FLQ crisis (Whitaker's essay; chap. 2) or the Air India bombing that primarily killed Canadians (Farson's essay; chap. 3), but from the insights of Canadians who believe in such things as "the right to protect" civil society (Beardsley's essay; chap. 8) or the "balance between freedom of expression and responsibility" (Firby's essay; chap. 5). Canadian public policy does not announce absolutes; it negotiates contingencies and navigates diversity. These essays do not make presumptuous pronouncements about the war on terror; instead, they urge the reader to tease out nuances in the notion of terror in relation to the "self" as well as the "other." The collection urges Canadians to *think* instead of relying on formulaic clichés of pundits. Because examination of the notion of terror cannot be left to a narrow group of experts, these essays collectively present a variety of perspectives characteristic of Canadian civil society. Nor are all contributors in this collection *experts* on terrorism in the conventional sense. Rather, the know-how of some contributors arises from direct engagement with terror while the expertise of other contributors provides a reflective consideration of terror as it manifests itself in multiple forms.

To achieve meaningful insights, a varied collection of individuals who have dealt with the issue of terror, such as journalists, scholars, and public policy experts, have participated to engage in a dialogue with the reader. Their essays are organized in a manner that alternates between examination of specific events and reflective consideration on how these events may be interpreted. *Understanding Terror* weaves diverse perspectives with a historical sense so as to allow an appreciation and contextualization of the notion of terror. Essays in this collection take a variety of forms. Some are explanations of historical events, while others are narratives of events in the first person; and yet others are analytical, exploring the implications of the narratives and historical events. Together, these essays peel away at the layers of the notion of terror.

The first essay is Gwynne Dyer's "Terror and its Boundaries." Dyer explains that the more powerful states have historically shown their willingness to use terror for their strategic interests. This balance of terror underpinned the Cold War. He describes the historical evolution of terror as a category of guerrilla war. He traces the development of guerrilla warfare and its use of terror as a form of resistance to, and liberation from, colonial rule. Dyer contrasts the development of rural and urban guerrilla war and the rise of "designer terrorism" in Western Europe and North America. Dyer illustrates that not only have terrorist movements been present in the West, but these powerful states have also made use of terror as a strategy both among their own societies and outside their borders. Dyer outlines the development that led to the use of terror by the African National Congress, the Irish Republican Army, the Palestinian Liberation Organization and more recently the Salafist movement that inspires al-Qaida. He concludes that the "war on terror" is misleading because terrorism has been present for a long time and will continue to exist as long as people have grievances.

Reg Whitaker, in "How Canada Confronts Terrorism: Canadian Responses to 9/11 in Historical and Comparative Context," compares the "Cold War" to the "global war on terror," revealing important parallels and differences. The comparison of "global war on terror" to the "Cold War" is significant because each has had a deeply polarizing effect on societies within the international system of nations. He explains that both wars were carried out on two fronts: without and within. The war within – that is among Canadians and Canadian civil society – has major implications for civil liberties. Compared to the Cold War, he argues that the "global war on terror" is a more populist struggle since the target of the terror is seen to be civilian. Therefore, this populist response poses a clear danger to visible minorities like the Muslim population of Canada. Whitaker also considers Canada's own home-grown terrorist movement, the Front de Libération du Québec (FLQ). The crisis in October 1970, resulted in the imposition of the War Measures Act. He illustrates the seeming paradox of how an illiberal response, namely the use of the power of the state, to crush opposition during the October Crisis ultimately led to the development of a liberal democratic Canadian public policy that increasingly safeguarded civil liberties while eliminating the threat of terrorism in Quebec. The FLQ failed because Canadians were able to develop democratic avenues to address the grievances of Quebeckers. Whitaker maintains that Canadian experiences arising from the Cold War and the October Crisis have significantly influenced policy direction resulting from the events of September 11, 2001. While the "War on Terror" is seen as primarily an American-led venture, Canadian support for it has underlying economic realities. Given the "global war on terror," Canada, Whitaker argues, has retained political distance from the United States primarily due to its response to the Cold War and the 1970 October Crisis. While not perfect, this unique historical and policy trajectory has resulted in a made-in-Canada solution to security.

Following Whitaker, Stuart Farson focuses on the events surrounding the downing of Air India flight 182. He examines the role of successive Canadian governments and media in not recognizing the destruction of Air India flight 182 as the largest civilian mass murder in Canadian history. In "In Accounting for Disaster: The Quest for Closure after Aerial Mass Murder – The Downing of Air India Flight 182 in Comparative Perspective," Farson considers the Air India bombing in light of the destruction of Korean Airlines, Iran Air, and Pan Am passenger liners. He provides examples of how state and non-state actors benefited from acts of terror. Building on Dyer's contention that state and non-state actors use the threat of terror to advance their strategic interests, Farson shows how the Government of the United States capitalized on the downing of a Korean Airlines flight to wage a propaganda war against the Soviet Union and advance its strategic military interests in Europe. Alternatively, he shows how the Pan Am disaster resulted from a private-sector decision to profit from the threat of terror. By advertising its security system as state-of-the-art in order to attract travellers and gain greater market share, Pan Am overstated its ability to protect its clients. The security system focused essentially on the wrong and ultimately ineffective aspect of passenger safety. Farson demonstrates that the families of the victims are consistently given the least consideration. In all cases, the concern for closure for the families was neither forthcoming nor a priority. The role of the Canadian government is particularly noteworthy with reference to the bombing of Air India flight 182 at the hands of Sikh separatists. Arguably

Canada's greatest civilian catastrophe, the downing of Air India flight 182 has remained, for decades, widely unacknowledged because it affected Canadians of Indian origin. Suggesting that for both policy makers and the public, the deep sense of loss felt by families of this ethnic minority of Canadian society is somehow less significant. However, building on Whitaker's assertion that Canada has a unique trajectory where public policy corrects historical injustices, the inquiry into the downing of Air India, while twenty-three years late, seeks to redress the concerns of the victims' families and find closure. Whitaker's and Farson's essays both illustrate that the tactical use of terror has diverse and context-specific origins. In the case of the downing or Air India, the origins lay outside of Canada but ended in the loss of Canadian lives.

While Dyer describes the boundaries of terror in a tactical sense, Melnyk in his essay "The Word 'Terrorism' and Its Impact on Public Consciousness" explores the term's metaphorical power. He illustrates how this politically charged word with implied morality sets the parameters of public discourse. He argues that as a result of media support and political sponsorship of the concept of "terrorism," the word has gained official and widely held meaning. This meaning of terrorism has established unquestioned legitimacy which stifles questioning and thoughtful analysis of its usage. As such, terrorism is beyond the pale of human conduct. This word effectively polarizes in order to identify enemies. It enables the separation between "them and us." It facilitates the dehumanization of individuals and criminalization of organizations. This uniform representation of the "other" through powerful media marketing has launched the so-called "global war on terror." Its heavy promotion and association with threatening images in the media has turned it into a powerful rallying cry, which cannot easily be challenged. A culture inspired by fear coupled with the spectacle of mayhem and death suits a profit-driven and sensationalist media's representation of the world. Melnyk argues that a striking feature of the war on terror is that it is perpetually self-justifying because those who can control public discourse can continue to label others as terrorists. A society can unendingly be on some form of alert. Reiterating the point made in earlier essays, Melnyk argues that the threat of terror is strategically used by media (non-state) and state actors. In other words, "the global war on terror" has economic and political currency. Having made a case for the usage of the word "terrorism" as political rhetoric, Melnyk proceeds to deconstruct the metaphor so as to facilitate public discourse.

Firby provides an illustrative case of representation of terrorism as a powerful metaphor in the media. The cartoons depicting the Muslim Prophet Muhammad as a terrorist demonstrate vividly the metaphorical dimensions of the word "terrorist." In "Groping in the Dark: How the Media, Absent a Frame of Reference, Fumbled the Danish Cartoon Controversy," Firby provides a rare glimpse into the process of decision making undertaken by editorial page editors. He explains the role of fear and intuition as factors that influence editors in the choice of news stories to cover. Generally, fear drives editors to make "safe" decisions, which are tantamount to imitating other media outlets in what they are choosing to cover. In the case of intuition, which depends on considerable experience, it may reinforce conventional wisdom. Both amount to the same result. He describes this phenomenon as "pack journalism." In other words, "if it bleeds, it leads." Furthermore, Firby explains how this type of reporting is vacant of nuanced analysis. In the case of the Danish cartoon controversy, Firby illustrates the exception, how a Canadian city's two leading newspapers chose not to publish the cartoons despite pressure resulting from the decision of the *Jewish Free Press* and outright taunts from the *Western Standard*. The decision to publish the cartoons depicting the Muslim Prophet Muhammad as a "terrorist" was framed as expression of the "freedom of the press" by these two (hitherto) lesser-known Calgary-based print media. Firby explains why editors need to have a historical sense in order to understand context and the ability to stay ahead of issues guided by a code of ethics when addressing dilemmas about what constitutes freedom of the press and the social consequences of that freedom. He argues that the decision not to publish material that is injurious to a sector of society may also be an exercise of the same freedom. Arguably, the choice by two of Calgary's leading newspapers not to republish the Danish cartoons is also an illustration of the sensitivity to the cultural and religious diversity that forms Canadian civil society. It is a resounding, but rare, example of the media choosing to act thoughtfully and reflectively.

To complement Firby's illustrative case, Kassam provides a contextualized historical analysis of terminology. Virtually every essay in the collection makes reference to the role of the media perpetuating an uncritical representation of terror for the purposes of spectacle. Reporting of terror in the media is often void of analysis and vacant of the historical context that gives rise to acts of terror. In the process of editing this volume, the issue of terminology arose to describe those who commit acts of terror. In the chapter entitled: "The Terrorist 'Other': The Fundamentalist and the Islamist," Kassam, examines the terms "fundamentalist" and "Islamist." He suggests that uncritical use of these terms obscures the issue of terror as solely inspired by religion. Attributing the causes of terror to religion is both vacant of understanding of grievances and dishonest. Framing the discourse of terror by some "experts" generates an (intended or unintended) monopoly where space for alternative and historically contextualized discourse is not possible in the mass media. To illustrate the dangers of uncritical use of terminology, Kassam shows the stark ideological contrast between the thought of two Muslim leaders, Muhammad 'Abduh and Muhammad ibn 'Abd al-Wahhab, who are credited with founding the Salafist movement. The Salafist movement is said to inspire organizations like al-Qaida. He illustrates how political motivations and legitimate grievances are disguised by religious rhetoric claiming to represent all of Islam. The characterization of Muslims as the violent "Other" has antecedents in Middle Age Christian discourse to facilitate unity among Christendom. In the twentieth century, this "Other" was replaced by the threat of communist evil from the East in order to sustain the Cold War. In the twenty-first century, the characterization of Muslim "Other" has returned. However, as Firby's case shows, for some media outlets, this uncritical characterization of Muslims is not acceptable in Canadian pluralist society.

James Lassoie begins with a unique and personal description of the anxiety generated by fear during the Cold War and its resurfacing in the so-called "global war on terror." In "Maintaining Environmental Priorities in the Age of Terrorism," he argues that decision making on environmental priorities is hijacked by the pervasive fear of terrorism in the public psyche. Using the statistical concept of "probability neglect," he shows how extreme emotional distress can cause people to ignore the probability of an outcome and focus instead on the unlikely but disastrous chance that it will occur. For instance, individuals may avoid swimming because of an overwhelming fear of shark attacks or avoid flying because of an overpowering fear of a plane crash. Lassoie maintains that as a result of probability neglect, citizens of Western democracies are afraid of the wrong dangers and subsequently ignore environmental concerns, which will have graver and longer-term consequences than an unlikely act of terror. He cites the role of the media in perpetuating the debilitating anxiety in public consciousness. The age of "the global war on terror" facilitates the advancement of not only certain political ideologies but also environmentally unsound business ventures. In other words, "the global war on terror" is profitable at the expense of the human habitat. Lassoie illustrates how the discourse of this war on terror prevents dialogue on the pressing issue of global climate change. The very distinction of the Western "Self" from the Muslim "Other" does not facilitate awareness of complex connectivity and deep interdependence between diverse human communities and their habitats on this planet. In essence, Lassoie is making a nuanced addition to the preceding essays, by arguing that pluralism is also intimately linked to biological diversity of all species (human and non-human). In other words, "the global war on terror" fails to take into consideration not only cultural diversity but also the complex connection of these cultures to their respective ecological environments.

In "Responding to the Terror of Genocide: Learning from the Rwandan Genocide of 1994," Major Beardsley speaks from a deeply personal and highly traumatic experience of the Rwandan genocide. He directly addresses the reader in a conversation about fear and subsequent fraying of the social fabric. He describes shrewdly calculated terrorization and savagely executed mass murder. Major Beardsley's account is ripe with immediate experience of horror. He explains how the ruling elite and the media are complicit in fomenting hatred. People as diverse as the disenfranchised youth of Kigali and a Christian pastor participate in committing crimes against humanity. Even the sanctuary of the Church is no longer sacrosanct. The case of the Rwandan genocide amply demonstrates the brutal and bloody consequences of the fragmentation of the "Self" from the "Other" in human society. The language of hate and fear perpetuated by the mass media does not allow for perception of interconnectivity and interdependence between cultures. Perhaps what is most significant is how genocide was carried out in Rwanda with clinical efficiency while the majority of humanity looked on with indifference. The names and the bodies of hundreds of thousands of human beings were effectively wiped out from existence. Such mass murder required a rational bureaucratic machine in order to be effective. Rwanda has the notorious reputation of being the most rapid genocide carried out in the twentieth century. In a matter of one hundred days, 800,000 men, women, and children were killed. His narrative reflects both the pain of Rwanda and a stark warning to humanity of the consequences of fragmentation of the "Self" fuelled by fear and hostility. Beardsley argues that the impulse of genocide needs to be dealt with first internally at the individual level and then externally at the level of the family, community, and humanity.

In the "Psycho-Dynamics of Terror: A Perspective on the Evolution of Western Civilization," Ron Glasberg takes up Beardsley's challenge to engage what is internal to the "Self." He wonders how the terror without blinds us to the terror within. Using the philosophical framework of the intrinsic and the extrinsic, he explores how the societal structure of Western civilization infused with repression of the "Self" results in fear and a sense of disconnection. Using three texts as representative of Western and specifically Christian civilizations, he contends that external (or extrinsic) terror is merely a manifestation of the repression of the failure to deal with internal (or intrinsic) fears. Using the Sermon on the Mount as the setting for an individual's desire to live life without fear, he examines the terror of fate faced by Oedipus in the play by Sophocles, the alienation between the "Self" (victimizer) and the "Other" (the victim) in Dante's *Divine Comedy*, and the powerlessness of the individual against a complex governing system in Kafka's *The Trial*. For Glasberg, the psycho-dynamics of terror are inherent in Western civilization. He explains that overwhelming fear results in disconnection of the "Self" from a greater whole. In turn, this alienation of the "Self" results in the stagnation of personal growth coupled with the nameless dread inspired by the seeming banality of an all-pervasive bureaucracy. The cumulative impact of persistent alienation, stagnation, and dread on the "Self" is an all-encompassing sense of terror. In short, fear inspires an endless cycle of alienation and ensuing feeling of terror. Glasberg links the alienation felt by the "Self" and the resulting personal terror arising from an individual identity articulated in the absence of connectivity with "other" human societies and cultures and their diverse ecological habitats.

The collection concludes with a discussion on over-determination of Islam as a source of a clash of civilizations. Given the change in U.S. administrations, there is a welcome sense of relief that the narrow "clash of civilizations" thinking will abate and reason will prevail. However, this type of thinking has become ingrained over a period of several decades in countries that exert considerable military and economic strength, and it is hard to change overnight the biases of civil servants who put such policies into operation. Furthermore, the recent economic crisis will merely exacerbate parochialism as it impacts countries that are affected both by terror and by poverty. Marginalization of people and their legitimate points of view will continue as humanity deals simultaneously with the economic crisis, the environmental and socio-cultural impact of climate change, and growing energy needs for livelihood and food security. The issue of terror is not going to leave us soon. Not only is it high time that we understand its multi-causal aspects, but it is our ethical responsibility as scholars to ensure there is thoughtful public discourse that avoids myopic thinking.

The motivations of the editor, who is Canadian and with Muslim heritage, teaching at an Ivy League institution in the United States, and undertaking research among indigenous communities in the Canadian, American, and Russian Arctic, as well as the Pamir Mountains of Afghanistan and Tajikistan, must also be disclosed. It is important to note that Canadian humanitarian and military activities are present in all these locations. These are not only regions where the Cold War played itself out, but strategic areas that are gateways for energy and other resources. These are also areas at the forefront of the damaging impacts of climate change, although the indigenous peoples of these regions did not contribute to its causes. It is at these extremes, where people are under social and environmental stress, that terror is felt and fomented. From the periphery, we can see the impact of our civilization, both its weaknesses and its strengths, and this can inform a pluralistic outlook that is uniquely Canadian.

Notes

1   For a more conventional examination
     of the subject, any online bookstore will
     provide material using the keywords
     "terror" or "terrorism." This work does
     not seek to be conventional.

CHAPTER 1

Terror and Its Boundaries

Gwynne Dyer
Journalist, Author, Lecturer

> *The ability to run away is the essence of the guerrilla.*
>
> – Mao Tse-tung[1]

1. Terror and the State

Terrorism is essentially a sub-category of guerrilla war, and indeed the conduct of guerrilla war almost always involves a good deal of terrorism. Most early guerrilla struggles were waged against foreign occupiers who had effectively decapitated the insurgents' state and destroyed its army, but they are now more commonly fought by political groups or ethnic minorities in rebellion against their own national government. Guerrilla war and terrorism are generally the only forms of warfare available to resistance movements or revolutionaries who do not control the resources of a state, and legitimate states have therefore consistently tried to paint them as immoral and illegal – except, of course, when they are sponsoring guerrilla war or terrorism on some other country's territory, as they have frequently done. Relatively recent examples of this phenomenon would include Libyan support for the IRA in Northern Ireland and American sponsorship of the Contras in Nicaragua and the Mujahedin in Afghanistan (U.S. President Ronald Reagan, who illegally provided financial aid to the Contras in Nicaragua, referred to the Mujahedin as "the moral equivalent of our own founding fathers.").

Most of the bigger states have shown no reluctance to use terror techniques themselves in war. The doctrine of "strategic bombardment" that underlay the construction of huge bomber fleets by Britain and the United States in World War II quite explicitly targeted the civilian population of enemy nations, arguing that their role as producers of weapons and war supplies made them legitimate objects of attack. Moreover, the theorists of air power like Emilio Douhet and Sir Arthur Harris openly argued that spreading terror among the civilian population by indiscriminate bombing would magnify the impact of air power far beyond the actual losses of life that it caused. The technological end-product of this logic was the nuclear weapons that were dropped in Hiroshima and Nagasaki in 1945, and in the years after the Second World War this approach was further elaborated into the "balance of terror" that lay at the heart of the Cold War.

For some forty years, from 1949 to 1991, the Soviet Union and the United States each sought to deter an attack by the other side by maintaining a credible threat to kill tens of millions of their opponent's citizens with nuclear weapons – what would be considered a war crime if committed on the battlefield mysteriously became morally neutral if done from a sufficiently great distance with high-tech weaponry. Wars of extermination are not unprecedented – Rome did it to Carthage, in the end, and the losing side in primitive warfare was often wiped out down to the last man, woman, and child – but the long premeditation and elaborate technological preparations for the mass killing of civilians that underpinned the strategy of "Mutual Assured Destruction" (MAD) had few precedents in warfare.

To be fair, the architects of American and Soviet nuclear strategy during the Cold War were faced with a problem that had no easy solution: how to deter the use of weapons whose destructive power threatened the survival of entire societies. If they had confined their efforts to various versions of the MAD doctrine, they could have offered the valid defence that the best way of deterring the use of these weapons by the other side was to ensure that there would be catastrophic loss of life if they were ever actually used. However, the West explicitly, and the Soviet Union implicitly, continued to cling to contradictory doctrines in which some act of aggression using conventional weapons by the other side would be punished by sudden escalation to the use of nuclear weapons. It is difficult to see the moral distinction between these "nuclear first strike" doctrines and the terrorist practice of targeting uninvolved civilians in order to bring political pressure on their governments. Governments always reject any suggestion of moral equivalence between their own strategies and the smaller-scale "terrorism" practised by non-state actors, but their protests in this regard may safely be dismissed as self-serving hypocrisy.

2. Terrorism as a Category of Guerrilla War

Very serious moral questions nevertheless arise with regard to guerrilla war, precisely because it does involve the large-scale terrorization and killing of civilians. While conventional armies seek contact with the enemy and decisive victory, guerrilla forces deliberately avoid fighting regular forces that they cannot hope to match and concentrate instead on 'soft' targets whose destruction may ultimately undermine the government's control over the country. In practice, this often means torturing local officials and slaughtering their families in front of the assembled community – and the counter-insurgency specialists are not too squeamish either. Operation Phoenix, the U.S.-run campaign of assassination to eliminate Viet Cong cadres after the Tet offensive in 1968, killed between twenty and fifty thousand people, most of them inevitably innocent civilians, but it also effectively gutted the Viet Cong infrastructure in much of South Vietnam.

For a time in the 1950s and early 1960s, guerrilla war seemed to be a virtually infallible technique for overthrowing governments. But like the first of the modern methods for seizing state power, the urban uprisings of nineteenth- and early-twentieth-century Europe that drew their inspiration from the French Revolution in 1789, guerrilla warfare proved to be a technique that flourished only in a specific environment.

> Wherever we arrived, they disappeared; whenever we left, they arrived. They were everywhere and nowhere, they had no tangible centre which could be attacked.
> – French officer fighting Spanish guerrillas, 1810[2]

Guerrilla warfare as a form of resistance to foreign occupation or an unpopular domestic government had been around for the better part of forever, but it gained particular prominence in the Napoleonic wars, when the Spanish who gave the technique its name (*guerrilla* = "little war") and the Germans waged large guerrilla campaigns against French occupying forces. As is almost normal in guerrilla war, systematic atrocities designed to terrorize the other side were routinely employed by the French army as much as they were by the Spanish guerrillas: the savagery of the struggle in Spain from 1808 to 1814 was indelibly captured in Francisco Goya's *The Disasters of War*. But guerrilla warfare was not generally regarded as a decisive military technique even as late as World War II, when it was widely employed against German and Japanese occupation forces, primarily because it lacked an adequate strategy for final victory.

So long as the guerrillas remained dispersed in the hills, forests, or swamps and indulged in only hit-and-run raiding against the government or the foreign occupiers, they could make an infernal nuisance of themselves. They could also carry out what would today be called "terrorist" attacks in the cities – but they could never clear their opponents out of the urban centres of power. If they came down from the hills and attempted to do so in open combat, they gave their opponents the target they had been hoping for, and the enemy's regular forces would smash them. Even the Yugoslavs, the most successful European guerrilla fighters of World War II, could not have liberated their country unaided; the Germans finally pulled out of Yugoslavia mainly because the victorious Red Army was sweeping through the Balkans toward them.

> By May 1928 … the basic principles of guerrilla warfare, simple in nature and suited to the conditions of the time, had already been evolved; that is, the sixteen-character formula: "The enemy advances, we retreat; the enemy camps, we harass; the enemy tires, we attack; the enemy retreats, we pursue."
>
> – Mao Tse-tung[3]

The one great exception to all the rules was Mao Tse-tung. After the Chinese Communist Party lost its urban Shanghai base in the massacres of 1927, he led the surviving communist cadres in an eighteen-year rural struggle against the

Nationalist government of China, and later against the Japanese invaders, that literally wrote the book on modern guerrilla warfare. It is unlikely that there has been any guerrilla commander of any nationality or ideology in the past seventy-five years who has not read Mao's works. However, there have not been many guerrilla commanders who have done what Mao did, which is to start with a handful of rural guerrillas and end up by overthrowing and replacing a well-established government with local roots. As time passed, his victory has come to look more and more like a one-of-a-kind.

This was not immediately evident after 1949, however, because rural guerrilla techniques were also deployed against the European colonial empires at a time when the imperial powers had lost their nerve and were in a gravely weakened economic condition. As in the occupied countries of Europe during the Second World War, the guerrillas in Asian and African colonies after the war had no difficulty in mobilizing many of their newly nationalistic fellow countrymen against their foreign occupiers. As in the occupied countries of Europe, they still had virtually no prospect of winning a military victory against the well-equipped regular forces of the imperial power, but they could turn themselves into an expensive and ineradicable nuisance. What was different was that whereas the Germans in Yugoslavia were fighting a great war in which the very survival of their own regime was at stake, and so were willing to bear the cost of fighting the Yugoslav guerrillas virtually indefinitely, the European powers had no such stake in retaining control of their colonies.

> You may kill ten of my men for every one I kill of yours, but even at those odds, you will lose and I will win.
> – Ho Chi Minh, ca. 1948 (to the French)

> The conventional army loses if it does not win. The guerrilla wins if he does not lose.
> – Henry Kissinger[4]

It came down in the end to the fact that if the guerrillas could make it very expensive for the colonial power to stay, and could go on doing so indefinitely, they didn't have to worry about gaining a military victory. The colonial power would eventually decide to cut its losses and go home. This was a reality that had already been demonstrated by the Irish war of independence in 1919–20 and the Turkish war of national resistance against attempted partition by the victorious Entente powers in 1919–22 (the struggle for which the Bolsheviks originally coined the phrase "national liberation war"). The pattern was repeated many times in the two decades after 1945, in Indonesia, Kenya, Algeria, Malaya, Cyprus, Vietnam, South Yemen, and many other places. In a few cases, like Malaya, the imperial power managed to hand over control to some local group other than the guerrillas themselves (but this depended mainly on the unusual racial split in Malaya). In most cases, it was the guerrilla leaders themselves who inherited power: Sukarno in Indonesia, Jomo Kenyatta in Kenya, the FLN in Algeria, and so on. And once the European imperial powers finally grasped their own fatal vulnerability to this technique, the decolonization process in most of their remaining colonies was achieved without need for a guerrilla war.

At the time, the apparently irresistible spread of rural guerrilla wars caused great alarm and despondency in the major Western powers – partly, of course, because it was their own oxen that were being gored. There was also an ideological element, however, in that most of the post-1945 guerrilla movements followed some version of the Marxist ideology that was also preached by the West's main international rival, the Soviet Union. (And naturally, being Marxists, the guerrillas attributed their successes to ideology, rather than to the particular environment they were operating in, and announced this conviction loudly.) This led to a belief in the West that it was Soviet and/or Chinese expansionism, and not simply local resentment of foreign rule, that lay behind these guerrilla wars. (A quite similar misapprehension today turns all the local manifestations of opposition to Western meddling in Muslim countries into a coordinated "Islamist" plot against the West.) This, in turn, led to the creation of special counter-insurgency forces, especially in the United States, and ultimately to the commitment of U.S. troops to Vietnam under a total misapprehension as to what the war there was about. Former defence secretary Robert McNamara, a leading architect of the U.S. war in Vietnam, later described it as "terribly wrong" and explains the mistake in his memoir, *In Retrospect: The*

Tragedy and Lessons of Vietnam (1995), as being due to the anti-communist climate of the times and wrong assumptions about foreign policy.

In fact, the guerrilla revolutionaries had adopted a Marxist ideology partly because of the powerful influence of Mao's successful example in China, but mainly because it was the principal revolutionary ideology on offer at the centre of the empires that ruled them: the Third World revolutionaries of the fifties and sixties learned their Marxism in London and Paris, not in Moscow. After all, they could scarcely be expected to adopt the liberal democratic ideology (for domestic consumption only) of the imperial powers they were seeking to expel. In opting for the leading opposition ideology that prevailed at the imperial centre, Marxism, they were following the example of an earlier generation of anti-imperialist revolutionaries who had borrowed the then-fashionable revolutionary ideology of liberalism from the European left and used it as the ideological basis for their own revolutions in Turkey in 1908, in Mexico and Iran in 1910, and in China in 1911. Nonetheless it did create the wrong impression in Western capitals.

The full-scale U.S. military commitment to Vietnam in 1965 was made not only for the wrong reason – to thwart perceived Soviet expansionism acting through the Chinese – but at the wrong time. For by 1965 the wave of guerrilla wars in what used to be called the Third World was coming to its natural end, as most of the countries there had already received their independence. Apart from Indochina, only southern Africa and South Yemen were still the scenes of active guerrilla campaigns against imperial rule by 1965. And although it had scarcely been noticed yet, the rural guerrilla technique hardly ever worked against a locally based government supported by the local majority ethnic group. The natural antipathy against foreign rule that would attract recruits to the guerrillas' cause was lacking, and, more importantly, a locally based government could not simply give up and go home if the cost of fighting a counter-insurgency campaign got too high. It already was home and had nowhere else to go.

The evolution of the African National Congress's strategy against white minority rule in South Africa illustrates how ideas about what was feasible and desirable changed over time. The ANC began as an organization committed to non-violent change and specifically to Gandhian tactics, but the rise to power

of the apartheid regime in 1948 and the wave of successful anti-colonial re-
bellions in the 1950s persuaded it that violence was necessary and might well
work. There were European settler populations in both Kenya and Algeria, for
example, but their presence did not much alter the basic equation: when the
cost of fighting a counter-insurgency campaign became too high for the imperial government in London or Paris, it gave up the fight and pulled out its
troops, and most of the settlers went home as well. The ANC faction (including
Nelson Mandela) that embarked on "terrorist" attacks against the white South
African authorities at the beginning of the 1960s assumed that they were in a
roughly similar situation, but the struggle in South Africa did not evolve along
the same lines at all. Twenty years later the apartheid regime was still in power,
and apparently as strong as ever, so gradually the ANC leadership reconsidered
its assumptions and its strategy. (A good deal of the rethinking was done on
Robben Island, the offshore prison near Cape Town where much of the ANC's
leadership was held.)

Although white South Africans were not a dramatically larger proportion
of the population than the French *pieds noirs* settlers in Algeria – whites accounted for only one-sixth of South Africa's total population in the 1960s, and
were down to one-eighth by the early 1990s – they were not "settlers." Most of
them were at least three generations in the country, and many had been South
African for ten generations or more. They held all the levers of power, and they
had nowhere else to go. Get a really large-scale guerrilla/terrorist insurrection
going and they would not "go home." They would fight with the desperation of
a local minority that has its back to the wall, and the consequence would be a
full-scale civil war of huge proportions: South Africa's population is about ten
times Lebanon's, and during the 1980s there were South Africans who began
to contemplate with horror the possibility of a civil war in their country at ten
times the scale of the ghastly Lebanese conflict. Mercifully, it did not happen.

Once the ANC's leadership recognized that they were not in a standard
"decolonization" situation, they backed off on the use of force within South Africa, putting more and more emphasis instead on non-violent resistance within
the country and the encouragement of external boycotts and sanctions against
the regime. At the same time, they stressed on every possible occasion that
there would still be a place within the country for white South Africans after

the end of apartheid. In the end, they succeeded in persuading the managers of apartheid that a negotiated surrender of white power was preferable to endless war, and the country came through the transition to majority rule relatively unscathed. It was a remarkable triumph of common sense over tribal instinct on both sides, but it was greatly assisted by the shift in thinking during those decades about what was possible to achieve by guerrilla war and/or terrorism.

The "decolonization" model is not totally dead: there are a few minority ethnic groups that are sufficiently large, cohesive, and determined that they can make it work against an independent Third World government. The Eritreans won their independence from Ethiopia in 1993, and the Tamil Tigers and the Chechens came close to success at several points in their struggles with Sri Lanka and Russia (though they have both now been defeated). However, most rural guerrilla movements who are seeking to overthrow their own national government have failed to solve the question of how to win final military victory in open battle against the government's regular forces.

> Make wiping out the enemy's effective strength our main objective; do not make holding or seizing a place our main objective…. In every battle, concentrate an absolutely superior force, encircle the enemy forces completely, strive to wipe them out thoroughly and do not let any escape from the net.
>
> – Mao Tse-Tung[5]

Mao was an effective guerrilla leader in the 1930s and the early 1940s, but he would never have issued those instructions then. In those days he followed the standard rules of guerrilla warfare: ambush small groups of the enemy, but never stand and fight against his main forces. By the time he gave the above orders, however, the Japanese had surrendered to the Allies and the Chinese Communists were moving into the last phase of their struggle with the Nationalist regime that still controlled all the cities and most of the population: open warfare using large regular formations. Between August 1945 and August 1947, the People's Liberation Army grew fourfold, to two million men, and came out into the open to beat the corrupt, divided, and incompetent Nationalist army in a series of full-scale battles. Indeed, it was a detachment of exactly the same

Chinese Communist army, using standard light infantry tactics, that crossed the Yalu River into Korea in late 1950, infiltrated rapidly between the numerically equal but more heavily armed and road-bound American and allied units that had advanced almost to the Chinese border, and drove them in panic down almost the entire length of the Korean peninsula. (American soldiers called it the Big Bug-Out; it was the longest retreat in U.S. Army history.) Mao achieved the Holy Grail of guerrilla war: he built his party cadres into an alternative government, turned his guerrilla soldiers into a real army, and then beat the existing government in open battle. And he did it with no support from outside and no help from ethnic grievances. It was a brilliant accomplishment, and innumerable revolutionary groups tried to follow his example, but only two succeeded: Fidel Castro's little band of brothers who came down from the Sierra Maestre in 1959, and the Sandinistas in Nicaragua in 1979. In both cases they benefited from having as opponents governments that were so extraordinarily iniquitous, incompetent, and politically isolated that they made even the Chinese Nationalists look good. They could also appeal to the anti-American sentiment that ran strongly in those countries after so much American intervention. Both the Batista regime in Cuba and the Somoza family in Nicaragua were widely seen by their fellow-countrymen as American puppets, and so the revolutionaries were not in a radically different position from those who waged successful anti-imperial struggles in the colonies of the European empires.

Even today the world remains littered with rural guerrilla movements, most of them representing minority ethnic groups and hanging on in the more rugged parts of Third World countries, but they generally have little prospect of success against local governments that can credibly invoke nationalism on their own side. If they ever try to move up from the low-intensity business of assassinations, car-bombs, and hit-and-run raids to more ambitious operations involving large units that stand and fight, they simply give the government forces the targets that they have been hoping for.

The most dramatic demonstration of how ineffective rural guerrilla warfare was outside the specific late colonial environment in which it had flourished was provided by the Cubans. They made a concerted effort in the middle and late 1960s to export the technique to the independent states of Latin America in the hope of bringing about Marxist revolutions there. Rural guerrilla movements sprang up in almost all the states of South America, Marxist in orientation and enjoying tacit or even open Cuban support. Without exception, they failed disastrously. The epitome of this failure was "Che" Guevara's own tragicomic attempt to start such a movement in Bolivia, which ended in his own death.

> Our isolation continues to be total; various illnesses have undermined the health of some comrades ... our peasant base is still underdeveloped, although apparently a program of planned terror will succeed in neutralizing most of them, and their support will come later. We have not had a single recruit (from the peasantry)....
> To sum up, a month in which all has evolved normally considering the standard development of a guerrilla war.
> – "Che" Guevara, Bolivia, April 1967.[6]

Six months later Guevara was dead and his little guerrilla band had been broken up – and the same fate eventually attended almost all the other attempts to copy the Cuban experience that had sprung up in Latin America. This is not to say that the technique can never work in independent countries, but rural guerrillas in Latin American countries had been eliminated or reduced to a merely marginal nuisance by 1970, except in Colombia (where they had their roots in a terrible civil war that had involved the whole country) and in Peru (where the Maoist "Shining Path" guerrillas drew their support from the ethnic Indian population of the highlands). Those two movements survive to this day, but another generation has brought them no closer to power. The inescapable conclusion – which was accepted by most Latin American revolutionaries – was that rural guerrilla warfare was another revolutionary technique that had failed.

3. URBAN TERRORISM

> It is necessary to turn political crisis into armed conflict by per-
> forming violent actions that will force those in power to transform
> the political situation of the country into a military situation [i.e.,
> carry out a military coup]. That will alienate the masses, who, from
> then on, will revolt against the army and police and blame them for
> this state of things.
>
> – Carlos Marighella, *Minimanual of the Urban Guerrilla.*[7]

The failure of classic rural insurgency in Latin America in the 1960s drove
numbers of disappointed revolutionaries into random terrorism (or rather,
urban guerrilla warfare, as it came to be known). In effect, the strategy of the
Latin American originators of this doctrine, most notably the Montoneros
of Argentina, the Tupamaros of Uruguay, and Brazilian revolutionaries like
Carlos Marighella, was aimed at driving the target regimes into extreme repression. It was what French Marxists have long called *la politique du pire* (the
policy of making things worse, in the hope of provoking a crisis and a decisive
break with the status quo).

By assassinations, bank robberies, kidnappings, hijackings, and the like,
all calculated to attract maximum publicity in the media and to embarrass
the government to the greatest possible extent, the "urban guerrillas" sought
to provoke the displacement of moderate, more or less democratic governments by tough military regimes, or to drive existing military regimes into
even stricter and more unpopular security measures. If the regime resorted to
counter-terror, torture, "disappearances," and death squads, all the better, for
the goal was to discredit the government and alienate it from the population.[8]

> First we kill all the subversives; then, their collaborators; later, those
> who sympathize with them; afterward, those who remain indiffer-
> ent; and finally, the undecided.
>
> – General Iberico Saint Jean,
> governor of Buenos Aires province during the terror.[9]

In a number of Latin American countries, the urban guerrillas did accomplish the first phase of their strategy: the creation of thoroughly nasty and brutally repressive military governments dedicated to destroying them. But what then happened was that those regimes proceeded to do precisely that. In Argentina, perhaps the worst-hit country, the military seized power from an ineffectual and discredited civilian government in May 1976, and instituted a reign of terror that ultimately killed between 15,000 and 30,000 people. Most of them were kidnapped off the streets or from their homes, tortured for some days in military bases, and then killed and their bodies buried in unmarked graves or dumped into the sea. The majority of those murdered by the military regime were innocent of any crime, a fact of which the soldiers were well aware. They, too, were pursuing a strategy of deliberate terrorism, but with all the resources of a modern state behind it. In every Latin American country where the urban guerrilla strategy was attempted, the vast majority of the revolutionaries ended up dead or in exile. Their principal achievement was to cause a military reign of terror that blighted the lives of a whole generation in a number of South American countries.

As in the case of rural guerrilla warfare outside the colonial environment, the fatal flaw in the urban guerrilla strategy was that it lacked an effective endgame. The theory said that when the guerrillas had succeeded in driving the government into a sufficiently repressive posture, the populace would rise up in righteous wrath and destroy its oppressors. But even if the population should decide that it is the government and not the guerrillas that is responsible for its growing misery, just how is it to accomplish this feat? By the urban uprisings that have rarely succeeded since the nineteenth century? Or by the rural guerrilla warfare that has just demonstrated its ineffectiveness?

4. Designer Terrorism

The faint and even more foolish echo of these Latin American terrorist strategies were the terrorist movements espousing mostly "Trotskyist" ideologies that flourished in Western Europe and North America during the 1970s and 1980s. Their main ideological guru was American academic Herbert Marcuse, who wrote about the need to "unmask the repressive tolerance of the liberal bourgeoisie" through creative violence that forced them to drop their liberal mask and reveal their true repressive nature – standard Latin American Marxist rhetoric from the previous decade – whereupon the revolutionary masses would rise up and overthrow them. As Richard Huffman wrote of the leading West German group of urban terrorists:

> The Baader-Meinhof Gang certainly didn't expect to win their war by themselves. They assumed an epic proletarian backlash would be the Revolution's true engine. They assumed their wave of terror would force the state to respond with brutal, reflexive anger. They assumed that West German civil liberties and civil rights would be quashed as the state turned the clock back 25 years. They assumed that the proletarian West Germans would react in horror as the true nature of their own government was revealed. They assumed that factory workers, bakers and miners would be inspired to smash their own oppressors. They assumed that they would be the vanguard of a movement where millions of Germans brought Revolution home. They assumed a lot.[10]

This was designer terrorism by celebrity terrorists, as much about radical chic as about real politics. The Red Army Faction (the formal name of the Baader-Meinhof Gang) was so well known for its preference for BMWs when stealing cars that their favourite model became popularly known in West Germany as the "Baader-Meinhof-Wagen." The urban guerrillas who flourished in the 1970s and 1980s in West Germany, Italy, the United States, and a few other countries in the developed world killed several hundred people and generated several hundred thousand headlines during their relatively brief moment in the limelight, but they never threatened any government anywhere. Leonard Cohen captured their naiveté and narcissism perfectly in his sardonic song "First We Take Manhattan":

> I'm guided by a signal in the heavens.
> I'm guided by this birthmark on my skin.

I'm guided the beauty of our weapons.
First we take Manhattan. Then we take Berlin.

From "Famous Blue Raincoat"

If the Baader-Meinhof Gang in Germany, the Red Brigades in Italy, the Symbionese Liberation Army and the Weathermen in the United States, the Japanese Red Army and the like had any influence at all on events, it was chiefly as bogeymen useful to right-wing governments seeking to vilify their legitimate left-wing opponents, but even in that humble role they were not very useful. Nationalist urban guerrillas operating from a religious or ethnic minority base like the Provisional Irish Republican Army in Northern Ireland and Euskadi ta Askatasuna (ETA) in Spain's Basque provinces showed greater staying power and killed more people – "It's not the bullet with my name on it that worries me. It's the one that says 'To Whom It May Concern,'" said an anonymous Belfast resident[11] – but they could almost certainly have made more progress toward their political goals in less time by the politics of non-violent protest. After decades of struggle, the IRA abandoned violence in 1997 in favour of a legitimate political role in Northern Ireland's affairs for its political wing, Sinn Fein. ETA, though it declared several cease-fires, is still fighting, but making no progress.

Political repression of Catholics in Northern Ireland generated enough popular resentment to support thirty or forty years of killing before the urban guerillas finally laid down their guns, and there is still enough resentment about Franco-era repression in Spain's Basque provinces to provide a limited base of support for ETA's campaign. But elsewhere, in places where there was no history of serious repression, nationalist urban guerillas found that they could not even get their project off the ground. The Quebec Liberation Front (Front de Libération du Québec – FLQ) was typical of these non-starters: a few dozen sub-Marxist intellectuals who believed that acts of exemplary violence would mobilize the French-Canadian masses behind their dream of a socialist republic of Quebec. They killed five people in all, and in 1970 they managed to panic the federal government into declaring a state of emergency, flooding the streets of Montreal with troops, and arresting several hundred innocent

Québécois nationalist intellectuals (standard *politique du pire* stuff). But in the permissive and law-abiding context of Canadian and Quebec politics they simply could not persuade many people that their resort to violence was legitimate. They almost all ended up in jail or in Cuban exile, and some of the ex-leaders are now to be found holding court at their favourite tables in various watering holes in Outremont, terrorists from a bygone age on display for intellectual tourists.

There have been two terrorist groups that did find a way to make an impact on events, however. Both of them made their mark with international operations, both had political aims that did not require the overthrow of the target governments – and both were Arab.

5. Palestine Liberation Organization

> Palestine is the cement that holds the Arab world together, or it is the explosive that blows it apart.
>
> – Yasser Arafat[12]

The Palestine Liberation Organization was founded by Yasser Arafat in 1964 as an umbrella organization that would coordinate a strategy for the many and ideologically disparate armed groups that were forming in the refugee camps that were home to most of the Palestinians who had fled or been driven from Israel in 1948. Most Palestinians had been politically quiescent for a long time, waiting for the Arab states to restore them to their homes by war, but in the aftermath of the catastrophic Arab military defeat of 1967 they recognized the hopelessness of depending on other Arabs for help. Arafat's key insight was to realize that while Palestinian armed groups stood no chance of defeating Israel and regaining their homes by force – they were even weaker than the Arab states and could do nothing except launch futile terrorist attacks – their energies might produce useful results if directed at a different goal.

Arafat and his colleagues had come to understand that their most important task was to re-brand the "refugees" as "Palestinians." So long as they were seen by non-Arabs (and even by some Arabs) as merely generic "Arab refugees," then they were only pawns in other people's games. They could theoretically be resettled – at least in the eyes of the West and in the insistent view of Israeli propaganda – anywhere in the Arab world. If they were ever to have any chance of going home, therefore, the first priority must be a campaign to convince the world that there was such an identity as "Palestinian" – for merely to call people by that name is implicitly to accept that they have some legitimate claim to the land of Palestine. Some Zionists seize upon this fact to suggest that the Palestinian identity is artificial, but it would be fairer to say that the transformation of the word "Palestinian" from purely a regional description to a genuine national identity was a result of the experience of loss and exile. It is probably also true to say that the Palestinians have come increasingly to resemble their enemy, as long-term opponents often do – longing for the lost land is a familiar theme in Jewish culture and a large part of Israeli identity.

So what kind of campaign might convince the world that there really are Palestinians? Not an advertising campaign, certainly, but a campaign of international terrorism might do the job. Carry out shocking acts of newsworthy violence and the media will have to report them – and to explain them, they'll have to talk about Palestinians. In September 1970, the Popular Front for the Liberation of Palestine organized the simultaneous hijacking of four airliners, which they then flew to a desert airfield in Jordan and destroyed before the world's television cameras after the passengers had been removed. Subsequent attacks cost many lives, but this was international terrorism with a rational and achievable objective: not to bring Israel to its knees, let alone the entire West, but simply to force everybody to accept that there is a Palestinian people and that they must be active participants in the discussion of their own fate. And once that objective was achieved in the late 1980s, the PLO called off the terrorists (though some maverick small groups continued to wage a private and pointless campaign on their own).

It wasn't pretty, but it was effective – and for almost a decade after 1988 the PLO essentially avoided terrorism while pursuing the goal of a negotiated peace settlement with Israel. Unfortunately, Arafat proved to be a maddeningly indecisive negotiator, and both he and his key negotiating partner, Israeli prime minister Yitzhak Rabin, found their freedom of action increasingly circumscribed by the "rejectionist" forces in their own community: Likud and the religious parties in Israel, Hamas, Islamic Jihad, and some of the smaller secular Marxist movements among the Palestinians. These parties and groups refused to contemplate the kinds of concessions (on land, and on the right of return for refugees) that would be needed for a peace settlement.

After Rabin was assassinated by a Jewish right-wing extremist in 1995, Palestinian terrorist attacks resumed, this time in Israel itself in the midst of an election campaign – but the authors of these attacks were the rising movements that flatly rejected the idea of a territorial compromise with Israel that would create a Palestinian state in only a small part of the former British mandate of Palestine. It was another terrorist operation with limited and achievable political goals, but this time directed as much at thwarting Arafat as at killing Israelis. The purpose of the Hamas and Islamic Jihad bombing campaign, which particularly targeted buses to produce high casualties, was to drive Israeli voters away from Rabin's successor Shimon Peres, who was widely expected to win easily on a sympathy vote after the assassination, and into the arms of the Likud Party's Binyamin Netanyahu, a closet rejectionist who could be counted on to stall indefinitely on peace negotiations with Arafat.

It worked: the bombs swung the election to Likud, and there was virtually no progress on a peace settlement for the next three years. While it would be wrong to talk of tacit collaboration between the rejectionists on the two sides to thwart the realization of a "two-state solution" where Israeli and Palestinian states live side by side between the Jordan River and the sea, it would be quite accurate to describe them (in the favourite term of the older generation of Marxists) as "objective allies" – and their principal tool for thwarting moves in that direction is violence.

6. SALAFISTS

The nations of infidels have all united against Muslims.... This is a new battle, a great battle, similar to the great battles of Islam like the conquest of Jerusalem.... [The Americans] come out to fight Islam in the name of fighting terrorism. These events have split the whole world into two camps, the camp of belief and the camp of disbelief.

– Osama bin Laden, October 2002

Terrorism is still not a useful tool for overthrowing governments directly, but it has been developed in recent decades into a quite flexible tool for achieving other, less sweeping political objectives. An appalling but very effective example of this was the terrorist attacks carried out against the United States by al-Qaida on September 11, 2001.

The Salafist project that animates al-Qaida and its many clones and affiliates starts from the proposition that the current sorry plight of the Muslim countries is due to the fact that they are half-Westernized and lax in their observance of Islam. This has caused God to withdraw his support from his people, and it can be regained only when Muslims are once again living their faith as God truly intends it to be lived – in the Salafists' rather extreme view of how Muslims should live.

On this analysis is built a two-stage project for changing the world. In stage one, all the existing governments of the Muslim countries must be overthrown so that the Salafists can take their places and use the power of the state to bring Muslims back to the right ways of believing and behaving. Then, once all of the world's Muslims are living properly, God will be on their side again, and it will be possible to move on to stage two and unite the whole of the Muslim world in a single, borderless super-state that will take on and overthrow the domination of the West. In the more extreme formulations, this will culminate with the conversion of the entire world to Islam.

Relatively few Muslims accept this analysis or support this project, but their numbers are greater in the Arab world than elsewhere because those are the countries where rage and despair at the current situation are strongest. As a result, there have been active Salafist revolutionary groups in most of the larger Arab countries for over a quarter-century already. Their first goal is to overthrow the existing governments and take power themselves in order to get on with stage one of the Salafist program, and their main tool is terrorism. Ever since the late 1970s, countries like Egypt, Saudi Arabia, Syria, and Algeria have been the scene of numerous terrorist attacks – and unsurprisingly, the Salafists have failed to win power anywhere. Terrorism on its own does not overthrow governments: it didn't work for the Tupamaros, it didn't work for the Baader-Meinhof Gang, and there is no reason that it should work for the Salafists either.

What *can* overthrow a government (apart from a military coup, which is an unlikely way for Salafists to come to power) is a million people in the street. Then a real revolution may happen, either in the old-fashioned violent way or even in the more recent non-violent style, but first you have to get the million people out – and for Salafists they just won't come. They simply don't like or trust the Salafists enough to risk their own lives to bring them to power. The result in several Arab countries has been a long and bloody stalemate between Salafists and governments, with most people sitting out the struggle and wishing a curse on both their houses. The deadlock was already well established when Osama bin Laden founded al-Qaida in Afghanistan at the beginning of the 1990s.

From the beginning, al-Qaida's goal was to attack not Arab governments – that could be left to the existing Salafist movements in the various Arab countries – but to go after the West directly. Yet we must assume that al-Qaida's militants have not forgotten that their real goal is still to bring about revolutions in the Arab and other Muslim countries that will raise Salafists to power and get stage one of the project – the reformation of their people in the true path of Islamic observance – off the ground. So how would attacking the West directly help to bring those revolutions any nearer? How will it get the mobs out in the streets?

Terrorists will never tell you their strategies, but almost certainly it was the *politique du pire* all over again, this time in an international context. Only a very ignorant person would have believed that a terrorist attack on the United States that caused three thousand deaths would make the U.S. government withdraw from the Muslim world and abandon all its client governments there, and there is no sign that bin Laden and his associates were either ignorant or stupid. Any sensible person would have known that the U.S. government's reaction was bound to be one or more large, armed incursions into the Muslim world in an attempt to stamp out the roots of the terrorism, and that it would not be too careful about who got hurt in the process. There was a reasonable chance that America's actions would alienate so many Muslims and drive them into the arms of their local Salafist organizations, especially in the Arab countries, that they might finally revolt against their pro-Western governments and bring the Salafists to power instead.

> Firstly, we stress the loyal intentions that fighting should be in the name of God only, not in the name of nationalist ideologies, nor to seek victory for the ignorant governments that rule all Arab states, including Iraq.
> – Osama bin Laden, just before the U.S. invasion of Iraq.[13]

If tricking the United States into marching into one or more Muslim countries was the strategic purpose of al-Qaida's 9/11 attacks on New York and Washington, it has to be conceded that bin Laden has had a reasonable return on his investment: within twenty months, the United States had invaded and occupied two Muslim countries containing 50 million people. The images that accompanied the invasions caused great distress and humiliation to Muslims, and the inevitable brutalities and mistakes of the subsequent military occupations of Afghanistan and Iraq produced a steady flow of further images in the same vein. The anger these caused no doubt pushed millions of Muslims, especially in the Arab world, into the arms of the Salafists revolutionary organizations, but at the time of writing this had not succeeded in producing any revolutions that actually brought Salafists to power in a Muslim country.

It is easy to overestimate the insight of the al-Qaida planners and the power that their mastery of terrorist techniques confers upon them. While they undoubtedly expected the United States to respond to 9/11 by invading Afghanistan to eliminate their bases there, they probably counted on a prolonged Afghan resistance of the sort that greeted the Soviet invasion of 1979. In fact, the United States rapidly conquered and subdued the entire country by making alliances with various local warlords who opposed Taliban rule and destroyed al-Qaida's camps without ever putting very large numbers of American soldiers on the ground as targets. This did not go well with the announced American aim of bringing "democracy" to Afghanistan, but it did minimize Afghan opposition to the occupation and also American casualties (always a major political consideration given the extreme aversion to casualties back home).

The loss of al-Qaida's bases in Afghanistan was a nuisance for the organization, no doubt, but not a disaster, as it was already a highly decentralized network with very small logistical requirements. Since it presented no further military targets of any significance after the occupation of Afghanistan, the logical thing for the United States to have done after the end of 2001 was to shift from military mode to a more traditional anti-terrorist operation: terrorists are civilians, not an army, and the appropriate tools for dealing with them are normally police forces, intelligence gathering, and security measures, not armoured brigades. Al-Qaida's planners could not have anticipated that the United States, instead of concentrating on terrorism, would then proceed to attack Iraq as well – al-Qaida began the process of planning 9/11 almost two years before the U.S. election of November 2000, and in any case its leaders were probably unaware of the neo-conservative agenda of those who would subsequently populate the cabinet of President George W. Bush. But it is that further invasion which may yet bring the balance sheet on the 9/11 operation into the black for al-Qaida.

7. "War on Terror" is Misleading

How big might the "international terrorist threat" get? So far, al-Qaida is still operating in the same technological universe that the PLO exploited thirty years before (although with radically different political objectives). It discovered a new use for hijacked airliners that depended on the unforeseen innovation of teams of suicide hijackers, including trained pilots, but that was a one-time-only surprise and there do not appear to be dozens of further unexplored techniques of similar power lying around waiting to be tried. All al-Qaida's subsequent attacks to date have been thoroughly conventional low-tech bombings that caused no more than a couple of hundred deaths at worst.

These attacks can have significant political effect when they are well-timed, like the bombs on Madrid commuter trains three days before the Spanish election of March 2004, which may well have swung the election outcome against the incumbent conservative government that had supported the U.S. invasion of Iraq. This is not exactly a brand-new tactic, however: two of the three major

North Vietnamese offensives were staged in the U.S. election years of 1968 and 1972, and the third was timed to take advantage of the aftermath of the Watergate crisis in 1975. As for the possibility of terrorism with so-called weapons of mass destruction, it is neither new, nor would it utterly transform the situation. It is known that one faction of the Baader-Meinhof Gang in Germany was experimenting with biological weapons in the 1980s, and in the United States a terrorist (now believed to be an American extremist rather than a Salafist) sent letters dusted with weaponized anthrax spores in late 2001; only four or five people were killed. The Japanese sect Aum Shinrikyo actually released sarin-type nerve gas on the Tokyo subway in 1995; only twelve people were killed. The practical problem with both chemical and biological agents is dispersal; the attackers listed above would all have got better results for less effort out of nail bombs.

A nuclear weapon in terrorist hands would be a much bigger problem, of course, and has been the subject of relentless speculation and dozens of novels and films over the past twenty years. But a single nuclear weapon is a local disaster, comparable in scale to the Krakatoa volcanic explosion of 1883 or the Tokyo earthquake of 1923. We should obviously strive very hard to prevent it, but even a nuclear detonation in some unhappy city some time in the future, if it were to occur, should not stampede the world into doing what the terrorists want – and what they almost always want is an overreaction of some sort. Terrorism is a kind of political jiu-jitsu in which very small, weak groups use the limited amounts of force that they can bring to bear in ways that trick their far more powerful opponents – usually states – into responding in ways that harm the opponent's cause and serve the terrorists' own purposes.

The world lived for forty years with the daily threat of a global nuclear holocaust that would have destroyed hundreds of cities and hundreds of millions of lives at a stroke. It can live with the distant possibility that some terrorist group some day might get possession of a single nuclear weapon and bring horror to a single city. The point is not to panic, and not to lose patience. The "war on terror" is a deeply misleading phrase, for wars can sometimes be won. It makes more sense if we regard it as a metaphor similar to the "war on crime" that is declared from time to time: it may succeed in getting the crime *rate* down, but nobody expects that all the criminals will come out with their hands up one day, after which there will be no more crime.

I'm afraid that terrorism didn't begin on 9/11 and it will be around for a long time. I was very surprised by the announcement of a war on terrorism because terrorism has been around for thirty-five years … [and it] will be around while there are people with grievances. There are things we can do to improve the situation, but there will always be terrorism. One can be misled by talking about a war, as though in some way you can defeat it.

– Stella Rimington, former director-general
of MI5, September 2002

Notes

1   Mao Tse-tung, *Strategic Problems in the Anti-Japanese Guerrilla War* (1939).

2   Walter Laqueur, *Guerrilla* (London: Weidenfeld and Nicholson, 1977), 40.

3   Mao Tse-tung (1936). "Problems of Strategy in China's Revolutionary War" (5.3). December. In vol. 1, *Selected Works of Mao Tse-tung* (Beijing: Foreign Languages Press Edition, 1965).

4   Henry A. Kissinger, "The Vietnam Negotiations," *Foreign Affairs*. January 1969.

5   Christon I. Archer, John R. Ferris, Holger H. Herwig, and Timothy H.E. Travers, *World History of Warfare* (London: Cassell, 2003), 558.

6   Bowyer J. Bell, *The Myth of the Guerrilla* (New York: Knopf, 1971).

7   Quoted in Robert Moss, *Urban Guerrillas* (London: Temple Smith, 1972), 13.

8   Ibid., 198.

9   First quoted in the *Boletin de las Madres de la Plaza de Mayo* (May 1985). Reproduced in Robin Morgan, *The Demon Lover: On the Sexuality of Terrorism* (London: Methuen, 1989).

10 Richard Huffman, "The Gun Speaks: The Baader-Meinhof Gang and the West German Decade of Terror 1968–1977," The Baader-Meinhof Gang at the Dawn of Terror, http://www.baader-meinhof.com/gun/index.htm (accessed March 31, 2007).

11 Quoted in *Time*, November 11, 1974.

12 Taped broadcast on al-Jazeera (February 12, 2003).

13 Broadcasting by Al-Jazeera, purported to be Osama Bin-Laden, as reported in *The Guardian*, February 12, 2003.

CHAPTER 2

How Canada Confronts Terrorism: Canadian Responses to 9/11 in Historical and Comparative Context

Reg Whitaker
University of Victoria

1. Introduction

To assess the impact of 9/11 on Canada, historical and comparative perspectives are helpful. I will offer two historical precedents in Canada, followed by some comparative context for Canada's post-9/11 actions in the experience of Canada's closest neighbours, the United States and the UK.[1]

When Canada joined the 'war on terrorism' after the attacks of September 11, the decision was not without historical precedents in the postwar world. The Cold War, especially in its initial stages from 1945 to the early 1950s, and the 1970 October Crisis in Quebec offer two intriguing parallels to the present situation, with a number of useful lessons to be drawn from these experiences.

2. The Cold War

In the late 1940s, Canada went to 'war,' called a Cold War, against Soviet Communism. Just as Canadian troops have found themselves fighting 'terrorists' on the front lines in Afghanistan, Canadian soldiers in the Cold War soon found themselves battling 'communists' in Korea. Both wars included a home front, and the identification of enemies within. Both wars involved Canada in ever closer integration with the Americans, the generals directing the conflicts. Both wars, especially in their initial, anxious, stages, raise issues of individual and group rights in contrast to the demands of the community for security.

The first public notice that the wartime alliance was about to break down into the inter-bloc rivalry called the Cold War occurred in, of all places, Ottawa. How this small, dull, rather provincial capital became the focal point for great power conflict in 1945/46 is part of Canadian mythology. Igor Gouzenko, the first important Soviet defector, exposed a spy ring operated by Canada's ostensible wartime ally, the USSR, exploiting the willingness of Canadians sympathetic to Communism to betray their own country on behalf of a higher loyalty to the Socialist motherland.[2] Canada, it was said, experienced a sudden wake-up call,[3] communicated this to its allies, and then settled in for a prolonged struggle on many fronts with the new enemy, once its senior partner had taken overall charge.

The struggle lasted four decades, and for most of this time, Canada was a very junior partner, toiling in alliance obscurity, very occasionally raising a cautious criticism, only to be quickly cuffed for its temerity. But it is important to understand that when the Gouzenko spy scandal broke, first in secret in September 1945 and then publicly in February 1946, Canada was, in important ways, on its own without clear models to guide it. It consulted and received advice from its close allies, but it had to work out the details itself. Its response stamped a distinctive 'made in Canada' look to Canadian Cold War security policy.[4]

Once the extent of Soviet espionage and Canadian complicity had become apparent from the documents and information Gouzenko brought with him, the government of Canada acted with what might be called the firm smack of Prussian command. There was a secret Order in Council, known only to three cabinet ministers, under the authority of the War Measures Act, even though the war had been over a few weeks before Gouzenko defected, empowering the government to act against the suspected spies with little or no regard for civil liberties, and outside the normal processes of the legal system. Armed with this, the government then bided its time, consulted its allies, studied the

2: HOW CANADA CONFRONTS TERRORISM

evidence, watched the suspects, and waited for the right moment to strike in light of the international scene.

When it did strike, in mid-February 1946, it was with a series of dawn raids by black-leather-jacketed members of the drug squad of the Royal Canadian Mounted Police (RCMP), who entered Ottawa homes and apartments without specific warrants and detained a dozen people (more followed in the days and weeks ahead), seizing papers and documents. The detainees were transported to the RCMP barracks, where they were interrogated for weeks on end. The detainees were not arrested under criminal charges; they were unrepresented by counsel; *habeas corpus* was ignored. Then they were brought before a secret tribunal, a royal commission of inquiry, a formidable establishment body, headed by two Supreme Court justices, with commission counsel being the president of the Canadian Bar Association. They were still without legal representation, told they had no choice but to answer all questions put to them, deliberately not informed that they had the right of protection against self-incrimination, and bullied and harried by the commission counsel.

At the end of these proceedings, the commission published a lengthy and widely read report in which it named some two dozen persons as spies and traitors to their country.[5] The detainees were then turned over to the courts, where various charges were brought against them, under various statutes, but particularly the draconian *Official Secrets Act*, which made communication of classified information to a foreign power a serious offence but did not distinguish between information that might be damaging and information that was harmless, and which laid the burden of proof upon the accused. Despite what appeared to be a stacked deck, only about half of the two dozen eventually charged with criminal offences as a result of the inquiry were ever convicted. Those who had incriminated themselves before the Commission were in all cases found guilty in court. Those who had resisted were mainly acquitted. Nevertheless, with one minor exception, all those acquitted were denied further employment with the government.

At the time, there was not a great deal of criticism of the government's methods. Public opinion approved, by and large, and important sections of elite opinion, especially within the legal community, seemed unperturbed. In retrospect, critics have described the treatment of the suspects as abusive of their rights and a serious violation of liberal democratic norms. Some have even compared Canadian behaviour unfavourably with the United States, which, even in the dark days of McCarthyism, did not round up suspects before dawn, hold and interrogate them incommunicado, and haul them before secret tribunals, which would later officially name them as traitors without legal recourse.

Although important, these criticisms do not get at the rationale for the government's methods. Contextually, this was a pre-Charter (and pre–Bill of Rights) era, and it followed immediately upon a war in which extraordinary state action against dissidents – detention without trial; search and seizure; censorship; even the forcible relocation of the entire Japanese-Canadian community from the west coast to camps in the interior, and the confiscation of their property – had been not only tolerated, but sanctioned by the highest authorities in the land. In this context, faced with clear evidence of espionage and betrayal of trust, government reached for the most expedient administrative method for protecting national security. A precedent was being set for a relatively low priority on civil liberties in peacetime, albeit the twilight peacetime of the Cold War.

There was more to the government's response than context alone. There was a consistent pattern, a single thread that ran through all its planning and execution with regard to how to handle the explosive spy affair. The government wished to maintain maximum control over the story, to frame it in the most appropriate manner, and to control its effects, both internal and external. In terms familiar to today's world, the government wanted to manage the 'spin.' There were good reasons for this. Externally, Canada found itself in a highly exposed position vis-à-vis the spy affair. At a time when the wartime alliance had not yet broken down publicly, a wrong move by Canada might precipitate grave consequences for East-West relations. Prime Minister Mackenzie King wanted no part of such a critical international role. That would be left to the big battalions of the Americans and the British. Thus the Soviet angle of the affair was systematically played down in the Commission report. Others might draw strongly anti-Soviet lessons, but Canada would not.

The other reason for keeping spin control under government wraps was domestic, and here the wisdom of the government became apparent only later. In downplaying the Soviet role, the government also chose to highlight the role of communism in subverting the loyalties of Canadians. There was genuine shock and dismay at the evidence that some Canadians held a higher loyalty to a foreign power and were willing to serve that power over their own country. The Commission report was an attempt at public education and public warning about the dangers of dabbling in extreme left-wing ideas. It could also be seen as an exercise in *political policing*, setting authoritative boundaries on permissible limits of dissent. But this could itself be a dangerous process, spinning out of control as rivals to the party in power sought to exploit the politics of loyalty. Without strict limits, and outside direct supervision by the Crown, the politics of loyalty could become divisive and socially and politically destructive.

Indeed, shortly after the Gouzenko affair had been put to bed, anti-communism in the United States threatened just this sort of anarchy. In 1947, the House Committee on Un-American Activities began its Hollywood witch hunt, and by 1950 Senator Joe McCarthy was launching his demagogic anti-communist smear campaign that gave the English language a dark epithet, 'McCarthyism.' Before McCarthyism had run its course by 1954, the integrity of such institutions as the U.S. Presidency and the Army was threatened. In 1946, the Canadian government did not foresee these developments, but by strictly controlling the Gouzenko story and its effects, they did pre-empt the emergence of potential Canadian McCarthys, one of whom was no less than the leader of the opposition by 1948, George Drew, who tried but failed to forge a demagogic anti-communist role for himself.

There was a direct link between the Gouzenko affair and the government of Canada's Cold War internal security policies. In its aftermath, the security screening system was set in place for civil servants, for immigrants and refugees, and for citizenship applicants. The screening system was also extended to defence industries and even to shipping on the Great Lakes. In all cases, the process was kept as secret as possible, with 'security' never being advanced as a reason for limiting a person's employment, or their admission to Canada or to citizenship. For many years, there was no appeal process for persons denied security clearance.

There were American pressures to step up security. The Americans were evangelical in their Cold War crusade, and from time to time thought it necessary to nudge, or push, their allies to shape up to appropriate (i.e., American) standards. Sometimes they were particularly insistent upon doing something that the Canadians deemed silly or excessive, and usually the Canadians complied, with weary resignation, on the principle that it would be more costly to provoke them. Yet, by and large, Cold War security policies were made in Canada. Canadians set their own rules for security screening and always sharply distinguished themselves from the United States by pointedly not referring to 'loyalty' or 'disloyalty,' but only to *risk*. What distinguished the two approaches were the secrecy in which the Canadian policy was administered, and its strict monopolization by the executive branch of the federal government. For the most part, it was Ottawa that prosecuted the Cold War on the home front, and Ottawa kept its cards well hidden. When opposition voices were raised to demand information, Ottawa tended to respond serenely (or smugly) that it was taking care of matters, that details were the business of the proper authorities, and that the operative principle was: 'trust us.'

Witch hunts wracked McCarthy-era America at all levels of government and throughout civil society. Not in Canada – at least, not publicly. In point of fact, there were purges, and there were victims. There was a witch hunt at the National Film Board (NFB), and scores of people lost their jobs and saw their careers suffer. But unlike the witch hunt in Hollywood, there were few headlines, and no names bandied about in the media. The government even denied there was a purge, insisting officially that only three persons had been removed. Behind the scenes, they gave the Security Service and a new, purged, NFB management a blank cheque to remove persons on suspicion, and by the end, some 35 permanent or contract employees were terminated or encouraged to depart before they were targeted, although the total number could only be confirmed by documents released under Access to Information requests many decades later.[6] The position of Canadian officials was that the politicization of security issues inherently risked illiberalism, and they could point to the U.S. example as confirmation. Some of the victims of these silent purges have different views in retrospect. The Hollywood witch hunt resulted in blacklists and blighted careers, but finally in the public vindication of those purged, who have been transformed from villains in the 1950s to virtual folk heroes decades later. The Canadian victims of the NFB purge received neither notoriety then nor public vindication later. For better or for worse, that was the Canadian Way.

Security screening of immigrant/refugee and citizenship applicants involved Canada in extensive and persistent application of a double standard with regard to potential New Canadians.[7] Applicants with left-wing backgrounds or associations were security risks, while those with right-wing backgrounds were generally welcomed as anti-communists. This had unfortunate implications for lax treatment of Nazi war criminals and collaborators – ultimately subject to a Royal Commission of Inquiry and a special section of the Justice department designated for retroactively tracking down war criminals and criminal collaborators who had passed through the security screen. It also meant that Canada put out the welcome mat for refugees from communism (Hungary in 1956/57; Southeast Asia in the late 1970s), while making it difficult for refugees fleeing right-wing violence (Chile in the 1970s, Central America in the 1980s). Apart from double political standards, Cold War immigration security firmly established a precedent of highly state-centred procedures. Immigration was deemed a privilege, not a right. Risk was determined by the state, and doubt must be resolved in favour of the state, not the individual. Moreover, procedurally, the deck was highly stacked in favour of the Crown, with non-disclosure of evidence and *ex parte* proceedings the norm in deportation cases.

Security screening has been an important tool for the political policing of Canadian society. The Security Service, first the RCMP and later the Canadian Security Intelligence Service (CSIS), has routinely used screening as an effective instrument for establishing sources within suspect organizations: the threat of lost employment, or worse, of deportation, is an effective persuader for cooperation. As an offshoot of this and of its preparation of threat assessments for the government, the security service amassed a remarkable volume of dossiers on Canadians and Canadian civil society. When the McDonald Commission of Inquiry investigated RCMP wrongdoing in the late 1970s, it discovered that the security service held files on no less than 800,000 individuals and organizations – a proportion of the population watched by the secret police that would have done credit to some less savoury regimes abroad.[8]

While Americans might be leading the Cold War charge, Canada was quite capable of setting and enforcing its own stiff standards for security. Even when pushed further in particulars than they might prefer by the Americans, Canadian Cold War policy was essentially made in Canada, according to Canadian imperatives, and in the end did not look that different from the Americans in content, although it did differ in style. What was most distinctive about Canadian Cold War security policy was its strict control by the executive branch of the federal government, and the zeal with which the federal government guarded its prerogatives. The federal government had responsibility for external relations and for peace, order, and good government within Canada. The differential, and sometimes invidious, effects of national security on individuals and groups in Canadian society were unfortunate by-products, but the security of the state and order in the community normally took precedence over individual and group rights.

3. THE OCTOBER CRISIS

When Canada faced the aftermath of the horrific attacks of 9/11, and the requirement to join in a new global war on terrorism, it did have an historical precedent. In October 1970, Canada faced its worst internal security crisis, when cells of the violent separatist group, *Le Front de Libération du Québec* (FLQ) kidnapped the British trade commissioner, James Cross, and kidnapped and later murdered the Quebec Minister of Labour, Pierre Laporte. Canada was thrust at this time into a harsh global spotlight amid a rising tide of anxiety and uncertainty at home, and conflicting calls for negotiating with the terrorists or for staring them down. To make matters more difficult for the federal government, this was primarily a domestic terrorist crisis (in spite of ineffectual attempts to link the FLQ to wider terrorist networks, or even to communism), with potentially serious consequences for Canada-Quebec relations. Faced with this mushrooming crisis, Canada acted – swiftly, forcefully, with no regard for civil liberties. Invoking the *War Measures Act* under a putative, but never proven, 'apprehended insurrection,' the federal government placed Quebec under what amounted to a state of martial law. Extensive use was made of the power to detain and interrogate without charge, without counsel, and without *habeas corpus*. The media were censored, and the FLQ was declared a banned organization, retroactive association with which could land someone in prison. In the aftermath of the crisis proper, the resources of the RCMP Security Service and the Quebec and Montreal police were mobilized to 'counter' and negate by virtually any means, fair or foul, the FLQ or its successors. In filling out the blank cheques issued them, the security and police forces so exceeded their lawful roles that their activities were subject to a series of federal and provincial commissions of inquiry.

However controversial the methods employed, the result was clear and unequivocal: the FLQ and, with it, the entire terrorist tendency of the sovereignty movement in Quebec was eradicated. From the early 1970s on, the sovereignty field was left entirely to the legitimate, lawful, and peaceful form of the Parti Québécois (PQ), and the contestation of federalism to democratic elections and referenda. Indeed, in surveying the contemporary history of terrorist movements around the world, the Canadian experience in stopping terrorism dead in its tracks and diverting the political energies that had helped drive the movement into constitutional channels, stands out as a quite remarkable success story. The FLQ also self-destructed with its wanton murder of Laporte, a senseless act that disgusted decent Quebecers. Above all, there were alternative, peaceful means of expression for sovereignist sentiment available. The PQ had just entered the National Assembly in Quebec elections earlier the same year. Force could be used successfully against illegitimate force, when legitimate channels existed.

Does the successful outcome of the affair offer retroactive justification to a government that in effect put liberal freedoms on hold and declared that the end justified the means? There are perhaps two answers to this question, and each has significance for how we understand the response of the government of Canada to 9/11.

First, it must be clearly stated that the Trudeau government during and after October 1970 was less than truthful or above board in its justification of its actions before Parliament and the public.[9] There was no 'apprehended insurrection': the failure of the government to follow up with supporting evidence for its claim in invoking wartime emergency powers was telling, for there was no such evidence, or at least nothing compelling. Moreover, the advice of the RCMP would have been against using emergency powers – if they had been consulted, which they were not. The government's retroactive justification leaned heavily on the alleged shortcomings of the intelligence on the terrorist groups provided by the security service that supposedly left them no choice but to round up all the usual suspects and sort them later. When I had documents on intelligence reports on the FLQ and other separatist groups declassified,[10] I discovered that this official rationale was seriously distorted. The distortions are unfair to the RCMP, who had in fact done a competent job of penetrating and reporting on violent separatist groups. They also constitute a reprehensible example of blaming the servants for the masters' misdeeds. The RCMP had even delivered a very clear warning in the summer of 1970 that the FLQ had adopted kidnappings as their priority tactic, and even specified diplomats and cabinet ministers as their likely targets. Yet the warnings were ignored, and potential targets were left unprotected (at the tragic cost of Laporte's life).

The RCMP believed that the crisis was essentially a criminal matter, to be solved by good, careful, patient police work. That was how, in the end, James Cross was liberated, and it might have saved Laporte's life. Instead, the government, or at least the prime minister and his close cabinet associates from Quebec (who in every instance of debate in cabinet proved to be the hawks), disingenuously citing an exaggerated threat they knew to be false, chose to perform a *coup de théatre*, a striking demonstration of the power of the federal government and the futility of violent resistance to it. From a liberal standpoint, the October Crisis offers a salutary warning about how the state can lie and use pretexts to aggrandize its power and crush opposition. From a Machiavellian standpoint, Trudeau skilfully manipulated a crisis not of his making to bring about a result that was in the national interest. It is ironic that Pierre Trudeau, whose historical reputation is that of the greatest Canadian liberal, the man who gave the country the Charter of Rights, should also be the man who presided over one of the more repressive state actions in our history. Some might argue that this experience gives the lie to his liberalism, while others might instead suggest that extraordinary challenges to liberalism require extraordinary defences.

Choosing between these alternative assessments is not easy. It is difficult to justify the Trudeau government's actions in misrepresenting facts and in shifting blame from themselves. On the other hand, a terrorist avenue that might have turned Quebec into an Ulster-style battleground was avoided, and the constitutional avenue for the sovereignty movement opened. Moreover, despite

2: How Canada Confronts Terrorism

dire predictions at the time that the fabric of liberal democracy had suffered irreparable harm from the arbitrary actions taken in 1970, the evidence suggests otherwise. As a long-term result of the crisis and its aftermath, the War Measures Act was later repealed and replaced with an emergency powers statute that is much more measured and balanced.[11] As a direct consequence of the post-crisis countering of the violent separatists by unlawful and improper means, the McDonald Commission recommendations led to the removal of the Security Service from the RCMP and the creation of a civilian agency with a specific legal mandate about what it is authorized and not authorized to do, and elaborate mechanisms of accountability, oversight, and review attached to its operations. These are positive gains for liberal democracy, which derive, paradoxically, from the violations of liberal democracy practised during the crisis. History, it should be remembered, does not always move in straight lines.

4. Keeping Up with the Neighbours? After 9/11

The war on terrorism differs from the two historical precedents in a number of particulars, despite certain *déjà vu* elements. Most significantly, 9/11 constituted a violent attack on American civil society, indeed the attacks appear to have been designed to spread fear throughout all levels of American life. Moreover, the targets have been publicly designated in al-Qaida pronouncements as *any* and *all* Americans, not being limited to state officials, military/security personnel, or corporate executives, as was the case with some earlier terrorist groups. The Cold War was only weakly felt as constituting a threat to the personal security of ordinary North Americans in their homes and families. The *subversive* threat of the communist 'enemy within' was largely a constructed abstraction that waxed briefly in the early, anxious, days of the Cold War, and then waned by the middle of the 1950s, when an uneasy stability took hold in East-West relations. The material threat to ordinary people in the Cold War was the spectre of nuclear holocaust, but this actually turned out to be a powerful factor pushing governments toward negotiating differences with the enemy and reducing the possibility of war. The diffuse threat of post-9/11 terrorism, on the other hand, works in the opposite direction, putting popular pressure on government to defeat and eliminate the terrorists, at whatever cost.

The war on terrorism is thus a somewhat more populist struggle than the Cold War, which was always primarily a matter of concern to states and state elites. The danger of populist authoritarianism is very real to vulnerable minorities – in this case, the Muslim and Arab communities – and to the fabric of liberal democracy. The Cold War witnessed a sustained assault on the civil liberties and democratic legitimacy of citizens singled out for their dissenting ideological views. The war on terrorism threatens entire minority communities based on their religion and ethnicity. States will no doubt always attempt to seize the opportunities offered by major security crises to enhance their coercive powers at the expense of individual and groups rights. Citing the 'wartime' terrorist threat, the Bush administration launched a series of assaults on the constitutional checks and balances that have traditionally curbed the excesses of executive power, even in wartime, while asserting a putative scope for unchecked presidential power unparalleled in American history. When governments have deep and enduring popular support in exploiting such opportunities, the long-term result promises to be bleak from a civil libertarian point of view.

9/11 was, however, not just an attack on civil society, but, in the first instance, an attack on *American* civil society. As a liberal, capitalist, 'infidel' democracy allied closely to the United States, Canada is obviously implicated as a target of terror attacks by extremist Muslim groups. A statement issued by Osama bin Laden in the fall of 2002 specifically threatened Canada along with other Western states associated with the United States. The train bombings in Madrid and the London Underground bombings of July 7, 2005, were grim reminders of how *any* Western society could be a target of terrorist atrocity. The Blair government in Britain and the former Spanish government at the time of the Madrid bombing had been leading allies of the United States in the invasion and occupation of Iraq, which may have particularly flagged the UK and Spain as targets. Even though Canada declined to join in the Iraq war, it has maintained, and under the Harper Conservative government stepped up, a military presence in southern Afghanistan in direct military confrontation with Taliban and al-Qaida guerrillas that may have identified it in the eyes of extremists as a leading Western enemy. In the spring of 2006, amid intense media attention, a combined RCMP-CSIS anti-terrorist unit announced the arrest of eighteen individuals from the Toronto area on charges under the post-9/11 Anti-Terrorism Act, with further arrests following in the UK and the United States. Authorities alleged a conspiracy to attack Canadian targets, including civilians. Just as the Gouzenko affair implicated Canada at the heart of the Cold War, so too the Toronto plot, if sustained in court, would seem to implicate Canada at the heart of the 'war on terror.'

Canada's apparent status as a terrorist target has not facilitated an easy partnership with the United States, any more than America's leadership of the West during the Cold War was absent of strains from time to time with America's northern neighbour. Canadians at the time of 9/11 sympathized with Americans and have continued since to support the general idea of the need for international co-operation to combat terrorism. Despite the successful coalition building activity of the U.S. administration around military intervention to bring down the Taliban regime in Afghanistan, the subsequent tendency of the Bush administration to pursue an aggressively unilateralist, 'America First' course put severe strains on a Western alliance that had remained relatively cohesive throughout the Cold War. The unsanctioned invasion and subsequent occupation of Iraq turned quickly into a fiasco, constituting perhaps the most colossal U.S. foreign policy error in the entire postwar era, and continues to be a festering sore in relations with the Muslim world, as did the inability or unwillingness of the Bush administration to force any amelioration of the position of the Palestinians under Israeli domination in the West Bank and Gaza. The Iraq War drew a sharp line of demarcation between Canada and the United States, involving critical Canadian public opinion as much as, if not more than, official government doubts about American judgment and intentions. The Liberal governments of Jean Chrétien and Paul Martin were seen by many in Washington as 'anti-American,' and the Conservatives under Stephen Harper as more favourably inclined to the Bush administration. The Harper government wants to be seen as following the lead of the popular new Democratic administration of President Barack Obama but ideologically is not on the same page as its American counterpart. Whatever the official stances of successive governments, the post-9/11 era has opened up serious differences between the two countries rather than deepening the closeness that has historically characterized the continent with the 'world's longest undefended border.' Canadians have thus tended to see the war on terrorism in practice as primarily an American, rather than a multilateral, struggle – a not unreasonable interpretation of the behaviour of the Bush administration, although less clear with regard to the more accommodative Obama administration – but one that constrains Canadian governments, whether Liberal or Conservative, in carrying out Canadian obligations in the war on terror.

Analysis of the policy response of the Canadian government to 9/11 suggests that Canada has actually been fighting a war on two fronts. One front is the public face of the war on terrorism, in which Canada fulfills its obligations as an ally in the broad coalition against terrorist movements and reassures its own citizens that it is doing what it can to protect their safety. The second front, less publicly acknowledged, is essentially damage limitation – not in relation to terrorist acts, but in relation to the potential collateral economic harm to Canadian interests caused by the U.S. interpretation of national security on its northern border. U.S. homeland security will be protected, either at the Canada-U.S. border or around a wider North American perimeter. If security is imposed along the border, it will be at an economic cost unacceptable to Canada, which sends more than 85 per cent of its exports to the United States.

Faced with a formidable big business lobby insistent on reopening the border for unimpeded commerce, at whatever political cost,[12] the Canadian government confronted an unsettling policy alternative: a North American security perimeter in which Canadian sovereignty would be seriously threatened by pressures to 'harmonize' its laws and practices along North American standards, which, given the disproportion of power between the two countries, would inevitably mean wholesale adoption of American standards. The Canadian policy dilemma on the second front has been how to reassure the United States sufficiently on border security so that commercial traffic can be maintained, while not surrendering a critical degree of Canadian sovereignty in the process.[13]

The two fronts are interrelated. Everything that Canada contributes to the war on terrorism, and to maintain strong security against terrorism within Canada, tends to relieve U.S. pressure on the border. The Canadian first front response has involved: substantially more resources for security and intelligence (close to $9 billion by 2006)[14]; development of a *National Security*

2: How Canada Confronts Terrorism

Strategy; a streamlined security decision-making structure within the federal government at both the political and bureaucratic levels, including the creation of a new umbrella ministry of Public Safety and Emergency Preparedness Canada[15]; new and expanded legal powers for anti-terrorist law enforcement and investigation; closer coordination and sharing of information with allies. All of these have helped maintain Canadian economic security by reassuring the United States that Canada is enforcing adequate security standards on its own. Yet they have not been enough.

Parallel to this track have been another series of initiatives by Canada under the rubric of the 'Smart Border' agreements.[16] These involve a series of ongoing negotiations with the United States on such matters as pre-clearance of container traffic at the point of origin; fast-tracking of safe persons and goods; collection and retention of a wide range of data on persons travelling by air across the border; the application of high-tech surveillance equipment along the border; expansion of Integrated Border Enforcement Teams; and, controversially, a 'safe third country' agreement to reduce the flow of refugees across the border. Critics in Canada, from those on the political right who have characterized border security measures as too little, too late, to those on the nationalist left who have tended to see them as sell-outs of sovereignty, have unanimously missed the point of the Canadian strategy. Rather than be trapped in sweeping negotiations on a mega-agreement over a Fortress North America perimeter security project (endorsed in the aftermath of 9/11 by a number of provincial premiers, the conservative opposition in Ottawa, and the influential Council of Canadian Chief Executives), the Canadian government engaged the Americans in a series of incremental negotiations, segmented but linked, which if successful would have had the cumulative effect of mollifying American security concerns, while keeping the flow of cross-border commerce more or less intact. The Canadian negotiators wished to minimize the larger loss of sovereignty necessarily entailed in any grander, macro-level integration and harmonization project. Unfortunately, although in many ways quite successful, this strategy has faltered in practice in the face of the obsessive 'security trumps economy' approach of the Americans, including the new Obama administration. The grand integration project, with all its inherent threats to Canadian sovereignty, thus remains on the table, a decade after 9/11.

Although Canadian governments have generally managed the second front of this two-front war with skill in the face of difficulties, it is a volatile process subject to unpredictable upsets. Certain politicians and journalists in the United States allude frequently to the alleged 'security risk' to America posed by lax Canadian security policies and a lamentably undefended northern border. An imagined Canadian Connection to 9/11 was doggedly investigated, but all leads came up empty. In fact, the U.S. State Department in its official report tracking global terrorist trends for the year 2001 explicitly denied any Canadian Connection and went on to describe Canadian co-operation in anti-terrorism as a model the United States would like to see practised with its other allies.[17] Yet as late as 2006, the same State Department produced a report attacking Canada for allegedly harbouring terrorists who exploit the "liberal Canadian immigration and asylum policies to enjoy safe haven, raise funds, arrange logistical support and plan terrorist attacks." As proof, the report named five "known terrorists" in Canada, but neglected to add that all five had been detained indefinitely by Canadian authorities (their detention being, presumably, how the United States had the names)![18] So absurd was this insinuation that the usually conservative *Globe and Mail* was moved to characterize the U.S. argument as "grotesque."[19] Nevertheless, when Canadian police prevented an alleged terrorist conspiracy with eighteen arrests in 2006, a number of U.S. politicians loudly demanded stiffer controls over the U.S.-Canadian border since Canada was obviously a refuge for terrorists. In fact, there is very little evidence that Canadian security is any less vigilant than American.[20] When Obama's new Homeland Security secretary tossed out the discredited canard about the 9/11 conspirators entering the United States across the northern border, Canadians, not surprisingly, were indignant. Although she eventually withdrew the false claim, Canadians were frustrated by the apparent lack of American progress in gaining a more realistic appreciation of the actual facts of the Canadian-American border. Although there had perhaps been a Canadian performance gap in the past, it was in enforcement and was attributable not to lower Canadian standards, but simply to fewer resources available to the Canadians relative to their U.S. counterparts. That gap had been closing even prior to 9/11, but certainly since that date, the gap has narrowed to negligible levels.

9/11's impact on Canada is by no means straightforward. Nor was the impact of the Cold War. Indeed, on the matter of Canadian sovereignty in North America, there is considerable continuity between the Cold War and the War on Terrorism. It is not a question of U.S. hegemony vs. Canadian resistance. Rather the lines are drawn within Canada, as they were during the Cold War, between those advocating greater integration with the United States and greater support for the American international position, and those wishing to limit that support and insisting on skepticism toward greater integration as a by-product of security co-operation. The latter camp must come to terms with the reality that there is underlying public support for the general stance of Canadian-American co-operation. During the Cold War, Canadians generally agreed that the communist bloc represented the chief security threat and accepted American leadership in contesting communism as appropriate. In the current crisis, Canadian opinion accepts that terrorism is the major security threat and supports Canadian participation, under American leadership, in confronting terrorism. Neither then nor now does this mean Canadian support for all aspects of American leadership or a willingness to follow the United States down any path – especially one entered upon in a unilateral fashion that ignores the UN and multilateral relationships. Yet underlying support, along with the inescapable economic realities of the existing degree of economic integration, limits the scope of open criticism of U.S. leadership, and fixes Canadian governments in the position of negotiating degrees of integration, rather than allowing the liberty of asking whether greater integration ought to take place.

Critics of government security policy after 9/11 charged that the anti-terrorist legislative changes brought before Parliament are largely a result of pressures to keep up with the American neighbour. Indeed, among these critics is the former director of CSIS, Reid Morden.[21] Yet on closer examination, there is rather less than meets the eye in this charge. Certainly some indirect pressure may have been applied on Canada to comply with a generally more stringent anti-terrorist regime that was falling into place after 9/11. In its centrepiece *Anti-Terrorism Act*,[22] Canada felt compelled to join in the multilateral anti-terrorist campaign by, for instance, developing a legal definition of terrorism that conformed to definitions in various international texts and in defining terrorist entities under Canadian law and listing them for the purposes of blocking the financing of terrorism, in conformity with international efforts sanctioned by the UN. Analysis of the *Anti-Terrorism Act*, as well as the *Public Safety Act*, discloses little that can be seen as directly responding to specifically American demands, as such, or reflecting American provisions and practices.

Upon reflection, it is not difficult to discern why the relationship between American and Canadian legislative initiatives is relatively weak. While the terrorist threat may be similar in all Western countries, each country has its own unique set of political institutions and processes, its own legal traditions, and its own specific political forces in play.

During the passage of the *Anti-Terrorist Act*, considerable controversy was generated by provisions for preventive arrest and investigative hearings: both were ultimately subjected to a sunset clause. Preventive arrest is strictly limited to forty-eight hours, although refusal to comply with terms of recognizance could result in imprisonment. At all times, however, a person held under preventive arrest is fully represented. Investigative hearings appear to be modelled to a degree on the U.S. grand jury system, but even where a person brought before such a hearing could be compelled to testify against others, Charter protection against self-incrimination is explicitly recognized. Yet neither of these extraordinary powers has ever been invoked. The projected use of the investigative hearing power during the Air India trial was sustained in the courts, which found that the power was constitutional, but in practice the government refrained from actually using the device. Surprisingly, when Parliament was asked to extend the powers beyond their original five-year life span, the combined opposition in a minority Parliament rejected the request, following a rancorous debate in which charges of being "soft on the Charter of Rights" were traded with charges of being "soft on terrorism" – a most un-Canadian spectacle in matters of national security where non-partisanship has usually been the rule. Ignoring the setback, the Conservatives simply reintroduced the two powers in the next session, apparently with greater chance of success the second time around. Yet even if returned to the anti-terror legal arsenal, the actual employment of these powers seems unlikely.

If this pattern persists, it will echo a precedent set during the early Cold War, when a series of amendments were made adding offences and stiffening penalties in the Criminal Code for treason, sabotage, sedition – all linked to the Cold War threat of communism. Critics at the time suggested, without evidence, that these changes had been initiated by American pressures. If so, pressure had been fruitless: no communist or communist sympathizer was ever charged under the amended provisions, which lay dormant for almost two decades, until the 1970 October Crisis, when a seditious conspiracy provision was dusted off and used against five people accused of being associated with the FLQ, newly banned under the *War Measures Act*. All such charges failed in court.[23] There is thus some precedent for tough-sounding legislative actions that prove to be more symbolic than substantive in intention.

The main reason for downplaying American pressures as a basis of Canadian legislation is that a great deal of the *Anti-Terrorism Act* is not directly related to 9/11 at all but answers to wider and deeper issues surrounding the legal and institutional framework for national security policy. Among the non-9/11 related elements of the *Anti-Terrorism Act*:

> The *Official Secrets Act* is replaced by a new *Security of Information Act*, including new offences, such as economic espionage.
>
> The Communications Security Establishment (CSE), the electronic eavesdropping agency, is for the first time given a statutory mandate, with its powers and limitations spelled out, and with an important additional power to retain Canadian communications related to terrorism (this is 9/11 related).
>
> Serious limitations are imposed on the *Access to Information*, *Privacy*, and *Personal Information Protection and Electronic Documents Acts* with regard to disclosure and retention of information relating to national security.
>
> Provisions regarding non-disclosure of sensitive national security evidence serve mainly to 'Charter-proof' existing evidence provisions following the *Stinchcombe* decision of the Supreme Court.[24]

Taken together with the *Canadian Security Intelligence Service Act* and the *Security Offences Act* of 1984 (the latter now augmented by An Act to Amend the Foreign Missions and International Organizations Act)[25] and the *Immigration and Refugee Protection Act*,[26] both passed just prior to 9/11, the latter itself amended by C-36, the Anti-Terrorism Act constitutes the basis for comprehensive Canadian national security legislation, augmented by the Public Safety Act in 2004.[27] The opportunity offered by 9/11 was alertly seized by the Canadian security and intelligence community, which ended up with much more than it would likely have achieved had 9/11 not happened. But most of these ideas for change were already in the pipeline, sometimes for years, in Ottawa, awaiting the political push that would bring them to the front of the policy agenda. The push came from al-Qaida, not from the United States, and the specifics of Canada's national security policy regime owes little to the model of the U.S. system; indeed, on many points, there are important differences from the American model.[28]

One controversial element of Canadian anti-terrorism policy has been Security Certificates, a pre-9/11 device imposed on non-citizens suspected of serious terrorist involvement who cannot be deported to countries that are likely to torture or kill them (there is a Supreme Court decision, *Suresh*, which denies deportation in such cases). Instead, five such suspected terrorists were kept in indefinite confinement on the basis of secret intelligence not revealed to the accused and their counsel, while the government was either unwilling or unable to bring criminal charges against them in open court. Amid an outcry by civil libertarians, the Supreme Court of Canada intervened by ordering changes to be made in the conditions imposed on the individuals, and in the disclosure of evidence against them.[29] The individuals were released under highly restrictive conditions, but under judicial review by the Federal Court, the government evidence supporting the certificates began to crumble. The high profile case of Adil Charkaoui collapsed completely when the government withdrew almost all of its evidence, and the judge freed Charkaoui, declaring his Security Certificate void. In two other cases, the Federal Court censured CSIS for being less than forthright about the reliability of its human source intelligence. Although CSIS apologized for its behaviour, its cases appeared to be failing under judicial scrutiny and, with them, the entire Security Certificate program.

The Security Certificate cases are all persons of Muslim and/or Arab background. The continuing controversy over what many see as heavy-handed and oppressive government treatment of these individuals has provided a counterthrust in public opinion against the initial post-9/11 attitudes of mistrust toward a suspect minority community. Many now see these 'suspects' as victims of state excesses in the 'war on terrorism.' This theme has also been highlighted by a series of well-publicized cases of Canadian Muslim targets of counter-terrorist measures now widely viewed as subversive of basic human rights.

The case of Maher Arar, a Canadian citizen of Syrian Muslim background, who was kidnapped by the American authorities while transiting a New York airport while returning home to Canada, and then sent to a Syrian prison where he spent a nightmarish year of torture and abuse before being released, offers the most remarkable example of how Canada is capable on occasion of breaking with its American ally's anti-terrorism priorities and preoccupations. Mr. Arar's moving account of his year in hell finally led to a Commission of Inquiry under Mr. Justice Dennis O'Connor, which produced an extraordinary report in the fall of 2006, which not only vindicated Mr. Arar as a innocent man, but brought Canadian officials to task who had demonstrated complicity in his fate by communicating false information about him to the United States.[30] The government accepted O'Connor's recommendations and paid Arar $10.5 million in compensation. Again, there is a contrast between Canada, where an innocent man could find official vindication, and the United States, which carries out what it calls 'extraordinary renditions' of terrorist 'suspects' to countries that routinely practice human rights violations. Worse, the United States at Guantanamo, Abu Ghraib, and other infamous centres for treatment of prisoners in flagrant defiance of international conventions has itself practised torture as a routine method of dealing with so-called 'enemy combatants.' The use of torture in interrogation was rejected by the incoming Obama administration, which also pledged to close Guantanamo. Yet the Obama administration refused Canadian requests to remove Arar from the U.S. no-fly list, and specifically indicated its intention to continue the extraordinary rendition program.

Coming out of the Arar inquiry, another inquiry looked at the case of three more Canadians of Muslim background who were detained and tortured in Syria and Egypt and concluded that Canadian officials, including CSIS officers, were to some degree complicit in the gross violation of their human rights.[31]

Two other cases echo the same pattern. Omar Khadr, the Canadian 'child soldier' held in Guantanamo on charges as an alleged 'enemy combatant' in Afghanistan has become a leading *cause célèbre* with the adamant refusal of the Harper government to ask the United States for his repatriation to Canada. With all the opposition parties in Parliament, civil liberties associations, the Canadian Bar Association, and leading newspapers, all calling on the government to bring Khadr home, the Federal Court ruled that the government was in violation of Khadr's Charter rights and ordered them to seek his immediate return.[32] The government appealed to the Supreme Court. The Harper government has chosen to play to its right-wing base in this matter, although public opinion, originally hostile to Khadr and to his 'terrorist' family, may have softened as evidence of torture at Guantanamo has been publicly admitted and regretted by the new Obama administration.

The final case to attract wide public attention also appeared to pit a government determined to take a hard-line stand against widespread public sympathy for a target of brutal anti-terrorist methods. Abousfian Andulrazik is a Canadian of Sudanese origin who was imprisoned by Sudanese authorities and, he alleges, tortured before being released. Named on the United Nations list of terrorists and on the United States no-fly list, Abdulrazik sought refuge in the Canadian embassy in Sudan, concerned that he would be subjected to continued persecution if returned to the Sudanese authorities. He appears to have been the object of American pressures on the Canadian government (partially inspired by alleged evidence against him gained by the repeated use of the notorious 'water-boarding' torture of an al-Qaida suspect at Guantanamo). There seems to be some evidence of Canadian complicity in his imprisonment. The Harper government for more than a year consistently refused permission for him to return to Canada, despite his Canadian citizenship, leaving him in a Kafkaesque limbo in the embassy compound in Khartoum. On June 4, 2009, a federal Court judge (recently appointed by Prime Minister Harper) issued a blistering indictment of the government's violation of Abdelrazik's rights and ordered his return.[33] After some delay, the government simply backed down and Abdelrazik returned to Canada at the end of June to a positive public reception.

There is a common thread running through all these cases: anxiety-driven public hostility to terrorism suspects and indifference to their treatment has changed over time into widespread sympathy for victims of ethnic/religious targeting and violation of human and constitutional rights, encouraged by grassroots campaigns of sympathetic Canadians. This change has never, of course, been unanimous; significant support remains in some quarters for a hard-line approach, to which the Harper government has intermittently appealed. It is, however, remarkable that in the course of a 'global war on terror' that began with deep public support for extraordinary measures, repressive if necessary, Canadian attitudes have shifted significantly. This shift is perhaps best symbolized by the public perception of Maher Arar, whose case initially met almost complete public indifference while he was still in Syrian hands, laced with some overtly hostile (and misleading) stories in the media. At the end of 2006, after the inquiry and his exoneration, Arar was named "Canadian of the Year" by the *Globe and Mail*. This movement of opinion in Canada has not to any extent been paralleled in the United States, where the shock of 9/11 remains vivid and Muslim Americans remain in many ways a suspect community subject to discriminatory treatment in the name of national security.

In both countries, though, it must be admitted that the objective effect of security policies has amounted to ethnic profiling of Muslims in practice. From a policing and security perspective, the targeting of high-risk people simply represents the efficient direction of resources; from the perspective of those flagged for particular attention, the policy represents ethnic and religious victimization. In the United States, apparent anti-Muslim bias in government policy is becoming increasingly public. Although targeting has focused on non-citizens, the line between aliens and Muslim-Americans is blurred – or is perceived to be by Muslim-Americans. A requirement for all aliens from listed Muslim countries to register with the Immigration and Naturalization Service sent a chill through the entire Muslim-American community.[34]

Canada does practise effective ethnic profiling in its own anti-terrorist security measures, but it typically does so in a more guarded, less public manner than the Americans. The Public Safety minister is advised by a Cross-cultural Round Table. Even when eighteen Muslim Canadians were arrested and charged under the *Anti-Terrorist Act*, every effort was made to avoid publicly pointing the finger at the Muslim communities as a whole, and indeed CSIS took the unprecedented step of alerting the Muslim community in advance of the arrests.[35] Criticism from some strident anti-immigration quarters[36] that Canada's 'liberal' immigration and multicultural policies were at the root of the emergence of a home-grown Muslim extremist threat were answered by Prime

Minister Stephen Harper when he addressed a UN conference in Vancouver and rejected the idea that liberal immigration was a cause of terrorism: "I believe, actually, the opposite is true," Mr. Harper declared. "Canada's diversity, properly nurtured, is our greatest strength."[37]

Another dimension that distinguishes Canada to some degree from its U.S. neighbour is its own history of relatively effective executive action to counter threats to domestic order. During the Cold War, Canadian authorities did contain the 'communist threat,' such as it was, without overt recourse to J. Edgar Hoover–like or McCarthyite tactics, and without banning the Communist party. In the 1960s and 1970s, the threat of the terrorist wing of the Quebec separatist movement was countered and crushed, while at the same time the way was kept open for the legitimate democratic expression of sovereignist demands. In both cases, liberal democracy was upheld, but this was accompanied by the application of an iron fist against those perceived to be the enemies of liberal democracy. Post 9/11, the same pattern seems to be repeating. With or without the additional emergency powers conferred by new legislation, the Canadian state has shown itself to be relatively agile in response to the new challenges. The reorganization of the architecture of national security policy making was accomplished with relative ease entirely within the confines of the federal executive and stands in sharp contrast to the protracted agonies that have publicly accompanied the creation of the Department of Homeland Security and the creation of the office of the Director of National Intelligence in the United States.

More impressive yet has been the capacity of the leading Canadian security and policing agencies to set aside, for the moment at least, their old turf wars and reconstitute their anti-terrorist efforts on an integrated and co-operative partnership basis. Two decades after the disastrous breakdown of co-operation between the RCMP and CSIS in the Air India terrorist tragedy of 1985,[38] the smooth and effective operation of the Integrated National Security Enforcement teams (INSETs), under RCMP direction, but including CSIS, other relevant federal agencies, as well as provincial and municipal police forces, has been demonstrated in the eighteen arrests of members of a suspected terrorist ring in Toronto in 2006. While turf wars continue to plague the U.S. anti-terrorist effort, pitting the CIA, the FBI, Homeland Security, and other bureaucratic actors in often awkward conflicts that spill out into public finger-pointing, Canada seems to have moved to a new level of integration which, if not entirely seamless, is certainly much more so than in the past. And this has been accomplished with little reliance on new and expanded powers, none of which were employed in the Toronto operation.

5. Concluding Reflections

Canada's response to 9/11 does indicate that keeping up with the neighbours is, to a degree, an important guide to public policy. Like the Cold War, the 'war against terror' is a multilateral effort, under American leadership, and as a participant in the alliance, Canada has to do many things to keep up its part. However, most of these things it would have done on its own, both to assure an anxious public concerned about threats to their security, and to pre-empt the Americans from taking more drastic measures that would directly threaten Canadian sovereignty. Ottawa recognizes that important, and influential, sections of the Canadian business, political, and media elites constantly push for greater integration with the United States and greater harmonization of Canadian policies with U.S. policies and that these pressures are more influential than usual during times of international crisis and high insecurity. At the same time, Canadian public opinion demands some distance from the appearance that Canadian policy is being dictated from Washington. This latter tendency is heightened when the U.S. leadership is perceived by many in Canada as immoderate and potentially dangerous, which was certainly the case under the Bush administration.

As historical precedents, the Cold War and the October Crisis demonstrate that Canada is capable of acting forcefully, and with relatively few restraints, in dealing with a perceived threat from within linked to a threat from without. The anti-terrorist legislation and the shift in resources towards national security enforcement in the wake of 9/11 come as no surprise. Yet the historical precedents are double-edged. If they suggest a capacity for repressive and illiberal actions in the name of national security, it is also the case that the long-term result of both these crises was to strengthen liberal democracy and the protection of civil liberties as a direct consequence of revulsion generated by repressive and unaccountable state actions. This too is part of the historical background to the present crisis. Canadians have learned from experience about the consequences of overreaction. There is a space between the Canadian and American responses, partly generated by the direction of the terrorist threat primarily against the United States and partly generated by differences in the political cultures. This space allows Canadians some critical distance, some room to develop made-in-Canada policies, and some capacity to resist American pressures, especially when these pressures come in the form of unilateralist, America First imperatives. Canada is always more comfortable keeping up with the neighbours when this is a multilateral enterprise.

Notes

1   This paper draws freely from Reg Whitaker, "Before September 11 – Some History Lessons. In Canadian Institute for the Administration of Justice," in *Terrorism, Law & Democracy: How is Canada Changing Following September 11?* (Montréal: Éditions Thémis, 2002), 39–54; and Reg Whitaker, "Keeping Up With the Neighbours? Canadian Responses to 9/11 in Historical and Comparative Context," *Osgoode Hall Law Journal* 41, nos. 2 & 3 (2003): 241–65.

2   Amy Knight, *How the Cold War Began: The Gouzenko Affair and the Hunt for Soviet Spies* (Toronto: McClelland & Stewart, 2005).

3   The characterization of a "wake-up call" is an exaggeration. Canada already had a lengthy history of official repression of leftwing activity since the Russian revolution, intensified during the social stresses of the Great Depression, and continued throughout World War II when the Communist party was made an illegal association and communists interned. The Cold War simply permitted more systematic anti-communist action.

4   Reg Whitaker and Gary Marcuse, *Cold War Canada: The Making of a National Insecurity State, 1945–1957* (Toronto: University of Toronto Press, 1994). See also Reg Whitaker and Steve Hewitt, *Canada and the Cold War* (Toronto: Lorimer, 2003).

5   *The Report of the Royal Commission Appointed Under Order in Council P.C. 411 of February 5, 1946* (Ottawa: King's Printer, 1946).

6   Reg Whitaker and Steve Hewitt, *Canada and the Cold War*, 47–50.

7   Reg Whitaker *Double Standard: The Secret History of Canadian Immigration* (Toronto: Lester & Orpen Dennys, 1987).

8   Ottawa Minister of Supplies and Services, "Freedom and Security Under the Law," *Commission of Inquiry Concerning Certain Activities of the RCMP, Second Report – Vol. 1,* 1981, 518. According to the 1971 census, the total population of Canada was 21,568,000: 800,000 files represent information on more than one out of every twenty-seven Canadians.

9 Even in retrospect, leading figures were evasive in their justifications. Immediately after the crisis, a prominent Quebec minister in the Trudeau government, Gérard Pelletier, published a memoir: Gérard Pelletier, *La Crise d'Octobre* (Montréal: Éditions du Jour, 1971). In Mr. Trudeau's own memoirs, his account of the affair raises many questions of both fact and interpretation: Pierre Elliott Trudeau, *Memoirs* (Toronto: McClelland & Stewart, 1993), 128–52.

10 Reg Whitaker, "Apprehended Insurrection? RCMP Intelligence and the October Crisis," *Queen's Quarterly* 100, no. 2 (1993): 383–406.

11 Elizabeth II [Canada], *The Emergencies Act*, RSC 1985, Chapter 29, chap. 22, 35–36–37.

12 Coalition for Secure and Trade-Efficient Borders, *Rethinking our Borders: A Plan for Action* (Thomas D'Aquino, December 3, 2001); Security and prosperity: the dynamics of a new Canada–United States partnership in North America. Presentation to the *Annual General meeting of the Canadian Council of Chief Executives* (Toronto, January 14, 2003).

13 Reg Whitaker, "Securing the 'Ontario-Vermont Border': Myths and Realities in Post-9/11 Canadian-American Security Relations," *International Journal* 1 (Winter 2004–2005): 53–70.

14 Reg Whitaker, "More or less than meets the eye? The new national security agenda," In *How Ottawa Spends 2003–2004: Regime Change and Policy Shift*, ed. G.B. Doern (Don Mills: Oxford University Press, 2003), 44–58.

15 Reg Whitaker, "Made in Canada? The New Public Safety Paradigm," In *How Ottawa Spends 2005–2006: Managing the Minority*, ed. G.B. Doern (Montreal: McGill-Queen's University Press, 2005), 77–98.

16 Department of Foreign Affairs and International Trade, "Manley and Ridge release progress report on the Smart Border Declaration and Action Plan," from June 28, 2002, DFAIT New Release: http://www.dfait-maeci.gc.ca/anti-terrorism/declaration-e.asp (accessed February 2, 2007). This link is no longer available.

17 The pre-9/11 case most cited by critics is that of Ahmed Ressam, apprehended in late 1999 attempting to enter the United States at Port Angeles, Washington, on his way to play a part in a planned millennium terror attack on the L.A. Airport. Yet in 2001, U.S. Attorney General John Ashcroft brushed off critics of Canadian security by insisting that in this case the United States had acted on information provided by Canadian authorities, with whom co-operation was "outstanding": John Ashcroft (December 4, 2001). Interview with *CTV News*.

18 Paul Koring, "U.S. blasts Canada on Terrorism," *Globe and Mail*, April 29, 2006.

19 "Arar Illustrates What?" *Globe and Mail*, May 5, 2006.

20 Reg Whitaker, "Refugee Policy after September 11: Not Much New," *Refuge* 20, no. 4 (August 2001): 29–33.

21 Reid Morden, "Finding the Right Balance," *Policy Options* 23, no. 6 (September 2002): 45–48.

22 49–50 Elizabeth II 2001, chap. 48. Even before its final passage, this legislative package received extraordinary academic attention in a book of essays, mostly critical: Ronald J. Daniels, Patrick Macklem and Kent Roach, eds., *The Security of Freedom: Essays on Canada's Anti-Terrorism Bill* (Toronto: University of Toronto Press, 2001). See also a special issue: Errol P. Mendes and Debra M. McAllister, eds., "Between Crime and War: Terrorism, Democracy and the Constitution," *National Journal of Constitutional Law* 14, no 1 (2002).

23 M.L. Friedland, *National Security: the Legal Dimensions*, Study prepared for the Royal Commission of Inquiry Concerning Certain Activities of the RCMP, (Ottawa, 1979), 22–30; Reg Whitaker and Gary Marcuse, *Cold War Canada*, 197–204.

24 R. v. Stinchcombe. [1991] 3 S.C.R. 326, ordered the production in court of criminal intelligence relevant to the defence. *Stinchcombe* was a criminal case, and its relevance to national security cases was unclear. The evidence provisions in C-36 are in the spirit of 'better safe than sorry.'

25 49–50 Elizabeth II 2001–02, Chapter 12 (assented to April 30, 2002).

26 49–50 Elizabeth II 2001, Chapter 27 (assented to November 1, 2001).

27 Canada, *Public Safety Act, 2002* [2004, c. 15], assented to May 6, 2004. This statute is mainly concerned with aviation and marine security and control over hazardous biological and chemical substances.

28 A notable example of institutional difference is the debate that has opened in Washington since 9/11 about the desirability of splitting the FBI into a counter-terrorist intelligence agency and an institutionally separate criminal law enforcement body. In Canada, this was done in 1984 with the CSIS Act separating the security service from the RCMP.

29 *Charkoui v. Canada (Citizenship and Immigration)* [2007] SCC 9.

30 Canada, Commission of Inquiry into the Actions of Canadian Officials in Relation to Maher Arar, *Report of the Events Relating to Maher Arar*. 3 vols., 2006; Reg Whitaker, *Arar: The Affair, the Inquiry, the Aftermath*, Institute for Research on Public Policy, IRPP Policy Matters, 9:1 (May 2008).

31 The Honourable Frank Iacobucci, Commissioner, *Internal Inquiry into the Actions of Canadian Officials in relation to Abdullah Almaki, Ahmad Abour-Elmaati*

and *Muayyed Nureddin* (Ottawa, 2008). See also Kerry Pither, *Dark Days: The Story of Four Canadians Tortured in the Name of Fighting Terror* (Toronto: Viking Canada, 2008).

32 Omar Ahmed Khadr and the Prime Minister of Canada, the Minister of Foreign Affairs, the Director of the Canadian Security Intelligence Service, and the Commissioner of the Royal Canadian Mounted Police, 2009 FC 405, April 23, 2009. On the Khadr case more generally, see Michelle Shephard, *Guantanamo's Child: the Untold Story of Omar Khadr* (Mississauga: Wiley, 2008).

33 Abousfian Abdelrazik and the Minister of Foreign Affairs and the Attorney General of Canada, 200 FC 580; Wesley Wark, "The exile is over, but the saga continues," *Globe and Mail*, July 1, 2009.

34 American Civil Liberties Union, "Immigrant Registration Program Pretext for Mass Detentions," Press release, December 19, 2002.

35 Omar El Akkad, "CSIS, RCMP Briefed Muslim Leaders Before Going Public with News of Arrests," *Globe and Mail*, June 9, 2006.

36 Linda Frum, "Q&A with Terrorism Expert David Harris on How Canada is Handling the Issue of Islamic Extremism," *Maclean's*, June 13, 2006. This so-called terrorism 'expert,' who had earlier called for a complete ban on all immigration to Canada, made the following astonishing juxtaposition: "2,700 people at CSIS vs. 230,000 people a year coming in" – as if every immigrant to Canada were a security threat!

37 Rod Mickleburgh, "Harper defends Canadian diversity: PM rejects calls to curb immigration, calls open society 'our greatest strength.'" *Globe and Mail*, June 20, 2006.

38 327 people, most of them Canadian citizens, died on board an Air India flight

that exploded off the coast of Ireland in 1985. No one has ever been convicted for this atrocity, and part of the problem is related to the breakdown in cooperation between the RCMP and the then fledgling CSIS. In 2006 a commission of inquiry under retired Supreme Court Justice John Major was created to fully review this deplorable chapter in Canadian history. It is expected to report in the fall of 2009.

CHAPTER 3

Accounting for Disaster: The Quest for "Closure" after Aerial Mass Murder — The Downing of Air India Flight 182 in Comparative Perspective

Stuart Farson
Simon Fraser University

1. Introduction

Two claims have often been made about the attacks perpetrated by Muslim extremists against the United States of America on September 11, 2001. One is that they changed the world inexorably. The other is that they ushered in an entirely new form of terrorism. While the first claim may yet be proven to be overblown,[1] it is difficult to dispute the fact that the attacks on New York and Washington fundamentally changed the way the international community responds to terrorism. Nation after nation introduced new legislation to fight the new twenty-first-century plague, often in the process limiting the hard-fought rights and freedoms garnered by their citizens. Traditional western allies now found "friends of convenience" with whom to trade information and intelligence about the new threat. And what had hitherto been primarily a phenomenon best fought by the police and security forces of individual states now became a global project described in the rhetoric of the day as a "global war on terrorism."

The second claim is largely false but yet has an element of truth. The organization said to be responsible for the attacks – al-Qaida – was not new, nor was its employment of so-called "suicide terrorists."[2] Furthermore, the United States was not a new foe. Its embassies and military serving abroad had been attacked on several occasions, sometimes inflicting simultaneously massive carnage on local communities.[3] What was new was the shift in the strategic orientation of al-Qaida to what Fawaz Gerges has called the "far enemy,"[4] the extensiveness of the damage caused to persons, critical infrastructure, and the economy, particularly the transportation sector, and the weapons used. Despite a vast U.S. intelligence network – with budgets larger than some national economies – civilian aircraft were successfully used for the first time as improvised explosive devices (I.E.D.s) in a well-coordinated attack against the U.S. heartland. Arguably, the results were more devastating, particularly in psychologically terms, than the surprise attack on Pearl Harbour by the Japanese fleet, which had brought the United States into the Second World War some sixty years before.

In many respects, however, the use of civilian aircraft as weapons was not itself new, just a progression in strategic direction. Aircraft, in fact, had a long history of being used as terrorist devices. With the dramatic increase in air transportation that occurred in the 1970s, particularly after the introduction of wide-bodied jets, a variety of groups and individuals around the world set about hijacking them with a view to extracting concessions from governments or to drawing attention to their cause. In the 1980s a new development occurred. Aircraft were ostensibly destroyed in flight to obtain redress against grievances both real and imagined. In at least one case, the plan encompassed the sabotage of two aircraft simultaneously, portending of developments to come. The attacks of September 11 thus can be seen as encompassing a development of both tactics – first a hijacking; then an act of sabotage.

This chapter focuses on the sabotage of aircraft in the 1980s and analyzes four disasters. As a possible precursor to the events of September 11, 2001, because of the coordinated nature of the attack strategy, the events of June 23, 1985, involving two Air India flights are compared with the downing of South

Korean, American, and Iranian wide-bodied aircraft. It also examines the events from a particular perspective. This chapter focuses on the largely forgotten entity – the victim – and the question of how "closure" might be obtained after incidents of mass murder.

2. OBJECTIVES

During the 1980s there was a lack of consensus at the international level about what constituted terrorism and about the labelling of individuals and groups as "terrorists." As a consequence it was difficult to obtain international agreements on how to prevent and respond to such groups. In the parlance of the times, today's "terrorist" was inevitably someone else's "freedom fighter." In part the lack of consensus was due to the fact that international law had traditionally dealt with preventing and resolving conflicts between states – not between states and non-state actors.

For those who looked at the world from the vantage point of a democratic state, Max Weber's notion that states possessed the monopoly over the *legitimate* use of violence often seemed to offer powerful guidance. However, for those who saw themselves as oppressed and unable to enjoy what they perceived as the reasonable rights and freedoms enjoyed by others, it held little suasion. But even where violence was deemed necessary and justifiable, it did not imply that the means were open-ended.[5]

The fact that states were said to have the monopoly over the legitimate use of violence also made issues of definition problematic for two other reasons. First, the notion tended to cause people to ignore situations where the state itself was involved in acts of terrorism against either its own people or those in another state. While this omission was more readily apparent in non-democratic governmental systems, such as that of the Soviet Union or Saddam Hussein's Iraq, it also occurred in states with certain democratic trappings, such as South Africa under the apartheid regime or Israel in its ongoing confrontation with the Palestinians. Second, the fact that states also tended to have ready access and influence, if not monopoly, over national media meant that they could with relative ease label a particular group as being "terrorist" and thus demonize and denigrate it in the eyes of public opinion. In the process, the distinction between rebels, revolutionaries, insurgents, guerrilla fighters, and others involved in civil wars was often lost and so too was sight of any legitimate grievances that might underpin their actions.

One form of political violence that was broadly condemned concerned attacks against civilian aviation. There were three primary reasons for this consensus. First, damage to the air transportation system eventually hurts all nations and their respective travelling publics, not just the carrier state. Second, international flights in particularly, and to a lesser extent domestic ones, tend to draw passengers from several different nationalities. As a consequence, while the target may, because it is often a national flag carrier, be readily identifiable with a particular cause, many of the victims will likely be truly innocent bystanders. And in cases where such incidents are driven by ethnic or religious extremism, they may even be members of the same ethnic group or religious faith. Recall that one in six of those who died in the September 11, 2001, bombings were Muslims.[6] Finally, air disasters tend to exacerbate the fear that many have of flying.

Obviously, in many instances where an aircraft is downed by an improvised explosive device (IED), the resulting crash may cause the death of all those on board. Where all are killed one might argue that victims fall into three categories: the deceased, their surviving family members and close friends, and all those who might have been on the aircraft that was downed – the potential victims drawn from the travelling public more broadly. To these separate entities one might well apportion quite different notions of closure. For the first, bringing those responsible before the courts indicates that justice has been done.

There is greater difficulty in defining what closure might imply for the second group as grief takes many forms and varies according to culture, family, individual personality as well as religious and spiritual beliefs and practices. While financial compensation may help to provide for surviving family members, it cannot hope to replace the loss of a loved one. There is also the question of responsibility to answer. Has the family member been given the funeral that is appropriate for his or her religious beliefs? Where bodies are not recovered this may not be possible. For this group the idea of justice needs to be taken a step beyond the mere application of the criminal sanction to concrete actions. This arguably includes needing to know what happened and why, as well as whether a government body or corporation failed in its duty to provide adequate security.

For the last group there is a need to feel safe and secure when travelling. This likely only comes from knowing that one's government, and the international air transportation system more generally, have taken all necessary steps to redress the flaws in the security system revealed by the disaster in question. Arguably, this requires that there has been a full and visible accounting of the events that led up to the mass murder. This also necessarily means that fair-minded criticism is levied in a transparent way against persons and organizations that failed to provide the necessary security where it was due.

While the primary interest of this chapter concerns the sabotage of Air India Flight 182 and the attendant mass murder of its passengers that occurred on June 23, 1985, it places this disaster in a comparative context with three other mass murders of civil airline passengers that occurred close to it in time. The purpose here is threefold. First, the chapter tries to establish whether governments of different political hues exhibit common traits in the handling of air disasters where political violence is concerned. Second, it examines the various independent inquiries to see what their primary findings were and whose interests they served. Of interest here is whether they were likely to provide some form of "closure" for the victim's families. Finally, it looks to see whether subsequent evidence changed either the initial portrayal of the event or the findings of the independent inquiries.

3. How the Four Disasters Occurred

The four disasters all took place within a few years of each other. The first occurred on September 1, 1983, shortly after President Reagan had condemned the Soviet Union as an "evil empire." Using a heat-seeking missile, a Soviet fighter plane shot down a Korean Airlines passenger jet near Moneron Island, located in the Tatar Strait in the northeastern section of the Sea of Japan. After making a refuelling stop at Anchorage, Alaska, the New York–originating flight

(KAL 007) had headed for Seoul, South Korea. When struck by the missile, the Boeing 747 was some 500 kilometres off course and had violated Soviet airspace over a considerable period. Though it was by no means the first civilian airliner shot down by a military aircraft in peacetime, it was the most deadly to date.[7]

The second case was in effect two events in one. On June 23, 1985, a bomb exploded at the New Tokyo International Airport (now Narita International Airport) in luggage destined for Air India Flight 301 to Bombay via Bangkok. Some fifty-five minutes later, another Air India aircraft disappeared off radar screens. Having taken off from Montreal, Canada, this Boeing 747 was scheduled to travel to Bombay (now Mumbai) via London, England. Instead, Flight 182 disintegrated over the Atlantic Ocean as it was closing on the Irish coast.

The third event involved an Airbus A300 flown by Iran Air on July 3, 1988. Flight IR 655 was en route from Bandar Abbas, a joint civilian-military airport in Iran, to Dubai in the United Arab Emirates, a journey of around 250 kilometres, when it was shot down in a civilian air corridor by the U.S. Navy guided missile cruiser USS *Vincennes* over the Strait of Hormuz. At the time, Iran and Iraq had been at war for nearly eight years. Initially, the U.S. Government, despite having had their embassy staff taken hostage in 1979, had been ambivalent towards supporting either party. However, from early 1982 U.S. policy began to tilt in favour of Iraq. This resulted not only in the provision of economic aid but also the issuance of high-tech export licences and high-grade military intelligence.[8] From the summer of 1987, U.S. Navy ships were deployed in the Persian Gulf ostensibly to protect Kuwaiti tankers making their transit through international waters. Though the United States was never officially at war with Iran, this military deployment had a covert component and resulted in military action. Special Operations forces were used to prevent Iranian forces from mining the Gulf and attacking shipping. After the USS *Samuel B. Roberts* was seriously damaged by an Iranian mine, U.S. forces responded by attacking Iranian warships, armed speedboats, and the oil platforms they used as bases. Dubbed "Operation Praying Mantis," this response constituted the largest engagement of surface warships since World War II.

The final event occurred on December 21, 1988, and also involved a Boeing 747. On this occasion, however, it was owned by a private American company,

Pan American Airlines. Pan Am Flight 103 was on route from London to Detroit via New York when it too was downed by a bomb near Lockerbie, Scotland.

4. Some Similarities and Differences between the Events

The four events exhibit similarities as well as differences. With the exception of the Narita bombing incident, each event resulted in the downing of a wide-bodied passenger jet causing the death of all passengers and crew. In the case of Pan Am 103, which was the only downing not to occur over water, the crash also caused the deaths of people on the ground, as did the bomb blast in Tokyo. The passengers killed on each occasion represented a variety of nationalities.[9] In each instance, relatives of those killed have eventually obtained financial redress through the courts or as the result of the perpetrating country acknowledging liability. In two instances – Pan Am 103 and KAL 007 – Americans were either the majority or a significant proportion of the passengers on board.[10] In the other two cases, they are not thought to be represented.

In two instances, Air India Flight 182 and Pan Am 103, non-state actors claimed responsibility for the disasters. However, the groups initially claiming responsibility were not subsequently thought to be directly involved. In the Pan Am case, a group calling itself the Guardians of the Islamic Revolution claimed responsibility for the disaster as retaliation for the earlier attack on the Iran Air Airbus. But though suspicions focused on this previously unknown group, a man said to be a member of Libyan intelligence would eventually be arrested, tried, and convicted of the crime. In the other two instances, state actors acknowledged responsibility for launching guided missiles against the aircraft.

The Air India and Pan Am disasters both were caused by IEDs being detonated in personal luggage placed in the forward cargo holds of the aircraft. Both led to the largest criminal investigations in Canadian and British history respectively. Only in the Air India and Pan Am cases were people brought to trial or guilty pleas received. However, in both cases some of the individuals who had been indicted were found not guilty and released. In the Pan Am case, a special court was established in a neutral country. Thus, the two Libyans initially accused of the crime were tried at Kamp Zeist in the Netherlands under Scottish law by a panel of three judges sitting alone. For the Air India trial, a specially secure courtroom had to be built in Vancouver, Canada.

The flight data recorders were recovered in three of the events, though in the case of KAL 007 the "black boxes" were not returned by the Russians until several years later and after the Soviet Union had collapsed. In only three of the cases were identifiable physical remains of those killed in the incidents retrieved. In none of the cases were all the victims retrieved.

Of the two privately owned airlines, only Korean Air survived, Pan Am, once the icon of international air travel, declaring bankruptcy in January 1991. Besides the 1988 Lockerbie disaster, it had earlier been the target of a deadly hijacking at Pakistan's Karachi International Airport. Pan Am's demise illustrates the problem airlines have striking the right balance between security and convenience. In 1986 it established a new subsidiary named Alert Management Systems. Depicted in advertising as one of the most far-reaching security programs in the industry, it did little to improve actual security.[11] Though a report presciently signalled the airline's vulnerability by suggesting that: "Pan Am [was] almost totally vulnerable to a midair explosion through explosive charges concealed in the cargo"[12] the unit was geared primarily to restoring and maintaining customer confidence. As this development required passengers to pay a $5 surcharge, it also became a profit centre. Financial considerations, in fact, led Pan Am to keep security procedures to a minimum as inconveniencing passengers was thought likely to hurt business. Ironically, the Lockerbie disaster on top of the Karachi hijacking led many air travellers and travel agents to consider Pan Am unsafe. Consequently, they sought alternative carriers, which had a disastrous impact on the airline's financial viability.

5. Accounts of Disasters

A central theme of much terrorism literature concerns the role that the media play in framing public understanding of state versus non-state conflicts. Most emphasis, in fact, has been placed on how terrorist groups use the media to further their own objectives and the mechanisms by which they draw attention to their particular causes. However, such groups are not the only ones to "frame" specific acts of political violence in a particular light.[13] Nor are they the only ones to commit acts of terror. Governments too may be guilty of perpetrating acts of state terrorism. How governments respond to both types of action in terms of the words they chose to describe them and the processes they select to analyze them can be particularly revealing. The four events chosen in this study provide an opportunity to garner a better understanding of the political cultures of the states involved, their approaches to international relations, and their systems of governance.

A. KAL 007

The central question for the world community, and for the United States in particular, was whether the Soviets had knowingly shot down a civilian aircraft. Certainly there was prior evidence that they had fired at and forced a civilian airliner to land where it had clearly overflown Soviet territory.[14] Not knowing the answer to this posed a dilemma for U.S. diplomats who were then engaged in a new round of arms control talks. They could either take a more cautious approach that permitted the Soviets an opportunity to explain their actions or an aggressive one that attempted to expose the ethical and moral flaws in the Soviet system. They chose the latter. George Schultz, the U.S. Secretary of State, claimed in a lengthy press conference covering the tragedy that the Soviets knew it was a civilian airliner and that they shot it down without giving prior warning.[15] Furthermore they had intercepted communications between the Soviet pilot and his ground station that proved it. Other senior diplomats referred to it as "wanton, calculated, deliberate murder." President Ronald Reagan himself best captured the thrust of the U.S. propaganda campaign with the question: "What can we think of a regime that so broadly trumpets its visions of peace and global disarmament and yet so callously and quickly commits a terrorist act?"[16]

While the initial response of Soviet spokespersons was to deny the story, this was subsequently followed by accusations in the Soviet press that KAL 007 was on a spying mission, had no navigation lights illuminated, did not respond to queries, and had ignored warning tracer shells fired by the Soviet fighter aircraft. Furthermore, the aircraft had violated Soviet airspace. There was no acknowledgment of any responsibility. Subsequently, the Soviets expanded on the intelligence-gathering angle by claiming that the plane resembled an RC-135, a type of surveillance plane that the United States had used on numerous occasions already that year to violate Soviet airspace. President Reagan responded to these accusations on U.S. television with excerpts from the tapes of the Soviet pilot. Significantly, he pointed to flaws in the Soviet position. Not only had the Soviet pilots failed to warn the South Korean aircraft but they lacked the means to do so. Their planes were not fitted with systems that allowed their pilots to communicate using international radio frequencies for fear of detection. In many respects, however, the *coup de grâce* was delivered by the U.S. ambassador to the United Nations, Dr. Jeane Kirkpatrick. Using techniques for the first time that would be echoed many years later by Secretary of State Colin Powell when he provided the UN with "evidence" of Iraq's continued development of weapons of mass destruction, she played a videotape on five TV screens before the UN Security Council that effectively drove home her key points: KAL 007 did have its navigation lights illuminated; the Soviet fighters did not fire tracer shells; no communication with the civilian aircraft was tried; and the Soviet fighters carried no equipment with which they could effectively communicate with planes of other nationalities. It was pure theatre. The videotape was a simulation with the translated intercepted audiotapes as backdrop.[17] Despite inaccuracies in the translations from Russian to English of the Soviet pilot's communications, the propaganda war was over. On the next day the Soviet government issued a formal statement acknowledging its part in the destruction of the Boeing 747. Based on its own inquiry, it at last expressed regret for the death of innocent people and the sorrow of their bereaved friends and relatives. The International Civil Aviation Organization (ICAO), a UN agency, was requested to conduct two investigations into the downing of KAL 007. The first took place shortly after the event and was completed in unusual haste by early December 1983 without the benefit of "black boxes." This study concluded that the plane had been brought down by a missile southwest of Sakhalin Island despite the fact that "the location of the main wreckage was not determined."

In Seymour Hersh's view, the commission's findings only further encouraged critics of the Reagan Administration to believe that the U.S. Government was withholding information about the true intentions of Flight 007.[18] Largely unexplored was the assertion made by the wives of the Korean pilots before U.S. attorneys representing many of the victims' families. They suggested that the navigational error was far from unintentional. To the contrary, they stated that the captain and co-pilot were specifically paid special bonuses by Korean Airlines to take the shortcut over Soviet territory and that their husbands had become particularly fearful and wanted to discontinue them, particularly Flight 007. This position is supported by Japanese radar data, subsequently made public, showing Flight KAL 007 changing course as it approached Soviet air space.[19]

The U.S. Government studiously avoided conducting its own inquiry into the disaster, despite having sixty-one of its citizens killed in the tragedy. For its part the State Department required the National Transportation Safety Board (NTSB) to hand over the information it had in its possession, saying that it would conduct an inquiry. It never did. In addition, various arms of government sought to make it difficult for those who wanted to conduct independent inquiries and, in some instances, actually threatened such people. Instead, the U.S. Government preferred to rely on ICAO's fact-finding report, which the State Department described as "the most authoritative account of the entire incident," despite the fact that it relied entirely on data volunteered by the various countries involved, which in each case held back crucial information.[20] At the time ICAO had little experience in making inquiries into aviation disasters, having investigated but one prior to KAL 007, the 1973 Israeli attack on a Libyan airliner. Furthermore, it acknowledged that its inquiry was not comprehensive and paled by comparison to state investigations.[21] In Congress, both intelligence committees conducted cursory investigations that concluded, as the ICAO report had done, there was no evidence to support the notion that

KAL 007 was on a spy mission. However, neither held public hearings, provided witness lists, or released summaries of evidence.[22]

The other ICAO inquiry was initiated some years later after the Soviet Union had collapsed. Boris Yeltsin, then president of Russia, decided to return the two "black boxes" to South Korea, but without the original tapes. ICAO's subsequent report would confirm that there was more than a little substance to R.W. Johnson's earlier claim that the Reagan Administration was marked by "a belief that events themselves [could] be shaped decisively by the way they [were] presented – that truth itself [was] a malleable quantity, a subject, like any other, for 'good management.'"[23] Alvin Snyder, who had been the Director of Worldwide Television for the U.S. Information Agency when that body had made the videotape presented at the UN by Dr. Kirkpatrick, concluded that he had been purposefully misled at the time by not being made party to the ground controllers' tapes. These showed that the Soviet pilot had tipped his wings and fired warning shots and that controllers were convinced that the aircraft was military.[24] At the same time five top-secret Soviet memoranda were published in the Russian press.[25] These had been prepared in the fall of 1983 and were primarily concerned with analyzing the flight and voice data recordings. They identified the exact location of the crash site and revealed that the inertial navigation system was not connected to the autopilot. Here the Soviets set out to mislead the United States and Japan as to the actual location by performing imitation search efforts. The documents strongly suggest that the Soviets believed that the South Korean aircraft had intentionally flown over Soviet airspace and that this was preplanned and part of a political provocation undertaken by the U.S. intelligence community. The second ICAO report, like the first, however, concluded that the Korean jet had inadvertently entered Soviet airspace.

More than a decade later, the pilot of the Sukhoi-15 who had shot down the Korean airliner personally acknowledged his part in the affair, saying that he did recognize it as being civilian and was sure it was not an RC-135 surveillance plane. However, he too remained convinced that it was on a spying mission.

B. Iran Air Flight 655

As with the KAL 007 disaster, accusations concerning the intent of those responsible for the downing of Iran Air Flight 655 were quickly levied. For its part, the Iranian government immediately accused the United States of a premeditated act of aggression and of "massacring" the passengers in cold blood.[26] By comparison to the response of the Soviet Government to the KAL 007 downing, the U.S. Government moved quickly to indicate its involvement. While its initial announcements expressed deep regret for the loss of life in what was said to be a proper "defensive action" against what was thought to be an F-14 by a U.S. naval vessel in international waters, they also suggested that Iranians were blameworthy. The airliner was said to be out of the normal civilian flight corridor, had failed to respond to repeated warnings, and had been heading straight for the USS *Vincennes* at a *decreasing* altitude.[27] It would subsequently be established that none of these allegations were true. In addition, the United States quickly offered to compensate the families of the victims of the disaster. The sum offered, however, differed significantly from that which would eventually be garnered from the Libyan Government following the Pan Am disaster. It would be made on a voluntary basis without any acknowledgment of liability or obligation. And payment would be made through third parties. No compensation to the Government of Iran for the loss of its airliner would be made.[28]

C. Pan Am 103

When Pan Am 103 disintegrated over Lockerbie just before Christmas in 1988, some observers immediately posited that the downing was in retaliation for the shooting down of the Iranian airbus by the USS *Vincennes* earlier in the summer. This notion was supported by the fact that one of the groups claiming responsibility for the aircraft's sabotage was a previously unknown Iranian group, the Guardians of the Islamic Revolution.

The British Government immediately assumed that the disaster was caused by an unlawful act. Several investigations were quickly started. The Dunfries and Galloway constabulary, then the smallest police force in the United Kingdom, commenced what would be the largest criminal investigation in the country's history. This would involve the collection and analysis of some 180,000 pieces of evidence, more than 20,000 name checks, and some 15,000 witness statements. Parts from the aircraft and its cargo were spread over a crash site encompassing some 2,190 square kilometres. Items thought to be part or contents of a suitcase were transferred to Royal Armament Development Establishment (RARDE) for forensic examination. RARDE established that a Samsonite suitcase contained an IED. This device consisted of a relatively small amount of Semtex plastic explosive placed in a Toshiba radio cassette player along with a timer manufactured by a Swiss company named Mebo. Further police investigation would trace materials in this suitcase to purchases from a store in Malta. A mole in the Libyan intelligence community would identify a member of that country's Jamahiriya Security Organization as being the head of security for Libyan Arab Airlines. His presence on Malta was established by the Maltese shopkeeper from whom the clothes had been purchased. Additional investigations would indicate that quantities of Semetex, similar Toshiba radio-cassettes and Mebo-manufactured timers had been sold to Libya. Interline baggage records from Frankfurt International Airport revealed that an unaccompanied case was shipped to Frankfurt from Malta and on to London where it was deposited on board Pan Am 103.

There was sufficient debris from the downed aircraft to allow the Aircraft Accident Investigation Branch (AAIB) of the Department of Transport to reconstruct a skeleton of the plane. An analysis of the materials would permit the AAIB to conclude in 1990 that an IED led directly to the destruction of the aircraft with the loss of all on board and some eleven residents of the town of Lockerbie.

Though the British Government has steadfastly refused to establish a public inquiry to this day, the American families of victims were more successful. They wanted an independent inquiry to provide answers to three questions: Who was responsible? How it could have happened? And how could such events be prevented in the future? Initially, the executive branch ignored their entreaties as well as those of Congress. Nevertheless, President George H.W. Bush did eventually respond to these pressures by establishing the Commission on Aviation Security and Terrorism in August of 1989 before the criminal investigation was completed. This commission was not intended to identify who was responsible for the bombing. Rather, it set out to evaluate the policy options for preventing future terrorist acts involving aviation. In particular, it was asked to evaluate:

> ... the adequacy of existing procedures for aviation security, compliance therewith, and enforcement thereof ... [to] review options for handling terrorist threats, including prior notification to the public ... [and to] investigate practices, policies, and laws with respect to the treatment of families of victims of terrorist acts.[29]

The commissioners held hearings between November 1989 and April 1990. In addition, their staff conducted over 250 investigative interviews and received sworn testimony from witnesses.[30] The Commission's findings were broad-ranging and were equally damning of the Federal Aviation Authority (FAA), and other departments of the U.S. Government, as well as Pan Am. A central finding was that the disaster might well have been preventable had existing FAA guidelines been followed. Having concluded that passenger/baggage reconciliation was the "bedrock of any heightened civil air security system," it noted that no one knew whether the plane was carrying any additional interline bags.[31] The aviation security system, which was still then designed more to thwart hijackings rather than bombings – now the preferred terrorist option – was found to be seriously defective. According to one member of the Commission:

> There were shortcomings in virtually all areas: the gathering, assessment and dissemination of intelligence; the Federal Government's oversight of airline and airport activities; counterterrorism research and development, our Government's response to tragedy; and in the area of negotiations and agreements with foreign government, a responsibility shared by the Departments of State and Transport.[32]

The Commission tendered its final report in May 1990. Among its sixty-four recommendations, which spoke broadly to all the concerns identified above, were several that directly addressed the bitter complaints levied by the families of victims against their own government's handling of the disaster. Equally significant were the series of recommendations that set out to elevate the role of aviation security within the bureaucracy of the U.S. Government and the airport system generally, as well as among air carriers.

A further inquiry was established by Scotland's chief law officer in October 1990. Known as a Fatal Accident Inquiry, this also concluded that an IED was responsible for downing of the aircraft. Significantly, it also underlined the importance of matching passengers with their luggage and the vulnerability of passenger/baggage systems that relied on X-ray machines alone. In the case of Pan Am, it specifically observed that their "reliance on X-ray screening alone in relation to interline baggage at Heathrow and Frankfurt was a defect in a system of working which contributed to the deaths."[33] Rodney Wallis has posited that the head of this inquiry would have known that the German police had broadly circulated a warning after they had raided premises in Neuss and Frankfurt in October 1988. These raids had led to arrest of members of the Popular Front for the Liberation of Palestine–General Command and the seizure of a number of IEDs. One of these was comprised of a Toshiba radio-cassette player and some 300 grams of Semtex explosive with a barometric trigger. This warning had clearly indicated that such IED's "would be very difficult to identify by X-ray procedures."[34]

Indictments were subsequently laid in both the United States and Britain. As Libya refused to tender the indicted individuals to the British and American justice systems, the U.S. and U.K. governments, supported by France,[35] pursued a United Nations Resolution that would both condemn Libya and impose sanctions. Once imposed, these had a significant impact on Libya's economy. To avoid extended damage, the Libyan government eventually agreed: to accept responsibility for what had occurred; to provide a compensation package for victims' families; and to have those indicted appear before a Scottish court situated in a neutral country. The subsequent trial found one of the accused guilty and one not guilty.

A UN-appointed observer was highly critical of the trial. He found it exhibited serious problems of due process and noted that the court's decision was "exclusively based on circumstantial evidence and on a series of highly problematic inferences. As to the undersigned's knowledge, there [was] not one single piece of material evidence linking the two accused to the crime."[36] It now appears that the verdict of the Scottish judges may be unsound. The lord advocate who originally issued the warrant against the convicted Libyan now has serious doubts about the veracity of the Maltese shopkeeper's testimony, describing the man as: "not quite the full shilling" and an "apple short of a picnic."[37] In addition, a former very senior police officer has testified that the U.S. Central Intelligence Agency planted the tiny fragment of circuit board that was crucial in gaining the conviction.[38] Equally damning is the claim that Scottish prosecutors suppressed "absolutely crucial" German police evidence from the defence.[39] In 2007, after a four-year investigation, the Scottish Criminal Cases Review Commission ordered a second appeal. It found that Abdelbasset Ali al-Megrahi's conviction "may be unsafe."[40] As a result, numerous alternative theories about who was ultimately responsible for the Lockerbie disaster have abounded, leaving the victims' families further from the truth. Since then, Scottish authorities have taken important steps. First, a decision was made to release al-Magrahi on compassionate grounds because he suffered from terminal prostate cancer. This has meant that his appeal now lies moot. Second, while the authorities have so far failed to respond to demands for a full public inquiry, they have revitalized the police inquiry. This will include a review of the forensic evidence.[41]

D. Air India Flight 182

Prior to June 23, 1985, Sikh radicals had often threatened to blow up Air India planes. It was therefore perhaps not surprising that sabotage was immediately suspected in both incidents and that someone claiming to be a member of the 10th Regiment of the All-India Sikh Student's Federation quickly acknowledged responsibility for the downing of Flight 182.[42] For their part, officials at India's High Commission in Ottawa immediately suggested that two Sikh fugitives who were wanted by the U.S. Federal Bureau of Investigation in connection with an alleged plot to assassinate Prime Minister Rajiv Gandhi during his visit to the United States earlier in the year were being sought in connection with the Narita bombing and the downing of Air India Flight 182.[43]

Though Canadian police immediately treated the events as potentially linked acts of sabotage, the public response of the Canadian Government was more circumspect. Though in the case of the Narita explosion Joe Clark, the Minister of External Affairs, immediately called it a "terrorist bombing," there was no immediate assertion that the downing of Flight 182 was a terrorist incident. Rather, the response of the Canadian Government took two general forms, neither of which did much to inform Canadians about what actions were being taken, except to obfuscate matters. For his part, Prime Minister Brian Mulroney wrote a letter of condolence to his opposite number in India. This was despite the fact that it had quickly been established that the vast majority of those killed were Canadian citizens, albeit of Indian heritage, with many being born in Canada.

Though he was immediately chastised for this initiative by associations representing Indo-Canadians,[44] it had the effect – either by design or by un-intended consequence – of suggesting that the issue was not fully a Canadian problem, but rather an Indian one. Some were thus led to question whether the reaction would have been the same if the victims had been primarily of Anglo-Saxon heritage. Though many media reports quickly suggested that the downing of Air India flight 182 was an act of sabotage because of the simul-taneous explosion in Japan, the government's response may have been partly due to there being insufficient evidence to conclude that the disaster had been caused by an IED. The other response was to say as little as possible about what was actually being done. The records of the House of Commons and govern-ment statements illustrate that several strategies were used to avoid the full accountability of ministers and the agencies for which they were responsible. It was claimed that, as a police investigation was underway, any discussion of the activities that led up to the bombing might jeopardize a future criminal pros-ecution. Similarly, the government raised national security grounds to prevent any debate over either the preparedness and capacities of security programs or what was known by the Canadian Government, the new Canadian Security Intelligence Service (CSIS), or the Royal Canadian Mounted Police (RCMP) about the threat posed by supporters of an independent Sikh homeland in the Punjab among the Sikh diaspora in Canada. And as a high-level panel had been formed to assess aviation safety, there was no need for any independent review.

Parliamentarians should wait until this had been reported before pressing for answers. Similarly, a public judicial inquiry was unnecessary because the Indian Government had initiated one.

Several inquiries were, however, undertaken by various governments. A coroner's inquest was conducted in Ireland immediately after the disaster as it was to this country that all bodies retrieved from the crash site were sent for autopsy. The coroner's report was completed on September 23, 1985, well before any clear evidence as to the cause of the disaster was available. As such, it did little more than identify the immediate cause of death of the 131 bodies that were recovered. Significantly, none of the bodies on which autopsies were conducted revealed any indication of fire or explosion.[45]

Canada was required by international agreement to investigate the disaster. This was conducted by the Canadian Aviation Safety Board (CASB) and completed by January 22, 1986. While the CASB concluded that there was no evidence of structural failure, it went on to note that:

> There is considerable circumstantial and other evidence to indicate that the initial event was an explosion occurring in the forward cargo compartment. This evidence is not conclusive. However, the evidence does not support any other conclusion.[46]

Part of the circumstantial evidence concerned the possible connection between the two events that occurred on June 23. Investigators discovered that a single person had purchased two tickets – one for a flight leaving Vancouver in a westerly direction that would make a connection in Japan with homeward bound Air India Flight 301; the other heading eastward making a connection with Air India Flight 182 in Montreal. In both instances interlined baggage was carried on the initial flights from Vancouver without being accompanied by the ticketed passengers. At the time, the CASB was unable to confirm that devices exploded in the interlined luggage. It did observe, however, that the Indian High Commission had sent a diplomatic note to the Department of External Affairs as early as May 17, 1985, concerning the threat posed by extremist elements to Indian diplomatic missions or Air India. Furthermore, in early June it had made requests to Department of Transport offices in Ottawa, Montreal, and Toronto and to RCMP offices in Montreal and Toronto for "full and strict security coverage and other appropriate security measures."[47]

As early as July 13, 1985, the Indian Government had decided to establish a court of investigation (rather than a commission of inquiry) under Justice B.N. Kirpal of the Delhi High Court. This inquiry published its findings on February 26, 1986. In addition to making several recommendations to improve aviation security, it also concluded that there was:

> ... circumstantial as well as direct evidence which directly points to the cause of the accident as being that of an explosion of a bomb in the forward cargo hold of the aircraft. At the same time there is complete lack of evidence to indicate that there was any structural failure.[48]

With regard to the interlined baggage, it observed that no lost-luggage claims were ever subsequently made.[49]

While the Canadian Government declined to establish a public inquiry, a number of investigations were initiated behind closed doors. Being cognizant of the possible connection between the downing of Air India Flight 182 and the explosion of an IED at Tokyo's Narita Airport in luggage emanating from Canada, Prime Minister Mulroney asked the Security and Intelligence Co-ordinator, Blair Seaborn, to lead a review by the Interdepartmental Committee on Security and Intelligence of aviation security in Canada. This report, which remained secret for some time, made several recommendations to improve airport and airline security.[50]

The Security Intelligence Review Committee (SIRC) is responsible for reviewing the activities of CSIS. Each year it is required to submit a report of such a review to the minister, who in turn must table it in Parliament within a set period. As such, it was at the time the only regular window through which Parliament could view the secret world. At some point during the late 1980s, SIRC initiated an investigation of CSIS's activities related to the downing of Air India Flight 182. This focused only on the activities of CSIS and was intended primarily to establish whether that organization had complied with its statutory obligations and policies. This report was not, however, completed until 1992, at which time there was still no clear evidence to confirm the exact cause of the disaster. While SIRC's report for the solicitor general, titled *CSIS Activities in Regard to the Destruction of Air India Flight 182 on June 23, 1985 – A SIRC Review*, remains classified as top secret, SIRC's annual report for 1991–92, which was tabled in Parliament, provided a summary of those findings it believed it could divulge publicly.[51] Careful scrutiny of its assessment suggests at best that it posed more questions than it answered.

The analysis is divided into two main parts: what happened before and after the downing of Air India Flight 182. Before the event, Sikh extremism was not high on CSIS's priorities. Certainly the Service had neither developed a comprehensive understanding of how it functioned nor identified what its objectives were. Furthermore, CSIS's work during this period appears to have been geared more to assisting U.S. intelligence agencies in identifying potential threats against Prime Minister Rajiv Gandhi prior to and during his visit to the United States in June 1985. In fact, the Service's physical surveillance of Sikh extremist leaders ceased immediately following his departure from the United States, some seven days before Air India Flight 182 was destroyed. Not having Punjabi speakers available meant that communication interceptions were not available in translated form until weeks, if not months, after the fact. To a lesser extent CSIS was also interested in threats to the Indian Government and its assets in Canada. In this regard SIRC acknowledged that the Indian Government did alert Canadian authorities about specific threats to Air India. But its report downplayed their significance by saying that none materialized or contained a specific warning about Flight 182. No mention was made of the fact that Air India's only flight from Canada each week was the Flight 182 departure from Montreal. However, SIRC did acknowledge that CSIS warned the government and qualified the threat as being "high."

The weakness in the security oversight system is revealed clearly by SIRC's analysis of the events prior to June 23, 1985.[52] Though SIRC claimed to have examined all the warnings forwarded by External Affairs and the RCMP, it seems to have been unaware of those received by the Department of Transport. Because SIRC is only permitted by law to review the steps CSIS took, the response of the RCMP and its minister, then the solicitor general, as well as the Privy Council Office and the departments of Transport and External

Affairs are not considered. And even where CSIS's response was considered, there was at best a certain naïveté or at worst an attempt to make excuses for what appears to have been a serious lack of initiative and co-ordination in the Service. Several fairly obvious questions appear not to have been considered. For example: given the fact that CSIS had on June 6 raised its assessment of the threat posed by Sikh extremists to "high," why was it that its monitoring of a single Sikh extremist leader (Talwinder Singh Parmar) was not expanded to a wider array of subjects rather being shut down altogether on June 17? In this regard, why is it that the person who accompanied Parmar and Inderjit Singh Reyat to a place near Duncan where they conducted a trial explosion has never formally been identified? Given the high threat level, why was there no sense of urgency in having the audiotapes of the extremist leader translated from Punjabi. And why was there no emphasis placed by SIRC in their report on rectifying this clear deficiency? Why was there by June 1985 no strategic intelligence on Sikh extremists? Did this reflect a shortage of strategic analysts at CSIS, a shortage of diplomatic reporting, a lack of foreign intelligence or shared intelligence from traditional intelligence partners? Furthermore, there is a disquieting discontinuity between CSIS's intelligence sources foretelling of "something big or spectacular" going to happen and SIRC's contention that there was nothing specific in the warnings provided by the Indian Government that would have enabled CSIS to predict an attack against Flight 182.

Several issues surfaced after the event. While SIRC acknowledged certain turf wars in the relationship between CSIS and the RCMP, it tended to believe that such eventualities were not of significant consequence and put them down to policies not yet being properly developed. On one issue, however, SIRC expressed serious concerns about both the extant policies and the handling of procedures. Apparently, CSIS had erased some 150 audiotapes of conversations between their principal target and other parties. It is clear from the SIRC report, though not explicitly stated, that at the time of the disaster CSIS had not translated the vast majority of the tapes recorded (some 210) between March and June of 1985. Furthermore SIRC was unable to establish whether they were ever translated. By 1992 it was, in the Committee's words, "impossible to say with any certainty that no unprocessed tapes were erased."[53] The issue of foreign government involvement in undermining the elements of the Sikh diaspora in Canada that favoured an independent Sikh homeland in the Punjab was first broached in a series of articles in the *Globe and Mail* in November 1985. Based on a four-month investigation using government sources, these suggested that India conducted intelligence operations both directly through its consulates and indirectly using agent provocateurs to infiltrate Canada's Sikh community with a view to discrediting the mainline separatist movement through extremist activity. These concluded that "as a result of its activities in Canada, India itself may have been *indirectly* responsible for the bombings." [54] At the time, both the Indian and Canadian governments officially denied any such responsibility. The Indian High Commission specifically denied that it had any intelligence operatives in Canada. [55] SIRC examined the claims subsequently made in *Soft Target: How the Indian Intelligence Service Penetrated Canada*, a book published by the author of the original articles and another reporter. [56] It concluded that the claims were without foundation while at the same time failing to acknowledge that at least three Indian diplomats had been asked to leave Canada in 1987. [57] It also appears to have been oblivious of the fact that Pakistan's Inter Services Intelligence was operating in Canada, [58] and that both Pakistan and China were alleged to be sponsors and supporters of Sikh extremism. [59]

Documents from the trial of two of the people who were charged with murder are revealing on a number of scores. The SIRC report, which even at that point was still being touted by the solicitor general as making a public inquiry unnecessary, came in for particularly harsh criticism. A memorandum from a senior RCMP officer, dated in February 1996, called it grossly inaccurate in several ways. Of critical importance was the claim that differences between CSIS and the RCMP had not led to a loss of evidence, a point given credibility by a CSIS officer subsequently acknowledging that he destroyed some of the tapes to protect the identity of sources. [60] Also of significance was the disclaimer concerning Government of India involvement. The claim that the RCMP had found no evidence to believe it was involved was false. According to Gary Bass, now an assistant commissioner, "the truth of the matter is that the RCMP never thoroughly investigated the issue, which means that apparently no one did." [61] It has also come to light that SIRC backed off from its original plan to conduct a broad review of CSIS's involvement in the investigation. Apparently, in 1989, senior officials in the solicitor general's office talked the Committee out of doing so on grounds that they would queer the prosecution. Ron Atley, then the chair of SIRC, admitted that "I guess with the value of hindsight, sitting in the year 2005, we should have been more aggressive."[62] Similar pressure was applied to the Special Committee of the House of Commons that reviewed the CSIS Act and Security Offences Act in 1989–90. While staff of that Committee had recommended examining the Air India tragedy in order to understand how well the relationship between CSIS and the RCMP was working, they were told that it was "not on the table."[63] Given the criticism that the Special Committee levied at SIRC's research capacity at the time, it is highly likely that, had SIRC's report been available in 1990, it would also have come in for severe criticism.[64]

The pressure by the victims' families, a few MP's, various media, and some academics eventually paid off once the Crown's case had failed to obtain murder convictions against two of the alleged conspirators.[65] In 2005, the Government appointed an "eminent person" to evaluate whether a public inquiry was viable more than twenty years after the fact and, if so, what form it should take. The report provided by Bob Rae, the former NDP premier of Ontario and former member of the Security Intelligence Review Committee, was released on November 23, 2005.[66] The approach and content of *Lessons to be Learned* differed in important respects from all those that had gone before. Significantly, it was victim-centric, reflecting the new government's attitudes[67] and emphasized the fact that it was a *Canadian* catastrophe, one that had never truly been understood as such. Rae met with the families of victims on several occasions with a view to understanding their objectives in holding an inquiry. His report's primary conclusion was that there should be a focused, fact-finding, policy-based inquiry that would pursue the public interest broadly by concentrating on lessons learned, not individual conduct. This would be done by Cabinet Order in Council – not under the *Inquiries Act* – would not have subpoena powers, would be less costly, and would report relatively quickly. He believed this should deal with four specific themes: the adequacy of the threat assessment provided by Canadian government officials concerning Sikh terrorism; whether relationships between government departments and agencies – most particularly CSIS and the RCMP – detrimentally affected the surveillance of terrorism suspects; the intelligence/evidence/enforcement conundrum; and whether Canada has adequately learned from the grievous breaches of aviation security that occurred.[68] The Rae report is also significant in two other ways. It was the first to identify several of the perpetrators specifically. This in part was made possible by the Justice Josephson's judgment in the *Queen v. Malik and Bagri*.[69] Second, the report was the first to identify both the aviation security regulations that Air India supposedly had in place prior to June 23, 1985, as well as the key changes that were undertaken by Canada immediately following the Air India tragedy.[70] If there is one serious weakness in this report, it is that it neither comments on Air India's enforcement of its regulations nor how quickly and thoroughly changes were made in Canada.

In the run-up to 2006 election, the Conservative party made a commitment to hold a full judicial inquiry into the Air India disaster. Once elected, they followed through on this commitment by establishing a commission under former Supreme Court Justice John Major.[71] The commission's terms of reference are broader than Rae recommended. In addition to the themes identified in *Lesson to be Learned*, it is to address questions relating to terrorist financing, the protection of witnesses against intimidation, and whether there are special prosecutorial needs relating to terrorism cases. In approaching the issue of aviation security policy, legislation, and related regulatory regimes, it is to work with the Independent Advisory Panel set up to review the provisions and operation of the *Canadian Air Transport Security Authority Act* for the Minister of Transport.[72] There are signs that this commission has run into the roadblocks, costs, and time-line problems that Rae forecasted in two particular areas. First, an examination of its document "Background and Summary of Facts" is short on facts.[73] There is, for example, no mention of Inderjit Singh Reyat, or to what he pled guilty. Nor is the conclusion reached by Justice Josephson concerning the involvement of Talwinder Singh Parmar recorded. Likewise, there is no mention concerning the intimidation and murder of potential witnesses. Second, the commission has shown signs of not being particularly victim-friendly. While it has spent several sessions taking testimony from the families of victims, it has chosen not to provide transcripts of these and other hearings available (as previous commissions of inquiry have done) because of the "horrendous translation costs" involved.[74] If it is true, as the Rae report suggested, that the downing of Air India Flight 182 has not been broadly seen in Canada as a *Canadian* catastrophe, this would seem to be a very short-sighted decision, given the opportunity it would have provided for the families of victims to tell their story of the tragedy and the impact it has had on their lives in their own words to Canadians from coast to coast to coast.

6. CONCLUSIONS

This chapter set out to establish whether government's of different political hues initially depict disasters in ways that are subsequently found to be false through either official accounts of events or as the result of information coming into the public domain through other means. In the case of the shooting down of KAL 007, the Soviets initially kept their own counsel. The release of intercepted communications between the Soviet air crew responsible for the downing and its base made denials no longer feasible and provided the United States with an opportunity to seek and achieve a significant propaganda victory over the callousness of the Soviet Union towards the lives of innocent civilians and civilian air traffic. It also provided a strategic victory regarding the deployment of Pershing missiles in Europe. While subsequent statements by the Soviet pilot himself indicate that he knew the aircraft was civilian, had navigation lights illuminated, and that he fired warning shots with his cannon armed with non-tracer shells,[75] Soviet officials remained convinced that KAL 007's deviation from its course was intentional and part of an ongoing spy mission that had been in place for more than a decade. International investigations completed by ICAO took a different approach and concluded more benign intentions on the part of the South Korean pilots. Both the Soviets and the United States governments initially showed little concern for the victims and their families, many of whom to this day are dissatisfied with the official explanations of events. In many respects, the most likely explanation concerns both the navigational inadequacies of Korean Airlines personnel as well as the incompetence and disarray of Soviet Eastern Asia air defence systems at the time. As a result, senior Soviet decision makers in Moscow did not have the full picture at hand and remained in a state of confusion for several days, and regional commanders lacked experience in dealing with serious violations of Soviet air space, while rules of engagement were not followed.[76]

The shooting down by the USS *Vincennes* of the Iranian Airbus was initially depicted and acknowledged as a terrible error in the heat of battle. The fact that subsequent international investigations showed that the U.S. ship had intruded into Iranian waters and that the Airbus was ascending on its normal course on its scheduled civilian flight path – not descending as argued by USS *Vincennes* crew members – suggests that the U.S. Navy was intent on covering up a gross act of incompetence, only offset by the fact that the tracking system on board was new. It is likely that this behaviour and the elongated way the Americans dealt with compensation for Iranian victims exacerbated the festering sore that exists between the Iranian and American Governments. It may even have given fresh impetus for terrorist attacks against the United States.

From the outset the downing of Pan Am 103 was depicted as a terrorist incident. Evidence collected on the ground confirmed that. But the British and American Governments differed considerably towards the holding of public inquiries. In the UK, despite pressure from victims' families, there was no inquiry, while in the United States a presidential commission was established. This inquiry was important in three ways. First, it reluctantly responded to the demands and interests of the families of victims. Secondly, its very existence demonstrated the flaw in the Canadian Government's argument that any inquiry into Air India would necessarily jeopardize the ongoing criminal investigations or be fruitless because nothing of significance could be revealed for national security reasons about aviation security. And thirdly, it indicated the fact that the existence of aviation security regulations did not necessarily mean that national airlines or foreign airports would follow them. A degree of enforcement was necessary. In addition, the recent revitalization of the police inquiry, following the release of al-Megrahi on compassionate grounds, may lead to a process that more profoundly questions who was ultimately responsible for the Lockerbie disaster.

The downing of Air India, which chronologically occurred second after the KAL 007 disaster, has been paradoxically a better studied disaster but also among the least well understood. As with most of the other cases, the interests of the victims and their families were the least well considered. Only recently have they come to the fore. Why it took so long for successive Canadian governments to recognize that the downing of Air India constituted the largest mass murder in Canadian history beggars belief.[77] As a result, it may not be surprising that many may share the view that the whole system let them down and that a multi-levelled failure occurred, one that covered: intelligence gathering and assessment, police investigation, the prosecutorial process, the review and oversight bodies of government, the witness protection system, to say nothing of aviation security provided by Transport Canada and Air India. In holding this view, the Canadian public may have certain unrealistic expectations. Intelligence operations necessarily fail on some occasions. Similarly, police investigations sometimes do not come to fruition because evidence that can be used in court is unavailable or cannot be established, even when the police "know" who was responsible for a particular crime. Likewise, prosecutions sometimes fail because they cannot meet the burden of proof required by Canadian courts to obtain a conviction. But what may realistically be hoped for is that when such failures occur, the government of the day will establish inquiries that provide an opportunity for the families of victims to garner some understanding and sense of closure. Similarly, it is to be hoped that independent review bodies and parliamentary committees will either not listen to government entreaties not to investigate such failures or, at the very least, identify publicly that they are doing so and provide reasons for a reasonable delay.

Notes

1 For arguments concerning how the risk of terrorism is exaggerated, see: John Mueller, *Overblown: How Politicians and the Terrorism Industry Inflate National Security Threats, and Why We Believe Them* (New York: Free Press, 2006).

2 Suicide terrorism began to manifest itself in a significant way in the 1980s. See: Robert Pape, *Dying to Win: The Strategic Logic of Suicide Terrorism* (New York: Random House, 2005).

3 For the origins of al-Qaida, see: National Commission on Terrorist Attacks Upon the United States, "The Foundation of the New Terrorism," in *The 9/11 Commission Report* (New York: W.W. Norton, 2004), 47–70.

4 See Fawaz A. Gerges, *The Far Enemy: Why Jihad Went Global* (Cambridge: Cambridge University Press, 2005).

5 Nelson Mandela, perhaps the classic example of someone who was imprisoned as a "terrorist," was instrumental in liberating his people and later became president of his nation. He came to support the use of violence by the African National Congress only as a last resort and, even then, tried to limit its use to military and government targets.

6 See Karim-Aly Kassam, "On Being a Canadian Muslim Post September 11th," In Karim-Aly Kassam, George Melnyk, and Lynne Perras, eds., *Canada and September 11th: Impact and Responses* (Calgary: Detselig, 2002), 185–193 at 187.

7 For previous incidents, see: Jin-Tai Choi, *Aviation Terrorism: Historical Survey, Perspectives and Response* (London: St. Martin's Press 1994), 155–57.

8 Kenneth M. Pollack, *The Persian Puzzle: The Conflict between Iran and America* (New York: Random House, 2004), 207.

9 Some 269 people from ten countries were killed on board KAL 007. The majority were Korean; 67 were Americans; 28 were Japanese. Thirty-eight of the 299 on board IR655 were non-Iranians drawn from six countries. The 270 people on Pan Am 103 came from 21 countries.

10 Of the 270 people on Pan Am some 189 (70%) were American citizens.

11 It did not even comply with the new Federal Aviation Administration guidelines in important respects. Sally J. Ray has noted that in December 1988 the Federal Aviation Authority fined Pan Am for numerous security breaches. See her chapter on Pan 103 in: Sally Ray, *Strategic Communications in Crisis Management* (Westport, CT: Quorum, 1999), 183–204.

12 Cited in Alan Gerson and Jerry Adler, *The Price of Terror* (New York: Harper-Collins, 2001), 30–31.

13 For a discussion of such framing in two of the events discussed here, see: Robert M. Entman, "Framing U.S. Coverage of International News: Contrasts in Narrative of the KAL and Iran Air Incidents," *Journal of Communication* 41, no. 4 (1991): 6–27.

14 For the earlier background, see: Seymour Hersh, *The Target is Destroyed: What Really Happened to Flight 007 and What the America Knew about It* (London: Faber and Faber, 1986). Past practice and the fact that little wreckage and no bodies were recovered from KAL 007 has led some to believe that the aircraft was forced down over Soviet territory and that the passengers were held in captivity.

15 At the time some members of the U.S. intelligence community doubted that the Soviets knew it was civilian.

16 The quotations are drawn from R.W. Johnson, *Shootdown: The Flight of 007 and the American Connection* (New York: Viking, 1986), 115.

17 The need to protect intelligence sources and methods is frequently touted. In this case the signals intelligence came largely from the Japanese SIGINT station at Misawa. It is not known how the Japanese Government felt about having their capacities revealed publicly or whether they were even consulted, especially when other sources responsible for collecting the ground controllers' contribution were kept secret.

18 Seymour Hersh, *The Target is Destroyed: What Really Happened to Flight 007 and What the America Knew about It* (London: Faber and Faber, 1986), 89.

19 David Pearson and John Keppel, "New Pieces of the Puzzle of 007," *The Nation* 17, no. 24 (1985): 104–10 at 110.

20 David Corn, "Fear and Obstruction on the K.A.L. Trail," *The Nation* 17, no. 24 (1985): 110–13.

21 Ibid., 112. ICAO's KAL 007 inquiry had five full-time and four part-time investigators for sixty days while the NTSB's investigation of the DC-10 crash at Chicago's O'Hare airport in 1979 had more than a hundred people for seven months.

22 Ibid., 113.

23 R.W. Johnson, *Shootdown: The Flight of 007 and the American Connection* (New York: Viking, 1986), 120.

24 Alvin Snyder, "The Truth about the Korean Airlines Flight-007," *Washington Post*, September 1, 1996.

25 The memoranda were published in October 16, 1992, *Izvestia*, http://www.rescue007.org/TopSecretMemos.htm (accessed December 6, 2006).

26 See: United Nations Security Council, Letter dated July 3, 1988, from the Acting Permanent Representative of the Islamic Republic of Iran to the United Nations addressed to the Secretary General.

27 See, for example, the Statement of Admiral William J. Crowe on the Destruction of an Iranian Jetliner by the United States Navy over the Persian Gulf on July 3, 1988, and the Letter to the Speaker of the House of Representatives and the President Pro Tempore of the Senate on the Destruction of an Iranian Jetliner by the United States Navy over the Persian Gulf of July 4, 1988.

28 See statement by Assistant to the President for Press Relations Fitzwater on United States Policy Regarding the Accidental Attack on an Iranian Jetliner over the Persian Gulf of July 11, 1988.

29 The Commission's terms of reference were established by Executive Order. See the United States, Executive Order 12686 *President's Commission on Aviation Security and Terrorism* , August 4, 1989.

30 United States, President's Commission on Aviation Security and Terrorism, *Report to the President* (Washington, D.C., May 15, 1990).

31 Ibid., ii.

32 United States Senate: Senator Frank Lautenberg, May 15, 1990, *Findings and Recommendations of the Commission of Aviation Security and Terrorism*. http://www.globalsecurity.org/security/library/congress/1990_cr/s900511-terror.htm (accessed November 29, 2006).

33 Cited by Rodney Wallis, *The Story and the Lessons* (Westport, CT: Praeger, 2001), 56.

34 Ibid., 21–23 and 56.

35 France too suffered the sabotage of one of its aircraft for which it blamed Libya. Flight UTA 772 was blown up over the Sahara desert in September 1989. It is often referred to as the "forgotten flight" as it was overshadowed by events related to Pan Am 103. See: Paul Reynolds, August 19, 2003, "UTA 772: The forgotten flight," *BBC News*, http://news.bbc.co.uk/2/hi/uk_news/3163621.stm (accessed February 3, 2007).

36 Hans Kochler, "Report on and Evaluation of the Lockerbie Trial Conducted by the Special Scottish Court in the Netherlands at Kamp Van Zeist. Santiago, Chile," February 3, 2001. http://i-p-o.org/lockerbie-report.htm (accessed December 2, 2006).

37 See: Mark Macaskill, "Fraser: My Lockerbie Trial Doubts," *TimesonLine*, November 30, 2006. http://www.timesonline.co.uk/article/O,, 2090–1839307,00.html (accessed November 30, 2006).

38 See: Marcello Mega, "Police Chief–Lockerbie Evidence Was Faked," *Scotland on Sunday*, August 28, 2005. http://news.scotsman.com/lockerbie/Former-police-chief-says-Lockerbie.2656612.jp (accessed October 15, 2006).

39 See: Macleod Murdo, "Lockerbie Retrial Demand Over New Evidence," *Scotland on Sunday*, October 15, 2006. http://news.scotsman.com/scotland.cfm?id=1526692006 (accessed December 2, 2006).

40 Anon., "Lockerbie bomber in fresh appeal," *BBC News*, April 28, 2009. http://news.bbc.co.uk/2/hi/uk_news/scotland/8021385.stm (accessed June 18, 2009).

41 See: Robert Mendick and Andrew Alderson, "Police relaunch Lockerbie bombing investigation," *Sunday Telegraph*, October 24, 2009. http://www.telegraph.co.uk/news/worldnews/africaandindianocean/libya/6425205/Police-relaunch-Lockerbie-bombing-investigation.html (November 2, 2009).

42 Thomas Walkon et al., "Sabotage Feared as 329 Die in Jet," *Globe and Mail*, June 24, 1985, 1–2. The Kashmir Liberation Army also claimed responsibility.

43 Zuhair Kashmeri, "Police Seeking Two Sikh Fugitives in Air Tragedies," *Globe and Mail*, June 24, 1985, 1–2.

44 Anon, "No Proof Yet of Terrorism Mulroney Says," *Montreal Gazette*, June 25, 1985, A7.

45 See: Canada, Canadian Aviation Safety Board, *Aviation Occurrence: Boeing 747-237B, VT-EFO Cork, Ireland 110 Miles West 23 June 1985* (Ottawa, January 22, 1986), 20.

46 Ibid., 58.

47 Ibid., 18.

48 India. Delhi. Court of Investigation. *Report on the Accident to Air India Boeing 747 Aircraft VT-EFO "Kanishka" on 23rd June 1985*, February 26, 1986, 159–60.

49 Ibid., 160–62.

50 Canada. Ottawa. Privy Council Office, *Security Arrangements Affecting Airports and Airlines in Canada*, September 24, 1985, 3. It does, however, indicate that measures to improve deficiencies were made after the disaster.

51 For this summary, refer to: Canada, Security Intelligence Review Committee. *Annual Report for 1991–92* (Ottawa: Ministry of Supply and Services, 1992), 5–14.

52 For an equally scathing assessment of SIRC's capacity, see the chapter by Robert Matas, the *Globe and Mail's* reporter who covered the Air India inquiry from 1987 onwards: Robert Matas, "Outside Canadian Intelligence," in *Inside Canadian Intelligence: Exposing the New Realities of Espionage and International Terrorism*, ed. Dwight Hamilton (Toronto: Dundern Press, 2006), 165–77.

53 Ibid., 13.

54 See: Zuhair Kashmeri, "Indian Spies suspected of trying to undermine Sikh groups in Canada," *Globe and Mail*, November 21, 1985, A1, A25. And: —(November 22, 1985), "Indian James Bond or Sikh Loyalist," *Globe and Mail*, November 22, 1985, A17 — , "Sikh Separatist Movement in Canada target of Indian spy game, sources say," *Globe and Mail*, November 28, 1985, A12. Emphasis added.

55 Canadian Press and Staff, "RCMP denies probers see India, bombs link," *Globe and*

Mail, November 22, 1985, A17. It should be noted that the *Globe*'s managing editor went on record as saying that the newspaper stood by its story.

56 Zuhair Kashmeri and Brian McAndrew, *Soft Target: How the Indian Intelligence Service penetrated Canada* (Toronto: James Lorimer, 1989).

57 Zuhair Kashmeri, "Three Indian Diplomats Identified as Spies," *Globe and Mail*, March 28, 1987, A1. According to Kasmeri and McAndrew, this information was leaked by CSIS. See *Soft Target*, 128. A former Indian intelligence official suggests that the entire Research and Analysis Wing of the external intelligence organization was made *personna non grata*. See Maloy Krishnan Dhar, *Open Secrets: Indian Intelligence Unveiled* (New Delhi: Manas Publications, 2005), 306.

58 Indian intelligence was apparently aware of this. See: Dhar, *Open Secrets*, 306.

59 See: Frank Camper, "The Sikh Terror Plot–Part 1," *Penthouse*, April 1986, 64.

60 Andrew Mitrovica and Jeff Sallot, "CSIS agent destroyed Air India evidence," *Globe and Mail*, January 6, 2000, AI.

61 Robert Matas, "Exoneration of CSIS assailed by Mountie," *Globe and Mail*, June 10, 2003, A1 and A8.

62 Campbell Clark, "Late in the day for a public inquiry," *Globe and Mail*, March 17, 2005, A11.

63 Communication with the author who served as the Special Committee's Research Director.

64 For criticism of SIRC's investigative capacity and other problems faced by the Special Committee, see: Stuart Farson, "The Noble Lie Revisited: Parliament's Five-Year Review of the CSIS Act – Instrument of Change or Weak Link in the Chain of Accountability," in *Accountability for Criminal Justice: Selected Essays*, ed. Philip C. Stenning (Toronto: University of Toronto Press, 1995), 185–212. Especially at: 203–5.

65 It is thought that there were between six and eight conspirators; at least three of whom are now thought to be dead.

66 *Lessons to Be Learned: Report of the Honourable Bob Rae, Independent Advisor to the Minister of Public Safety and Emergency Preparedness on outstanding questions with respect to the bombing of Air India Flight 182*, November 23, 2005 (Ottawa: Air India Secretariat).

67 These were best reflected by Prime Minister Paul Martin in both words and deeds. He was the first prime minister to meet with the victims of families, to visit the crash site memorial in Ireland, and to designate June 23 as a National Day of Remembrance for Victims of Terrorism.

68 *Lessons Learned*, 22.

69 See: Canada. *Regina v. Malik and Bagri.* [2005] BCSC 500. *Reasons for Judgement*, dated March 16, 2005.

70 *Lessons Learned*, 18–21.

71 At the time of writing, the commission had completed its work but its report has not been published.

72 Its report has recently been published. See: Canada, Transport Canada, "Flight Plan: Managing the Risks in Aviation Security," *Report of the Advisory Panel*. http://www.tc.gc.ca/tcss/CATSA/Final_Report-Rapport_final/chapter1_e.htm#Intro, especially section 1.1.2–3 (accessed December 17, 2006).

73 See: Canada, Commission of Inquiry into the Investigation of Bombing of Air India Flight 182. *Background and Summary of the Facts*. http://www.majorcomm.ca/documents/FINAL_Facts_dossier_EN.pdf (accessed December 17, 2006).

74 Correspondence between the author and staff of the commission, dated November 7, 2006.

75 Michael Gordon, "Ex-Soviet Pilot still insists KAL 007 was spying," *New York Times* (December 9, 1996), A12.

76 Christopher Andrew and Oleg Gordievsky, *KGB: The Inside Story of its Foreign Operations from Lenin to Gorbachev* (London: Hodder and Stoughton, 1990), 497–501. See also: Jonathan Haslam, "The KAL Shootdown (1983) and the State of Soviet Air Defences," *Intelligence and National Security* 3, no. 4 (October 1988): 128–33. The landing of a Cessna light aircraft outside the Kremlin in 1987 by a young West German pilot provided further evidence.

77 One should note that members of the media were sometimes equally guilty of this misperception, frequently citing such other tragedies as the 1989 "Montreal Massacre," in which fourteen women were shot at l'Ecole politechnique.

CHAPTER 4

The Word "Terrorism" and Its Impact on Public Consciousness

George Melnyk
University of Calgary

> Terrorism means an ideologically motivated unlawful act or acts, including but not limited to the use of violence or force or threat of violence or force, committed by or on behalf of any group(s), organization(s) or government(s) for the purpose of influencing any government and/or instilling fear in the public or a section of the public.
>
> *– Terrorism clause added to author's Home Insurance Policy 2006*

> The prevailing ideological keyword of our present is "terrorism," a word that slices acts out of the historical contexts that gave them birth, reframing them as spectacles that can be understood only as outbursts of fanatical irrationality.
>
> *– Stephen Henighan,[1] A Report on the Afterlife of Culture*

> For worse *and* for better, therefore; for the worst *and* the best, the worst, that, it seems, *is* also the best. That is what remains terrible, terrifying, terrorizing; that is, on earth, *in terra*, in and beyond territories, the ultimate resource of all terrorisms.
>
> *– Jacques Derrida[2]*

In the spring of 2009 Bob Rae, the former Premier of Ontario and now a Canadian Member of Parliament, went to Sir Lanka to investigate the humanitarian crisis facing Tamils after the final, bloody defeat of the Tamil Tigers, a longtime insurgent movement seeking Tamil independence. At the time the Sri Lankan military was purging the formerly encircled Tamil civilians of any guerillas that might have been hiding amongst them. Rae was ejected from the country because the government accused him of supporting terrorists and terrorism by seeking to investigate what was happening. The Canadian government expressed outrage. Nevertheless, this is an example of how the words "terrorists" and "terrorism" have come to be used by authorities around the world. The state is the one that controls the terminology and its use. It defines who is and who is not a practitioner of terrorism and it never accuses itself of such acts. So when the State of Israel invaded Gaza in 2008 and killed over a thousand people and caused several billions of dollars in war damages, it defined the de facto authorities of that territory as "terrorists" while excusing its actions as legitimate, justified, and proper. This was not an act of terror even though its violent methods were meant to terrify the Palestinians living there and overthrow their authorities. This sounds very much like the goals of "terrorism" listed in the insurance policy quoted above. The insurance policy and the Canadian cultural commentator, Stephen Henighan, use the term "ideological" in order to politicize both the actions and the language associated with terrorism. Thus these terms are politically charged and motivated. And as the philosopher Jacques Derrida points out, it is "the resource of all terrorism," including that of the state, to designate what or who is the worst and what or who is the best. The terrorist is the worst and a huge number of acts are listed as terrorist, including launching mostly ineffective homemade mortar shells from Gaza or planting a bomb on a subway or placing an IED under a military convoy in Afghanistan. The state is the best and so the national saviour. In reverse, the insurgent sees his movement as the best and his opponent as the worse. The discrepancies in power between the labeller, the labelled, and the labels used in public discourse is the focus of this article. It seeks to deconstruct a terminology that has become counterproductive in resolving political issues because of its increasingly rhetorical nature and decontextualized ahistoricity.

1. Defining Terrorism

Between the legalism of a clause in a Canadian home insurance policy and the philosophical wordplay of a renowned European thinker exists a broad field on which public discourse is played out in contemporary societies. At one end stand the goal posts of financial implication, where those seeking compensation and those denying it struggle on, while at the opposite end stand the goal posts of philosophical dialogue, where an ordinary term is deconstructed in order to wring out some hidden meaning. The general public seldom plays at either of these ends. Instead it is stuck in midfield, bombarded by messages coming at it from various directions, as it tries to make up its mind which meaning to embrace. It is a cultural struggle that is played out every day in the media, as Henighan reminds us.

A major source of understanding the meaning of political language is the media, which regularly adopts the usage offered by government leaders and repeats it endlessly. Because governments are ideologically motivated entities with economic and social interests and political goals, the terms they use are usually loaded with those interests. These interests are given a patina of morality that is meant to weigh on public consciousness. The result is the creation of a public morality, defined in terms of "good" and "bad." Once a government-sponsored term has reached the level of obviousness in media discourse (the words "terrorism," "terrorist" or "terrorist act" come to mind), debate becomes severely restricted. The media creates a general agreement over the basic meaning of a term that suggests its connotations are real and permanent. Once a meaning is considered widely held, the term itself can be applied here and there with impunity because of its established credibility and the authority of those who use it. Occasionally there is a "grey" area that is presented as being good for some and bad for others, but in general the implied morality in certain politically charged words sets parameters for public discourse. Even if there are different viewpoints on how to deal with an issue to which it is applied, the use of the term itself and its validity are not debatable. Because politically sponsored, media-supported definitions establish moral boundaries for public discourse, the public prefers to adopt the prevailing usage, thereby aligning itself with official and widely held meanings. Once this occurs, public terminology takes on a vicious life of its own that makes it seemingly morally indestructible. That indestructibility creates a "black and white" or "for and against" character to discussion of persons and acts. If something is labelled "terrorist" by government sanction, media usage, or the law and the term has been accepted as the descriptor of a heinous moral persona, anyone challenging that usage or application becomes smeared with the label. The term is meant to preclude debate. This is the process of demonization.

For example, the meaning of the term "criminal," when used in the media, has implications for all public discourse, whether or not one favours or opposes harsher prison terms for certain crimes. Simply using the term "criminal" creates an accepted understanding and identity that is seldom debated because the term is considered an obvious designation of unlawfulness and so is closed to further discussion. Who would support criminality (or criminals) as a valid way of being without being totally marginalized? The taken-for-grantedness of this particular term obscures the fact that a criminal is someone that the law and the authorities have designated as such.[3] The word "crime," when used by the media, implies a level of serious wrongdoing and moral turpitude offensive to public morality. But the term itself can be found applied to numerous, less serious situations and in a very general way. Clearly the public does make distinctions among various levels of crime, as does the law. This ability on the part of the public to differentiate serious from non-serious "crimes" is notable, and yet the term itself has come to be used in political and media discourse to carry a heavy moral and anti-social meaning wherever it appears. Being "tough on crime" and criminality becomes a catchword, a motivator for simplistic and undifferentiated thinking about illegality, which is welcomed by certain politicians who seek to use the term to their advantage. The use of the term "crime" in public discourse is similar to a discussion of how the term "terrorism" is used in the media and, in turn, how it plays out in public consciousness.

The use of the word itself in North America by both politicians and the media reached a crescendo after the events of September 11.[4] Over time, the term, which had been sanctified in the American slogan "War on Terror" became less noticeable because events designated as "terrorism" declined in the West. While terrorism is a concept that comes up frequently today in relationship to war situations such as Afghanistan or other conflict zones, the fear and loathing instilled in the public over the term has diminished because of the perceived lack of immediate threat to North America that occurred post-9/11. By 2009 and the election of the Obama administration, the "War on Terror" terminology had been sidelined to some degree because of its association with the rhetoric of the previous Bush administration, though it was not dropped from presidential political vocabulary completely. The political language of terrorism continued unabated in public discourse. The fact that a new administration has found it necessary to tone down the Bush rhetoric was meant to indicate to the public that there was now a political shift in thinking. Announcing the shift also acknowledged the political motivation behind the use of the term in the first place and its continued use in specific circumstances.

Repeated headlines and broadcast language using a certain word create validity and legitimacy for that word and indicate to the public what is acceptable and what constitutes normative values. Because the word and its implied meaning come to be accepted as a not-to-be-debated norm, its inherent power to mould an issue in a certain direction is not discussed. Words like "terrorist" and "terrorism" have come to connote such serious malfeasance that they generate an extreme level of approbation among those that see themselves as a right-thinking and moral public. In the process of achieving this level of acceptance, the ideological underpinnings, state agendas, and interest group strategies attending the term are quietly ignored. All that is allowed is an outright condemnation of the actors, their acts, and their thinking – terrorism and terrorists are the epitome of evil. Because the term has entered a kind of "forbidden zone" of unquestioned legitimacy, this powerful signifier is used to stifle critical examination, thoughtful analysis, and legitimate public discussion in order to hide the goals of manipulative rhetoric.

So what are the now-established meanings implied in the word "terrorism" that residents of Western countries, especially in North America, have come to associate with the term? For the public, terrorism is a violent act against an innocent population perpetrated by heartless, fanatical enemies of that population or its government, whose only goal is death and destruction. Terrorism is an act of aggression and war and must be opposed at all costs. This is the understanding of terrorism that political leaders have been eager to promote.[5] Those associated by the media and politicians with "terrorism" are thereby stripped of any legitimacy: any political or moral justification for their acts or their rationale. Terrorism becomes a mantra to be invoked by politicians and the media to spread fear and loathing. In other times and other places, political elites have used other identities, persons, or peoples to foment animosity. Because terrorism in this view is without any merit whatsoever, it is outright evil and monstrous and beyond the pale of human conduct.

2. DINING WITH DEFINITIONS

In contrast to this general understanding, British journalist Phil Rees, in his provocatively titled book *Dining with Terrorists* (2006), states that defining "terrorism" has been something that the United Nations has been unable to do in spite of repeated efforts.[6] This is not because of a lack of literacy; it is a result of the deep political nuances associated with the word, which in turn suggests that terrorism is not an obvious idea. The political divisions in the United Nations and ongoing insurgencies, liberation struggles, and guerrilla wars make agreement probably impossible because of the various interests and attitudes of opposing states whose political leaders use the term when their interests are threatened. As has been said often, one man's terrorist is another man's freedom fighter.[7] This very lack of agreement points to the fundamental nature of the term – its political and ideological parameters. It is a word that mobilizes, that polarizes, that identifies enemies, that dehumanizes individuals and criminalizes organizations. But it is not a term that is very informative because it paints its canvas with a uniformly monochromatic certainty. Even as the global political community cannot agree on how and when to use it properly and objectively, those who have studied the phenomenon either theoretically or first hand have come to even more radical conclusions about the word.

Rees, who has covered wars and insurgencies for twenty-five years, says he never uses the term.[8] Based on his experiences in the field and from his observations of global politics, he concludes that terrorism is "a word that has no precise or agreed meaning ... [and yet] has become the lynchpin of an ideology that is dividing the world."[9] Likewise, Louise Richardson, an American academic authority on terrorism, makes the following candid observation:

[T]he term [terrorism] has been bandied about so much that it has come to lose all meaning.... if you can successfully pin the label [terrorist] on your opponent you have gone a long way towards winning the public relations aspect of any conflict."[10]

Because of how the term has come to have non-debatable moral implications and legitimacy as a meaningful concept, it is a useful part of political rhetoric. It has gained a powerful and far-reaching currency, especially after September 11, 2001, when the United States experienced its first attack since Pearl Harbor. That event launched George Bush's "War on Terror" and with it a national agenda preoccupied with terrorism and terrorist acts. Paul Rutherford, in his insightful *Weapons of Mass Persuasion: Marketing the War Against Iraq* (2004), makes the following point about the nature of American public discourse:

It is hard to exaggerate the significance of hype in the political as well as commercial life of the United States. Nothing really big, no new product meant for the millions enters the marketplace unless heavily promoted to feed the demand, the desire to possess.[11]

Rutherford's observation can lead to the conclusion that the term "terrorism" is just so much hype. But that would be a mistake. Propaganda is an area rich in nuance, information, associations, and relationships. When terrorism is used as propaganda, it is not a thoughtless or unimportant act. Because of the innate sense of monstrosity associated with the label (the destruction wrought on September 11 has become its iconic representation), the concept of a war on terrorism implies a holy crusade against a monstrous creation, which requires the mobilization of a society against an enemy that threatens it. In order for a term like "terrorism" to be so all-pervasive, it must be heavily promoted, properly associated with threatening images in the mind of the public, and so turned into a rallying cry that is too powerful to be challenged.

The links between the news media in the United States, that country's ruling elites, and state-sponsored propaganda have been well explored by American thinkers such as Edward Herman and Noam Chomsky, who have focused on the defining role played by the media in supporting American imperial goals. It is through the media that terms associated with anti-terrorist activities by the state, such as "national security" and "freedom" or "the public good" and even "the American way of life" create a web of understanding that binds broadcasters, politicians, and the public into a community of believers with a common language. The generators of these beliefs, and their motivations and goals, are often left unquestioned because questioning removes oneself to the outskirts of the community and its sense of assured knowing. One has stopped affirming the known. Rutherford makes the point (with reference to Jürgen Habermas's *The Structural Transformation of the Public Sphere*) that the "quality of debate and dialogue" in the mass media is highly constricted.[12] One of the disturbing observations made by Rutherford and others is how the language of war, which was created around the concept of an appropriate response to terrorism, results in an instant polarity that suits the media's sensationalist presentation of the world. The result has been called "war porn," which includes the media's exaggerated and detailed portrayal of death and destruction caused by "terrorists" as well as its opposite – the eroticization of American weaponry and the virtualization of its use (no body parts please – just bright explosions and distant noises).[13] Rutherford concludes that the end result of the war on terror as a slogan, a policy, and reality-TV is the creation of a powerful spectacle that undermines democracy because of its disembodied images and its confident language.[14] It is totally one-sided because terrorism as an event and a concept is not open for discussion.

The views of academics like Richardson and Rutherford do have significance because of their research and theoretical understanding, but their ideas have practically no circulation in the public sphere. It is professional journalists who feel the contradictions of one-sided labelling the most. A practising journalist like Rees argues that in his experience the word "terrorism" is used by politicians and propagandists because it creates fear – an emotion that allows manipulation.[15] The threat of terrorism is magnified so that the political leadership's demand for anti-terrorist action is readily accepted, whether it is torture, extra-judicial murder, or kidnapping. The focus on terrorism suits an agenda in which those who identify someone as a terrorist can parade themselves as anti-terrorist and fundamentally innocent, while those whom they label are turned into non-humans against whom all actions are justified. The magnitude and immediacy of the threat associated with terrorism, whether real or hyped, becomes the perfect excuse.

The war metaphor is used in fighting terrorism because war is such a serious state in the mind of the public that its existence allows all kinds of questionable actions. The really fascinating aspect of the war on terror is that it is perpetually self-justifying because those who label others as terrorists are the ones who control public discourse to a large extent. They can keep on naming terrorists and terrorist organizations. They create alerts and they excuse their own immoral or illegal actions as necessary for self-defence.[16] The definition of the enemy is in their hands. Currently the list of terrorist organizations includes hundreds of organizations and thousands of individuals. New names are added constantly to keep the threat alive. Rees sees terrorism and the war on terror as metaphorical, meaning that it is more about association than reality:

> Metaphorical war [such as the war on terror] ... necessarily creates an enemy. The language of war ... demands duty and urgency. The culture of the society shifts toward glorifying violence. There are also many casualties of war, including the accountability of government, the freedom of the media and legal rights of a nation's citizens.[17]

When terrorism is put at the forefront of public concern, forces are unleashed that are profoundly anti-democratic. The word creates a demagogic atmosphere in which fear reigns supreme and that fear must be refreshed from time to time with real actions in the real world. When events labelled "terrorism" recede into memory and are not refreshed with fresh events so labelled, the term loses its potency as political explanation and mobilization.

French philosopher Jean Baudrillard wrote about terrorism in the 1970s, the era of the Red Brigades, political kidnapping, and airplane hijacking, but his work *A l'Ombre des majorités silencieuses* (1978) was not translated into English until 2007, an indicator of his growing stature in North American intellectual circles and the relevance of the subject matter. While decrying terrorism of his day as a "non-representative act," meaning it represented only a small clique or group rather than a social movement, he acknowledged that there was a symbiosis between "the masses, the media and terrorism" in that they were all relating to each other in a "violence of intake and fascination, a violence of the void."[18] He saw terrorism as a product of a media-centric universe in which everything was about representation and not reality. So the political use of the term contributes to the irreality of the concept and a certain level of social alienation. The world of public discourse is ruled by metaphors.

Rees's concept of the war on terror being a metaphoric war is supported by Richardson, who asks how it can make sense to declare war on an emotion (terror) or on a tactic (terrorism).[19] The terms are simply metaphors for anyone designated an enemy. The entities so designated are real and identifiable, but no other identity that they may have matters. The power of a metaphor rests in its sublimation of the real into a vast imaginary that holds the public enthralled. That imaginary requires a term that matches its import. It must be the size of a monster and it must clearly denote a monster. And so the metaphorical power of terms such as "terrorism" can reach sublime heights because of their elasticity and substantive emptiness. In the July 2006 case of Israel's incursion into Gaza, the killing of fifty Palestinians – including innocent civilians – in the initial foray is never equated in the media with terrorism because Israel is an ally of the United States, but the kidnapping of one Israeli soldier is called a terrorist act because the Palestinians have long been tarred with the brush of terrorism by Israel. It is precisely because terrorism is a politically motivated term that it ends up so empty, while at the same time having such a powerful impact on public consciousness. Thus a suicide bomber on a bus is a terrorist to be condemned for killing civilians, while a pilot in a helicopter gunship who kills women and children is a legitimate actor in a war who may or may not have made a mistake.

Michael Ignatieff, when he was director of the Carr Center for Human Rights Policy at Harvard University (before becoming the leader of the Liberal Party of Canada in 2008), wrote a book titled *The Lesser Evil: Political Ethics in an Age of Terror* in which he concluded that arms "without argument are used in vain."[20] In other words rhetoric is required to ensure meaning for a war such as the war on terror. By subtitling his book with the phrase "an age of terror," he accepts the validity of terrorism as a key definition of the contemporary world and supports its usage. As a result he takes the position that "necessity may require us to take actions in defence of democracy which will stray from democracy's own foundational commitments to dignity."[21] But in the end he believes that if the democratic process is kept alive "there is no reason to fear that a war on terror will lead us to betray the values we are fighting for."[22] This is an interesting and dangerous contradiction. By accepting the general meaning of terrorism as presented by political leaders and the media, Ignatieff in his current role as a political leader and his previous role as an academic in the United States has made terrorism an important, one-dimensional reality, which may lead to some state excesses, which he justifies as the "lesser evil." In other words, for Ignatieff there is a "war of civilizations" going on with legitimate states on the one side and terrorists and their friends on the other. It is precisely this polarization that Rees and Richardson challenge. And they are not the only ones.

3. The Politics of Terminology

The American-based academic writer Faisal Devji calls wars such as the war on terror and their languages "metaphysical" rather than metaphoric.[23] While he is referring specifically to the concept of "*jihad*" (originally the ideological epitome of terrorism in the eyes of the U.S. government), he shows how the "war" of the "war on terrorism" is meant to be a mirror of the war claimed by American interpreters of *jihad*. The war of *jihad* begets the war on terror because *jihad*, so they argue, is a terrorist war and can only be fought off as a war. War becomes an expression of an endless exercise in morality struggling against evil powers. The war on terror, as metaphor and metaphysical statement, has religious connotations. It pits one side against another in an epic battle to the death even though this battle is a self-created one. Even Ignatieff confirms that this is a total exaggeration and that no liberal democracy has ever been overthrown by terrorist acts,[24] which is Baudillard's point. Real terrorism is unconnected to the people and so is powerless. Anti-government or state violence associated with popularly based movements does have the power to overthrow regimes but unpopular terrorist groups cannot. The public does not support them. So when the Sri Lankan government terms the Tamil Tigers terrorists, it ignores their popular following, as does the Israeli government in regard to Hamas or the Canadian government in regard to the Taliban and so on. The blurring of the line between popular resistance movements and small terrorist cells is one of the damaging aspects of political rhetoric. The naming of something as terrorism results in a defined course of obliterative action; if it were named something else, something less apocalyptic or metaphysical, other responses could be possible. When the foreign powers that are occupying Afghanistan today finally decide that they want to negotiate a settlement with the insurgents in that country, then the rhetoric of terrorism in use today will stop and the same insurgents will be legitimized as government players. The label will be removed. Such a label cannot be removed from isolated non-state actors like the Red Brigades.

The apocalyptical overtones given to terrorism in the post-9/11 world are part of a metaphorical (i.e., rhetorical) power rather than any precise military or political reality. That an organization like al-Qaida was presented as a profound military threat to the United States has been proven to be absurd by the ease with which its actions and leadership were curtailed after 2001, and yet its threat was the *raison d'être* for the invasion and occupation of Afghanistan and, less centrally, the invasion and occupation of Iraq. This is only possible when terms such as "terrorism" take on a metaphysical quality of a life and death struggle. It is not that metaphorical wars are not real. It is precisely the opposite: they are the most potent wars of all. And those wars, which take on metaphysic attributes of fundamental morality, are ones that millions live by. In *The New End Game: Blood and Oil in Central Asia*, Lutz Kleveman writes about how the use of political concepts such as the war on terror "has allowed the Bush administration to massively extend American influence in Central Asia."[25] The term became so universal and all-pervasive that it took on a global character that allowed it to be shifted wherever the labellers wanted it used.

Current public discourse in the West today has moved away from the heightened tension and all-pervasiveness of the concept of "terrorism" while retaining its fundamental definition as a violent attack on civilians, who are considered by the community in which those civilians reside as innocent victims. This is a common working definition that excludes governments and their military, except for the phrase "terrorist states." The existence of this contradictory phrase (terrorists are usually considered non-state actors) suggests that terrorism has been expanded to encompass a very wide arena. The term has taken on the dimensions of the once prominent terms "communist" or "communism," which became endowed in the United States with such fear and hostility that they were used indiscriminately against anyone who opposed government positions. If a state can be termed "terrorist," we can conclude that "terrorism" has become a generic term of vilification that can be applied indiscriminately by those in power and can be used to quiet opposition. So from a specific meaning, "terrorism" has been expanded to embrace any and all enemies of a state. When a term has reached this status, its only future is either further debasement through proliferation or decline because of irrelevance.

Louise Richardson, who accepts the use of the term against groups and individuals, actually lists seven characteristics of the term, which support a non-government application. She says that 1) terrorism is politically inspired, 2) it is violent, 3) it makes a statement, 4) its acts and victims have a symbolic significance, 5) it is used by sub-state groups, 6) its victims and audience are not the same, and 7) it deliberately targets civilians.[26] The more general definition accepted by the public, a violent act committed against innocent civilians, lists only two of her seven points. It also focuses purely on the consequences of the act – the death and injury of the victims of violence. Far from this level of public discourse, the isolated and arcane universe of academic discourse provides all sorts of understandings of terrorism, but without any real public impact because these understandings are not part of mainstream media usage.[27] For example, in a recent article titled "Terrorism and Art: Don Delillo's *Mao II* and Jean Baudrillard's *The Spirit of Terrorism*," academic writer Leonard Wilcox states that both writers he is discussing see "terrorism as a canny adaptive response to the Western regime of image proliferation, sign exchange, and spectacle ... their acts are staged for the media."[28] Now, this is quite a long distance in both vocabulary and conceptualization from the one-dimensional definition that political leaders offer in their moral crusade or even Richardson's more complex listing of characteristics. What is radical about Wilcox's perception is its seeking to understand the motivation behind acts usually labelled as terrorist. It is input- rather than impact-oriented. He suggests that the society of the spectacle that is media-saturated North America is not just a victim of terrorism but a player in the creation of terrorism. Terrorism as a concept and as an act makes an appealing form of popular media representation. That is definitely heretical and oppositional to most political narratives about terrorism.

Drawing on the neutral tone of social science jargon that seeks to create a universal standard or definition, Richardson prefers to see the causes of terrorism – a disaffected individual, an enabling community, and a legitimizing ideology – from the side of the victims.[29] She clearly suggests that terrorism is the fault of those with grievances, of their collective identities and the ideology that excuses or rationalizes their acts. She considers this list of causes as scientific compared to the usual, simplistic identification of terrorists as psychopaths and criminal gangsters.[30] But she does not challenge the use of the term; instead, she validates it by giving it more substance than popular discourse and state propaganda can. Rees, on the other hand, questions the whole semantic exercise underlying the term. He makes a telling point when he points out how the American administration terms Colombia's FARC rebels, who had an 18,000-strong army and governed a quarter of the country during a period of truce, as terrorists.[31] FARC fit into the definition of a revolutionary movement that sought to control a territory to implement its agenda. To call it "terrorist" or "narco-terrorist" was to deprive it of any legitimacy, which was the very point of the political rhetoric. There can be no dialogue with criminality, only war. Likewise, how is it possible to consider Hamas, the legitimately elected government of the enclaved Palestinian territories, solely a terrorist organization as Canadian and American governments do in following Israel's lead, when Hamas has popular support in spite of Israel's use of massive violence as a way of cowing the population into rejecting Hamas. If a large population votes for "terrorists" then it must surely have some powerful reasons for doing so. Is it voting for "terrorism"? Is it voting for or against something? And even if it is voting for armed struggle, which governments term "terrorism," why is it doing so? The Hamas and FARC examples point to an inherent hollowness of the term as it is widely applied to democratic elections or territorial governance. Rees's observation about Colombia is bolstered by the observation that 30 per cent of the value of Colombia's exports come from cocaine, meaning that "the collaboration of important figures inside business, government and the military" is absolutely crucial.[32] In short, if FARC is a terrorist organization funded by drug money, so is the government of Colombia. The same may be said of Afghanistan, where the multi-billion-dollar heroin trade is the country's only export and exists with the support and collaboration of the governmental structures and the complicity of the occupying Western powers. In short, those who claim to be victims of terrorism can often be viewed as active participants in the development of terrorism, not just as part of political rhetoric but as creators of the conditions that maintain belligerency, which the drug trade informs. Be it political strategy; be it complicit funding; be it military actions against civilian populations – the role of state entities in the terrorism game is crucial. Those who label others as terrorists know that. They seek a self-fulfilling prophecy. They don't want terrorists to go away. The enemy must remain in the public mind justifying their political course of action.

4. The Universal and the Particular

The legitimization of terrorism as a global threat to Western civilization has allowed the doctrine of pre-emptive strikes in self-defence to be articulated by the United States and Israel. It has allowed the inclusion of all insurgencies that threatened existing nation-states. So from Russia to Sri Lanka, governments cry terrorism to keep the global meaning of the term constantly reinforced. Wherever in the world today there is armed conflict, the word "terrorism" gets used. The result is a radical bipolarity – the *us versus them* model. And the "them" in the current climate is often Islam and its adherents. Faisel Devji, in his critically insightful text, *Landscapes of the Jihad: Militancy, Morality, Modernity* (2005), moves beyond the narrow concerns of strategy and security found in most books on the topic[33] toward the broad fields that make up cultural studies. He calls this the "invisible world of ethical, sexual, aesthetic and other forms of behaviour."[34] His purpose is to make visible the underlying reality of "jihadism" or what former President Bush calls "terrorism." The fact that the same phenomenon can garner two different terms is not unusual. What is interesting is how generic or general the term "terrorist" is, while the term "jihadist" is culturally and religiously specific. It is the opposition between the specific and the general that reveals the problems associated with the universal application of a universal term to specific people and ideology. It is specificity that brings understanding, while generality tends to obfuscate.

The difference in naming is significant. Devji's prime object of study is the ideology of al-Qaida, the source of the September 11 attack. He argues that al-Qaida, as a proponent of *jihad*[ism], or holy war, has created "new patterns of belief and practice" in Islam.[35] So he looks at the impact of this organization on a widespread religious community of a billion adherents. He claims that al-Qaida's marginality to Islamic traditions (Baudrillard's argument) has resulted in its becoming a metaphysical power with global reach because it can create its own form and its own content, taking bits and pieces from here and there. The result is an ideology that combines Islamic terminology and postmodernist understanding. According to Devji, the postmodern global reality is one in which there are all sorts of accidental, unintended effects resulting from actions that are aimed at a universal, media-influenced audience. The postmodern, global universe with its media-saturated, virtual-reality consciousness is a room of endlessly bouncing balls, whose motion never stops, and whose causal actors spend as much time understanding the results of their actions as performing them. In defending this interpretation, Devji points out that the Arab Middle East is not the homeland of *jihad*, as is commonly perceived, and that the Middle East is often the target of *jihad*'s holy warriors. He sees jihadism as "a global movement ... [that] depends on the erosion of traditional religious and political allegiances [within Islam] for its very existence."[36] There is no territoriality for *jihad*, making it "metaphysical." It is everywhere and nowhere. It seems to thrive in geographic peripheries but many of its adherents come from the centre. It is not based in one culture (Miami is as possible as Peshawar). Nor is it interested in any territorial successes except as temporary bases for the all-encompassing battle with the United States, which itself is everywhere, present, and alive. "Jihad's global character," he writes, "is manifested in its abandonment of the freedom struggle for the religious wars."[37] National liberation and other insurgencies fighting in a particular area and for control of a territory are nothing but the fertile ground in which it seeks to operate and flourish but to which it owes no allegiance. Its battle is postmodern in its rejection of place and it welcomes people from all over the world to its side. This is the globalism it posits against U.S. hegemony.

Devji's radical thinking offers "terrorism" the very specific identity of "jihadism," which is far beyond the simple calculation of deaths and destruction that Western politicians associate with terrorism. Devji sees jihadism as a mystical movement that is transforming Islam, clearly undermining traditional forms of authority and fragmenting Islam. Jihadism achieves its universality primarily through the mass media with which it is constantly engaged. Osama bin Laden, the founder of al-Qaida, addressed the American people on the eve of the 2004 presidential election in an effort to influence the vote. "The jihad's world of reference," Devji goes on to explain, "is far more connected to the dreams and nightmares of the media than to any traditional school of Islamic jurisprudence or political thought."[38] Of course, this has a bearing on the use of the word "terrorism" by al-Qaida's opponents because it is in the media that this word most often appears. To refer to bin Laden as a "jihadist" rather than by the epithet of "terrorist" automatically gives a modicum of validity to his organization, philosophy, and actions, which encourages reflection on its pronouncements and demands. Why? Because *jihad* has a religious grounding, no matter how misled, while terrorism has no grounding except criminality. To think "'holy warrior'" rather than "'terrorist'" creates a certain equality between the two opposing causes that the latter term refuses. What that validity would entail is an acknowledgment of the political demands that jihadism makes. But terrorism as a concept cannot do this because it denies any and all validity to the terrorist cause or its explanation. There is no justification for the terrorist, while there may be some for the jihadist. "Jihadism" has some sort of political dimension denied to the term "terrorism." Because of the continued use of terrorist terminology to include "Islamists" and "Jihadists," the jihadist struggle takes on characteristics that are both contradictory and complementary. Devji describes the result in this way:

> What makes Islam universal [in television, for example] is the forging of a generic Muslim, one who loses all cultural and historical particularity by his destruction in an act of martyrdom ... [which] achieves meaning only by being witnessed in the mass media.[39]

This generic Muslim is a desired product of jihadist ideology as well as a desired product of its opponents, who want to tar all of Islam with the same brush. It suits both sides very nicely. Devji explains how martyrdom witnessed by the media is a central tenet of jihadism because Islam is then universalized through this collective witnessing in the mass media. Every act of death and destruction by a suicide bomber becomes an affirmation of this identity for both sides. Calling martyrdom an act of terror may prevent us from seeing the morality or ethical motivation that the actors carry within themselves, such as dying to resist government attacks, but the suicide bombers, a.k.a. martyrs, are one and the same and their role is recognized and prompted, albeit in opposite ways, by both sides. Again there is a rhetorical complicity between martyrdom and terrorism, and when this is acknowledged one steps outside the one-dimensionality of the term as it is used by political leaders in the West.

Devji is convinced that there is a powerful ethical dimension to terrorist thought, at least as ethical as that of their opponents, in the sense that both sides base their actions and pronouncements on a sense of morality. Jihadism presents itself to its followers as an ethical enterprise involving duty, honour, etc., much like Ignatieff's choice for a "lesser evil" is argued as being ethical. Devji even believes that jihadism could transform itself out of being a violent movement to a non-violent practice in the not-too-distant future.[40] This implies that jihadism is much more than terrorist acts or acts of war. This bringing jihadism into dialogue with the human community and so into human history is beyond even the most liberal of Western commentators. It is the rejection of the all-encompassing nature and simplicity of the term "terrorism" that is refreshing about his analysis. By using "jihadism" to replace "terrorism," Devji allows room to breathe intellectually and so move forward from the do-or-die paradigm of North American public discourse on the subject.

5. Beyond the War Metaphor

In 2006 there was a little book, which appeared on the checkout counters of independent bookstores in the UK, titled *Making Terrorism History*, which was written by peace activists seeking to eliminate the causes of terrorism.

Like activists everywhere, they present a catalogue of actions and approaches that are alternatives to the military and police actions of states. They argue that the military approach to eliminating acts of terror is doomed to fail because it is predicated on the furthering of war and occupation that lead only to powerlessness and humiliation for its victims, who then fight back. They insist that terrorism be approached in a non-violent way, in a spirit of respect and with genuine dialogue. They reject the criminalization of insurgents and insist on a dialogue with those who have political demands. For them, the war option, which is the only one proposed and implemented to date, is a lose/lose situation. They point out that the victims of war are not just those attacked, but those who remain behind and end up being subverted by its rhetoric into being vocal supporters of the war machine. They claim that the very "fabric of society" is undermined by the war on terror, be it in Iraq or in the UK.[41] That undermining occurs because of the power of the media to give pre-eminence to a concept to the detriment of other values in a society. An obsession with terrorism becomes a black and white neurosis with an inquisitorial aspect.

While *Making Terrorism History* has a laudable goal and its appearance is valuable, it still accepts terrorism as a fundamentally meaningful term, however much it questions the strategy used against it. What would be even more powerful would be to stop using the term altogether, except in very specific cases. One would then undermine its use as political rhetoric. One could replace the all-encompassing term "terrorism" with a plurality of terms that give some level of validity to its proponents, thereby making negotiation possible. If the now defeated Tamil Tigers were nothing but terrorists, then there was little room for negotiation. If they were "nationalist revolutionaries" there would have been a place to start. Only when the discussion moves beyond the one-dimensionality of the term "terrorism" can new doors open up to ending the cycle of violence. A diverse and nuanced vocabulary is better for non-violent solutions. Why is this so?

Terrorism as a concept today is totally deed-oriented, morally charged, simultaneously so narrow in its meaning, and yet so general in its application, that the designation removes most choices and possibilities. The unrelenting negativity associated with the term closes doors to dialogue and understanding. The granting of the slightest legitimacy to opponents, which non-terrorist terms do, allows fresh perspectives to appear that can lead to solutions. For example, the word "soldier" carries a designation of validity that the term "enemy combatant" does not. The latter is a variant on "terrorist" in North American political parlance. With a new language, the humanity of the other or the enemy re-emerges and the monstrosity associated with terrorism is diminished. The continued uncritical use of the term by the media and even the critical use of the term by others only ensures further death and destruction because war is the only solution that that term acknowledges.

Specifically, the connotations of the term "terrorism" are dissipated when it is not used in a general way. They are replaced by more neutral and less apocalyptical connotations. They develop content. For example, the connotation of "sneak attack" that is associated with terrorism is not present in a word like "jihadist" or "insurgent." The connotation of "indiscriminate killing of civilians" is not associated with the term "revolutionary." Likewise, the symbolic or metaphoric status accorded terrorism in political rhetoric is not present in these other terms, whose moral dimension is more ambiguous. Ambiguity should not be viewed as a failing, but rather it ought to be seen as a valuable resource that can be explored in the interests of dialogue and insight. Putting a moratorium on the word "terrorism," when no terrorist acts have occurred for some time and the public may have wearied of the concept, would lead to a different response the next time. We would be responding to a different meaning for a similar act because a new language presents it differently and that new meaning would guide our response. By not using the term, except in very specific and limited instances, we free ourselves from its chilling embrace. As a result the *us versus them* model implied in the word breaks down and the equation between a specific religion (Islam) and armed struggle against the West is shown to be complex, non-universal, and as much a creation of our own political imagination as that of others. By using other terms, we are acknowledging that the continued use of the term "terrorism" is a disservice to public awareness and a contribution to continued violence and destruction.

On that broad field of public discourse mentioned at the beginning of this essay, where legalism and philosophy exist at either end, the main play is in mid-field. Since the mainstream media takes its cues from the political terminology created by politicians and their advisors, there is little likelihood of terrorism disappearing from contemporary rhetoric and being replaced with a more nuanced and conflict-specific vocabulary. In the struggle for the hearts and minds of the public, the critical viewpoint only rises to prominence when it gets adopted by the ruling elite. This occurs only when the contradictions in using a term like "terrorism" become so profound and unmanageable that a new language is adopted. The most recent Canadian example is Canada's participation in the Western occupation of Afghanistan since 2001, first as a small contingent of special operations troops, then a player in the UN-sanctioned role propping up the Karzai government in Kabul, then a move to full battle in Kandahar under NATO auspices, and now a planned redeployment to less dangerous roles because of the take-over by U.S. troops. As the war drags on and has migrated to Pakistan as the Vietnam war migrated to Cambodia and Laos forty years ago, there is a new call for negotiation with the Taliban, who are still most commonly referred to as "terrorists." First, there is reference to "moderate Taliban elements" as a replacement for the generic "terrorist" term. Then there is reference to "tribal leaders." Then there is a new emphasis on "reconstruction." And so it goes. As political will wanes, rhetoric modifies. The removal of terrorist language from public discourse allows for dialogue, for negotiation, for peaceful settlement. This can never be the case with "terrorism," which always requires the rhetoric of war and destruction. Talking about a "War on Tribal Leaders" is absurd, rather than apocalyptic. Realizing we are discussing the same people with the same goals and same methods but using different terms, we expose the emptiness of the earlier use of the term "terrorism." That rhetorical emptiness has led to innumerable deaths and mass destruction. The power of metaphoric and metaphysically charged terminology is the real terror because of its consequences.

Notes

1   Stephen Henighan, *A Report on the After-life of Culture* (Toronto: Biblioasis, 2008), 46.

2   Jacques Derrida, "Autoimmunity: Real and Symbolic Suicides – A Dialogue with Jacques Derrida," In *Philosophy in a Time of Terror: Dialogues with Jürgen Habermas and Jacques Derrida*, ed. Giovanna Borradori; trans. Pascale-Anne Brault and Michael Naas (Chicago: University of Chicago Press, 2003), 124.

3   It can be argued that the law and the authorities are representative of public wishes and so there is a seamlessness between public desire and public discourse created by the media and elected officials. In a counter-argument, it may be said that the law and officials represent certain interests and ideologies that do not represent the commonweal as a whole.

4   For a discussion of the Canadian response to September 11, 2001, see Karim-Aly Kassam, George Melnyk, and Lynne Perras, eds., *Canada and September 11th: Impact and Response* (Calgary: Detselig, 2002).

5   George W. Bush, "America is Winning the War on Terrorism," August 14, 2003. Speech reproduced in Lauri S Friedman, *Are Efforts to Reduce Terrorism Successful?* (New York: Thomson Gale, 2005), 9–13.

6   Phil Rees, *Dining with Terrorists* (London: Pan, 2006), xxiii.

7   An obvious example is the recent history of Afghan insurgencies. The *mujihadeen* were terrorists to the Russians who were fighting them and freedom fighters to the Americans who supported them. When the Americans began fighting there in 2001, the *mujihadeen*, now renamed the Taliban, became terrorists.

8   Ibid., xv.

9   Ibid., xxii.

10   Louise Richardson, *What Terrorists Want: Understanding the Terrorist Threat* (London: John Murray, 2006), 19.

11   Paul Rutherford, *Weapons of Mass Persuasion: Marketing the War Against Iraq* (Toronto: University of Toronto Press, 2004), 8.

12   Ibid., 141.

13   Ibid., 174.

14   Ibid., 184.

15   Rees, *Dining with Terrorists*, 2.

16   For a discussion of American treatment of Iraqi prisoners of war and the media, see Henry Giroux, *Against the New Authoritarianism: Politics after Abu Ghraib* (Winnipeg: Arbeiter Ring, 2005), 109–20.

17   Ibid., 91.

18   Jean Baudrillard, *In the Shadow of the Silent Majorities*, trans. Paul Foss et al. (Los Angeles: Semiotext(e), 2007), 69 and 73.

19   Richardson, *What Terrorists Want*, 214.

20   Michael Ignatieff, *The Lesser Evil: Political Ethics in an Age of Terror* (Toronto: Penguin, 2004), 170.

21   Ibid., 8.

22   Ibid., 81.

23   Faisal Devji, *Landscapes of the Jihad: Militancy, Morality, Modernity* (London: Hurst, 2005), 74.

24   Ignatieff, *The Lesser Evil*, 80.

25   Lutz Klevemann, *The New End Game: Blood and Oil in Central Asia* (London: Atlantic Books, 2004), 257.

26   Richardson, *What Terrorists Want*, 20–21.

27   From time to time, an academic idea is popularized such as Samuel Huntington's "clash of civilizations." This is usually done by the media because it is easy to digest and fits into the already established norms of discourse.

28   *Mosaic*, 39, no. 2 (June 2006): 90–91.

29 Richardson, *What Terrorists Want*, 14.

30 Ibid., 6.

31 Rees, *Dining with Terrorists*, 96.

32 Ibid., 113.

33 Books on terrorism fall into three broad categories: accept the threat and talk about what to do or glorify the struggle against (the majority of books); question the seriousness of the threat and debate what ought to be done to deal with it (the minority of books); and finally, books that try to step away from the topic and analyze it from a less immediate or pressing perspective.

34 Devji, *Landscapes of the Jihad*, xvi.

35 Ibid.

36 Ibid., 25.

37 Ibid., 74.

38 Ibid., 90.

39 Ibid., 94.

40 Ibid., 132.

41 Scilla Elworthy and Gabrielle Rifkind, *Making Terrorism History* (London: Rider, 2006), 92.

CHAPTER 5

Groping in the Dark: How the Media, Absent a Frame of Reference, Fumbled the Danish Cartoon Controversy

Doug Firby
Calgary Herald Editorial Pages Editor

1. Pack Journalism

They were a curious collection of images: mildly amusing in some cases, lame in others, sharply provocative in at least one. It was clear they all depicted a man, or men, in traditional Arab attire, often bearded. To the uninitiated, they could have been images of anyone at all.

These cartoons, however, weren't intended to depict just any Arab. They were depicting the Prophet Muhammad. And their publication in one Danish newspaper, and later a number of European newspapers, caused an international furor, pitting some Muslims against the secularized press in a dispute that was alternately characterized as deliberate blasphemy, a provocation, and a courageous act in defence of free expression.

But, it wasn't really about any one of those issues. The dispute was rooted in much larger themes that hark back to the September 11, 2001, terrorist attacks that reshaped global relations. The attacks provided a convenient instrument for several conflicting agendas, ranging from anti-immigration Islamophobia to fuelling the extremist-driven sense of Muslim victimization.

In the hours and days following the attacks, the "instant analysis" – often based on incomplete information – significantly altered the way many North Americans perceived Muslims, at home and around the world.[1] As the commercial news media strained to provide instant answers based on incomplete or incorrect information, followers of Islam broadly fell under suspicion in North America. In time, media analysts became more emboldened in their assaults on Islam in general.[2] And many Muslims, mostly innocent second or third-generation Canadians and Americans, would come to endure years under a cloud because of the impressions created by coverage and commentary related to the attacks.

Much has transpired in the years after the attacks in New York City and Washington, D.C. – most notably two U.S.-led wars on totalitarian regimes suspected of harbouring terrorists – but the degree of ignorance and general lack of sophistication among the media about the Arab population in general and Islam in particular remains appalling. The consequences of that ignorance – commonly found among the very reporters and editors upon whom we rely for credible information – is reflected in the cliché-laden tone of coverage that has so much power in shaping the attitudes of North Americans.

It is easy to think of the "media" as monolithic, marching in lockstep in both the choice of daily "news" events and in the way those events are packaged and presented. But they are not. Instead, the media are directed by a diverse collection of individuals who make decisions based on unwritten conventions that are widely accepted in the communications industry. Those practices, combined with some commonly held assumptions, are what lead most media to reach remarkably similar conclusions on what constitutes news, and what the audience is interested in. They also form the root of many of the faults in content – the shallowness, lack of insight, absence of context – that news consumers most often complain about.

A review of a typical day's news line-up illustrates the similarities in choices among the various media outlets. To see how similar, I've appended a list of "skeds" – actual news line-ups – from Canada's three major television networks, and several newspapers from a typical news day (see the Appendix). Readers should note the manner in which those priorities are suggested (by the provider, the Canadian Press), and the assurance from the provider that the issue is "covered." It is pack journalism writ large. Reviewing the lists, two things jump out: the repetitiveness of the word "covered" and the overlap in topics judged to be the top news items of the day. As the "skeds" are distributed on the news wires from eastern Canada to the West, editors in each time zone have a chance to review decisions made by others. This gives them the opportunity to take the "safe" route, by matching what others have done. Knowing that something is "covered" offers them assurance that they too will have access to similar news copy. By this process, the distribution system reinforces imitation over originality in news selection and presentation.

Any journalism text will give you a list of news criteria, the conventions developed over more than a century of practice that help editors decide what is important. These include timeliness, impact on the reader, proximity to the audience, and so on. But these criteria often do not truly guide real-world experience. In the real world, I have time and again seen senior editors in the news media make decisions on the basis of: a) fear, and b) intuition. Editors often express the fear they will somehow miss a big event that some other media outlet will get and the editor responsible for making the choice will be humiliated (or worse, punished) for being "scooped." The other driver, intuition, is rooted in accumulated experience and input from one's predecessors. As an editor apprentices through the news hierarchy, he is infused with a sense of values passed on from generation to generation of editors; not unlike the way oral culture has passed along the myths and legends held by Canada's aboriginal population.

The problems created by these two drivers are obvious. Fear drives editors to go with "safe" decisions. For example, if an editor is pondering whether to run a front-page feature on a local issue (e.g., the effects of urban sprawl on urban planning in Calgary) or to match the priorities being chosen by other major outlets (e.g., a story out of the Ottawa bureau on a cabinet meeting), the safe decision is to do what the other outlets are doing, which is to go with the "he said/she said" national story. It's true an editor can look bold and smart if he chooses a separate path, but it's a high-risk strategy with uncertain rewards. The editors I have known often expressed the fear they'll make an embarrassing miscalculation. If their choice is out of sync with those they answer to, their bosses are much more likely to say they made a poor judgment than they are to say they made a clever or interesting choice.

Similar issues arise around the reliance upon one's "intuition." The problem with that is the context within which such "conventional wisdom" is absorbed. An editor who has been fully tutored inherits the values, attitudes, and beliefs of his predecessors. And, while some wisdom is indeed passed on from those elders, many of the assumptions are outdated and untested in the modern world. Such conventional wisdom may dictate, for example, that readers are more interested in crime or tragedy – in "the business," it's often referred to as "ambulance chasing" – than they are in issue-oriented stories or insightful features. There was certainly some truth to that in the past (supported by the commercial success of tabloid-style police and gossip publications), but today most market research suggests the needs of news consumers are evolving. Research tells us that most news consumers keep up to date on the news headlines from electronic media or the Internet, and they turn to print for more reflective and insightful reportage. Yet, contrary to the business strategy that might be inferred from such knowledge, the majority of the popular press continue to be driven by the old maxim, "If it bleeds, it leads."

There are a number of manifestations of these factors: The news media are structurally impeded from finding nuance; their editors have short attention spans, unable to follow news events through their full cycles (remember, for example, how quickly the tragedy of the New Orleans flood dropped down the priority list); they consistently underestimate the ability and willingness of their audience to assimilate complex issues; they equate "conflict" with news; and, of course, they are driven by commercial imperatives.

Fred Brown, a member of the Society of Professional Journalists Ethics Committee, and former political editor at the *Denver Post*, spoke of this compulsion to rely upon the familiar eye-grabbing content. He said the media tend to play up sensational stories, especially those with star appeal or involving lurid crimes, because agenda-setters (such as he, in an earlier incarnation) *know* sensational content attracts readers or viewers.[3]

But, contrary to the apparent assumptions of content decision makers, the media are only fooling some of the people some of the time. The most astute news watchers quickly identify inconsistencies in stories and superficial research. A variety of credibility measures over the last two decades show a steady decline in news consumers' willingness to believe what they read. Research released by the Pew Center in the United States in 2004, for example, found:

> Half of those surveyed ranked the newspaper they are most familiar with as believable (i.e. 1 or 2 on a scale of 4). That is down a full 13 points from 1998.
>
> Only 17 per cent gave their newspaper the highest credibility ranking, down from 27 per cent eight years earlier.
>
> Network and cable news fared somewhat better – ranging between 54 and 65 per cent – but is also steadily falling.[4]

In a discussion on National Public Radio, on April 7, 1997, Andy Kohut, of the Pew Center, bluntly identified what he saw as the causes for the unbroken slide. Asked about a growing perception that journalists interfere with politicians' ability to do their jobs, he cited three reasons: "sensationalism, bias, and inaccuracy."

"And they're all interrelated," he went on to explain. "There's this sense that the press is covering these people in an excessive way not because it's interested in revealing the truth about this scandal but because it wants to exploit it for the sake of audiences, or for the sake of career enhancement, or for advancement."[5]

It does not require a large leap of imagination to see how this process plays out in the treatment of news stories around terrorist acts. The decision makers in the media are conditioned to look for conflict, drama, and violent events – often branded as sensationalism. So, when a terrorist act occurs, there is a great deal of reporting of the "what" – sometimes in intense and graphic detail – but comparatively little explanation of the "why." When the western media write about Osama bin Laden, for example, he is portrayed in almost cartoon-like dimensions. Very little content in the mainstream media has attempted to explore the psychology, motivations, and social conditions that would explain how a once-bright youth from a wealthy family could be turned into a dangerous radical who loathes western values. Attempting to understand his motivations almost seems like an act of disloyalty. So, the media opt for the safe approach – to portray him as Public Enemy #1, an evil entity whose motivations are irrelevant.

As extreme an example as he is, bin Laden is far from the exception. In its inaugural April 2006 edition in Canada, the *Muslim Free Press* explained why its founders felt it was necessary to establish a newspaper that would challenge many of the common misconceptions to be found in the popular media. The newspaper's first editorial declared, "Sadly, much of how Islam is portrayed in Canada and around the world is negative, inaccurate and threatening."[6]

This analysis began with an observation that mainstream media display a lack of sophistication – and in some cases blatant ignorance – in reporting on people who follow Islam. This phenomenon reached its apex with the transmigration in the winter 2006 of what was essentially a regional European controversy – the Danish cartoon controversy – to North America. Let's review some of the facts around this event.

2. Danish Cartoons as Freedom to Injure

The dispute began in Denmark in September 2005, where tensions between the majority Danes and minority Muslim immigrant population had been building for some time. Newspapers were being accused of engaging in self-censorship by showing "excessive" sensitivity to the Muslim population. In response, Jyllands-Posten – which *New Yorker* cartoonist Art Spiegelman noted is well-known for its anti-immigrant bias – commissioned editorial cartoons which depicted the Muslim Prophet Muhammad in various commentaries, some largely inoffensive, but others clearly heretical to Islam.[7] It published twelve of those cartoons on September 20, 2005.

Muslims took deep offence to the initiative, protesting that the act of publishing the cartoons was itself Islamophobic and the cartoons blasphemous. As the controversy grew, newspapers in about fifty other countries – most notably France, Norway, and Austria – reprinted the cartoons, rationalized in most cases as an act of solidarity in defence of freedom of the press. As violence and vandalism grew, Denmark's Prime Minister Anders Fogh Rasmussen described the crisis as the worst for his country since the Second World War.

Knight-Ridder Newspapers reported: "The fierce reaction to the cartoons reflects not just anger over Europeans poking fun at the revered prophet, but years of pent-up fury by Muslims who feel alienated in the West and oppressed in their home countries, according to Muslims in several nations."[8] Muslims destroyed churches in Nigeria, a Catholic priest was murdered while praying in a church in Turkey, and embassies were razed.

Much of the reporting observed while this issue developed remained highly superficial and almost totally devoid of context. But there were a few exceptions. One of the more insightful pieces was a report by Nelly van Doorn-Harder, written for the *Christian Science Monitor*, and distributed March 2, 2006:

> Much of the discussion has centred on Muslim perspectives and sensitivities, but few people realize this affair erupted from a crisis in leadership of European Muslim communities, where radical imams are battling to gain the religious authority. As European Muslims seek new identities and voices, they form a target for radical leaders. And because of the competition for followers among these Danish radical-minded Muslim groups, the 'cartoon war' that could have been battled out on Danish grounds, grew into an international episode. Radical groups have vested interests in what the Swiss-Egyptian Muslim philosopher Tariq Ramadan refers to as "couching socioeconomic problems in religious terms," and fostering a "minority obsession."[9]

The issue remained largely isolated to Europe and the Middle East until well into 2006 when the cause was taken up by two Calgary-based publications. They became the first periodicals in Canada to go beyond reporting about the Danish cartoons, to running the images themselves. Both publications adopted the freedom-of-the-press mantra as a rationale.

The 2,000-circulation *Jewish Free Press*, based in Calgary, published them on February 9 under a headline, declaring: "First they came for the cartoonists...." The paper also featured portraits of the Prophet Muhammad printed over the last two hundred years, suggesting that Muslims who objected to a portrayal of the image of the prophet were not supported by history. The Calgary-based *Western Standard* biweekly magazine, with a claimed national circulation of 40,000, published eight of the twelve cartoons a week later.

"I'm not trying to flaunt the cartoons" to anger Muslims, *Jewish Free Press* publisher Richard Bronstein told the *Calgary Herald*. "But, hey folks, surely we have a right to see what this is all about. It's not anti-Muslim or pro-Muslim. We have a duty to be informed, so we can decide whether the cartoons justify all the rampaging around the world."[10]

The *Jewish Free Press* also published a selection of anti-Semitic cartoons that had appeared in Muslim countries – like a cartoon of hook-nosed, diabolical Jew tunnelling under Jerusalem's Temple Mount – to call attention to what they considered a double standard.

This created an interesting ethical dilemma for Calgary's two daily newspapers, the broadsheet *Calgary Herald*, where I was Editorial Pages Editor, and the *Calgary Sun*, which, as a tabloid, bears the image of a more highly sensationalistic publication. Conflict is news, and what we understand to be the economic imperative would seem to indicate that publishing the cartoons would result in higher readership, improving each paper's position within the marketplace. Further, extreme free-speech advocates argued that readers are entitled to see what the images were all about so they could judge for themselves whether they are offensive.

But neither newspaper did, and both offered explanations to the public. In a February 11, 2006, editorial page column, I compared the controversy to an elementary school yard squabble, in which a poke in the eye was rightly considered an invitation to a fight.

That analogy, I wrote, exposed "what looks like a flaw in the logic of the people who argue we should insult Muslims by running blasphemous cartoons of their most revered spiritual figure, just to prove that we are free." I went on to ask whether being free didn't also mean we could make a free will decision not to run the cartoons.

"Just who are we asserting our rights over?" I asked. "None of the extremists we read about in Europe and the Middle East are likely to subscribe to the *Calgary Herald*. The people we'd be insulting are the moderate, kind and sensible Muslims who belong to Calgary and who are helping to build and enjoy a great city." As I review those words, I would add, freedom of expression is not licence to diminish the dignity of another.

Further on in the column, I raised the issue of unintended consequences, just as the embattled editors of *Jyllands-Posten* had discovered to their regret, after the rioting began. "Should this newspaper, in asserting its right to publish-and-be-damned, not pause to consider the possible chain of events that such action might trigger? Is our job now to act as our own agents provocateurs?"

On the accusation of censorship, I noted, "we only control this publication, nobody else's, and make no effort to influence any other source of information. As I said to one caller, if you want to ridicule the Prophet Muhammad on your bumper sticker, the *Calgary Herald* isn't going to tell you that you can't."

I argued that there is a clear differentiation between censorship (telling people what they can't see) and exercising an editor's right to make choices about what will appear in a publication:

> There is a wondrous spectrum of offensive material we choose not to publish every day – because it is judged to be too offensive, too sexually explicit, libellous, racist, beyond the limits of taste, obscene or culturally insensitive. We don't tell other publications what to do with such material – and, indeed, anyone who visits the local variety store or knows the word "Google" can find all the offensive, sexual, racist, tasteless material they want.
>
> It's a free country. And, in a free country, we have the right to say, 'No thanks.'[11]

Licia Corbella, then editor of the *Calgary Sun*, also wrote about her experience. She noted that after the *Sun* indicated it would not run the cartoons, callers labelled her everything from a "coward" to "brave" to a "pathetic appeaser," a "wise person," a "sycophant," and "someone who calls 'em as I see 'em."

Corbella gave several reasons for the *Sun*'s decision not to run the cartoons: "My main reason for not publishing the cartoons is because to do so would be disrespectful of our Muslim readers."[12]

In a subsequent column, she elaborated:

We looked at the cartoons in question and determined that we would not have run these cartoons prior to this controversy and therefore we won't now.

Why? Because they are in very poor taste. They are offensive to the religious sensitivities of Muslims, and just as we wouldn't knowingly run cartoons that are crudely disrespectful to Christians, Jews or any other religion, we will not gratuitously insult Muslims either.[13]

In an explanation that closely echoed my own, Corbella added: "Every day, we make thousands of judgment calls as to what we cover and don't cover.... That's not censorship, it's editing."[14]

Noting the paper does not make a determined point of offending readers, she concluded, "That doesn't make us brave or cowardly – just discerning."[15]

Readers who phoned or wrote to the *Herald* endorsed our decision not to run the cartoons by a ratio of about three to one. Meanwhile, reaction to the two niche Calgary publications that ran the cartoons was curiously divergent.

The *Jewish Free Press* ran into unexpected opposition from its own community. The Calgary Jewish Community Council dissociated itself from the paper and said it wouldn't have published the cartoons since "they are offensive to Muslims," according to spokesman Nelson Halpern. He compared them to "anti-Semitic cartoons which have appeared in Western and Middle Eastern media." Editor Bronstein had to appear before the council and "explain" the paper's actions to avert a threatened boycott.[16]

The *Western Standard*, however, remained defiant, holding "mainstream" media up to ridicule, and accusing the two Calgary dailies of cowardice. Publisher Ezra Levant, a prominent pro-Israel activist in Calgary, accused the papers of censoring and acting "out of fear."[17]

He told the *Calgary Herald*: The media "mock Christians and Jews, and they're not afraid of offending them, because they know Christians and Jews won't cut off their heads." Levant also argued that the media would be failing readers if it didn't show them the images that had created all the fuss. He also called the depictions "relatively innocuous," in comparison to the mockery Christians and Jews routinely experience in the press.[18]

Not content to let the chips fall where they might, the *Western Standard* devoted much of its subsequent (March 13) edition to the issue, proclaiming with almost childlike glee: "WHAT WERE WE THINKING?"[19] Although there were anecdotal reports that some readers cancelled their subscriptions in protest, the publication acknowledged no such reaction and ran only letters that supported the decision to publish.[20] The *Western Standard* also ran a series of supportive columns from regular contributors.[21] Dismissing the CBC and other media as "organs of correct thought," columnist David Warren unleashed his invective:

> Elsewhere, I have called them cowardly in their defence of press freedom, but this is too vague. It would be more accurate to say that Canada's cultural establishment does not want a free press. They would actually prefer regulation by kangaroo "human rights" tribunals, hate literature commission and thought police. This would spare them the effort of even pretending to think about fundamental principles of anything.[22]

Such intemperate language effectively cast the *Western Standard*'s writers as the new *agents provocateurs*. One wonders whether they were secretly disappointed that they were unable to trigger the violent protests that had shaken Europe. Instead, Calgary Muslims, like those across Canada, reacted with restrained indignation and a genuine sense of hurt.

In a statement only the most paranoid could construe as threatening, Syed Soharwardy, founder of Muslims Against Terrorism, said publication of the Danish cartoons was "completely unacceptable." Contrary to the assertions of columnists in the *Western Standard*, Soharwardy said Muslims don't expect the right to stop portraits of Muhammad in Western publications because they are non-Muslim and not under Sharia law. "But these cartoons of the Prophet are deliberately hateful." He added: "If I make fun of the Holocaust, is that freedom of speech?"[23]

Canadian academic and Muslim activist Mohamed Elmasry, national president of the Canadian Islamic Congress, spoke of the subtle racism promulgated by the so-called free speechers, as they defend their right to offend

Islam's most holy figure while concurrently mocking those who choose not to. In a speech to the Canadian Association of Journalists on May 15, 2006, he refers to publication of the cartoons as an act that "incites hate, or which spreads negative stereotyping about a Canadian minority," frighteningly similar to the most notorious racism of the twentieth century – the pre-Holocaust dehumanizing of Jews.[24]

"The issue here goes beyond the boundaries of free expression," Elsmasry told the journalists. "It is about the power of 'free speech' to dehumanize fellow citizens and depict them as 'not like us.' Unfortunately, that consideration did not deter publications like the *Western Standard*."[25]

I asked publisher Levant whether he had considered how offensive the cartoons might be to Muslims. As outspoken and provocative as ever, Levant's response was both sharp and telling: "I say again that most Muslims don't give a damn about this. It's a noisy few – the Al Sharptons of the Muslim world, always hustling some grievance. They're hucksters, claiming to represent all Islam. Frankly, most Muslims I know are embarrassed by these buffoons, who do not have a mandate to speak on behalf of anyone."[26]

Although there are signs of anti-Islamic attitudes in some national columnists – the *Globe and Mail*'s Margaret Wente, for example, returned frequently to the theme of Muslim extremism in the years following the September 2001 attacks – the niche media are the most outspoken. For example, in an e-mail he distributed in an appeal for financial assistance to fight the human rights complaint lodged against his magazine, Levant picked up the jargon, referring to Soharwardy as a "radical Calgary Muslim imam" (March 30, 2006).

Soharwardy, a 50-year-old engineering consultant from Pakistan, is no doubt a complex individual who shows an arguably excessive degree of sensitivity to western treatment of Islam. But Levant's self-righteous self-aggrandizing, of course, is not only complete nonsense, it's an insidious act of singling out one element of the Canadian social fabric for apparently hurtful motives.

"One does not have to be a Muslim to feel the pain and betrayal these pictures convey," Elsmasry told Canadian journalists. "It is the same kind of pain felt by descendents of Holocaust survivors when confronted with the illogical ranting of those who deny it ever happened; or the pain of Black citizens faced with the spectacle of white supremacists marching down the main street of their town."[27]

It is perhaps surprising that, even though most publications in Canada did not publish the cartoons, seven out of ten journalists surveyed by the Compas Inc. research firm in February 2006 said they believe the media should have published the cartoons and they would do so now if the decision were theirs.

The reason? The respondents told Compas they believed not publishing the cartoons would strengthen the hands of the Saudi-based Wahhabists. Three-quarters of respondents said non-publication strengthened the position of such extremists within the Muslim world.

"I think the greatest, and most disturbing, reason [for not running the cartoons] is that many reporters and editors in North America have lost touch with those liberal values, emanating from the Enlightenment, in which journalism is grounded.... Journalism is a product of Western liberalism and we should not be afraid to defend it on that basis," one respondent told Compas.[28]

3. Dilemmas and Ethics

While readers might not be surprised that, as the largest-circulation family newspaper in Calgary, the *Herald* chose not to publish the cartoons, what of the racier tabloid, the *Sun*? Licia Corbella, of the *Sun*, and I did not talk about the decision of whether to publish the cartoons at the time, although we read each others' published explanations. So, some months later, I sat down with her to compare notes. What was going through her head at the time? How closely did her reasoning correlate to mine? How did our ethical reasoning compare? And, in hindsight, does the reasoning hold up? Or were we, as our detractors suggested, merely cowards acting out of fear?

It was somewhat surprising to me that both of us made the decision not to run the cartoons almost instantaneously. It was an immediate, intuitive reaction – curiously counter-intuitive, if you consider that both of us are products of traditional newsroom culture that is driven by conditioned learning and awareness of the economic imperative. Both of us looked at the cartoons and questioned the merit of running them. We knew they would be offensive to a significant number of readers and therefore could not find a justification for doing so. In both cases, we then consulted with other senior editors, who reinforced the decision.

In other words, the initial decision was not the product of a prolonged ethical debate, even though such debates are not uncommon. In fact, debates occur on a daily basis at newspapers. Most news outlets are guided by ethical codes (most major dailies have their own, or rely upon universal codes, like the Society of Professional Journalists Code of Ethics).[29] Among the values mandated in the code is one that requires journalists to "examine their own cultural values and avoid imposing those values on others."

In an article in the April 2006 *Quill* magazine, Fred Brown, a member of the SPJ Ethics Committee, said editors must seek a balance between two of the Code's key clauses: "seek truth and report it" and "minimize harm."

"It probably doesn't matter much where a story is placed," Brown said. "If it damages someone's reputation or puts someone at risk, it will do so whether it's on 1-A or 17-C." On the question of photographs or other visual elements, he said: "an ethical editor must consider whether it's really in everyone's interest to play them large and in colour on the front page."[30]

It is only with the benefit of time that I can now look back on the incident and pass judgment on my actions and on those of others. To the question of whether I was motivated by fear, I can honestly say that was not the case. As I review the conversations and thoughts that went through my mind during the height of the controversy, my personal safety and the safety of the newspaper and its staff did not once cross my mind as a potential concern. Someone might accuse me of imprudence for not having such thoughts, but I think it is more likely that such danger was so remote in my mind it was beyond consideration. I thought then, as I do now, of the Muslims I know – gentle, fair-minded people; neighbours, friends, businesspeople – members of the Calgary mosaic. Not apart from us, as their accusers would suggest.

I recall a conversation I had about the issue with a group of journalism students I was teaching at Mount Royal College in the winter of 2006. I had asked them how they felt about the *Herald*'s decision not to run the cartoons, and I got a broad range of views, from those who felt strongly that we should have run them, to those who commended us for our restraint. I noticed that one young woman, a modern Muslim who was normally the life of the class, had become quiet and withdrawn. After class, I pulled her aside because I was curious about her reaction to the discussion. She looked distraught. "I just wanted to leave," she said. "I have never felt so much like I didn't belong." The issue had made someone who normally fit so comfortably into the group suddenly an alien entity.

So then, if it was not fear, what was my motivation for not publishing the cartoons? Fortunately, the decision was made before I heard from those who would later chide me and the media outlet I work for. In that sense, it was a clear-headed decision, untainted by doubts about my own motives. As I have searched my heart over the ensuing months, I remain convinced I was acting out of a genuine conviction that running the cartoons would amount to nothing more than an inconsiderate act of rudeness – lacking any genuine motive. In that sense, to do so would be an act of provocation that would invite a response.

I also wrote at the time that one could not ignore the rioting and other disruptions that the publication of the cartoons had triggered in Europe. The *Sun*'s Corbella told me she did not cite that reason at the time in her public explanations, but it was on her mind. There were those who argued that in so doing the media were capitulating to Muslim pressure, but they are labouring under a deep misapprehension. It was simply a matter of showing some social responsibility. Free-speechers must truly feel insecure about their rights and powers if they must constantly be asserting them just to prove that they can, regardless of the hurt or havoc that might result from their actions.

Advocates for publishing the cartoons almost invariably cite what they consider a double standard, asserting that Christians are treated much more poorly in the media than Muslims would ever be simply because the media know Christians are more tolerant of such abuse. Often, they refer to a controversial art object from a few years ago entitled "Piss Christ," in which the figure of Christ is shown submerged in urine. Why, they ask, would newspapers publish such a heretical image of a holy Christian figure but not the comparatively milder images of Muhammad?

But coverage of that heretical art item has been subject to some revisionism; in fact, treatment of that story was not so different than the way the cartoon controversy was handled. Although it is often asserted that the media carried photographs of "Piss Christ," a check of major databases shows that very few actually did. Instead, news outlets wrote or spoke descriptively about the artwork, just as those reporting on the Danish cartoons described them in detail but did not show them. The treatment is extremely similar.

Fundamentalist Christians, in particular, have become highly sensitive to the treatment of stories about their faith since the cartoon controversy. The *Calgary Herald* ran a cartoon, done by staff cartoonist Vance Rodewalt, that illustrates the sensitivity. It showed Preston Manning, a Christian and then-possible candidate for the leadership of the Alberta Progressive Conservative party, standing on a mount looking towards the heavens and saying, "Hellooo! I'm waiting for a sign down here".

To someone like me, who was raised in a fundamentalist Christian family, it seemed to be a gentle, playful treatment of the relationship between Manning's faith and his political aspirations. Certainly, it was no depiction of the Supreme Being, although it's worth noting Christianity has many images of the Supreme Being personified in Jesus Christ. Yet, publication of the cartoon drew an angry response from several readers, who identified themselves as Christians and demanded to know the difference between that cartoon and those that mocked Muhammad. Of course, there is all the difference in the world.

The *New Yorker*'s Art Spiegelman comes closest to the truth when he observes that the mainstream media's reluctance to publish the Danish cartoons reflects a much broader trend in the media to generally avoid offence. "In recent decades newspaper editors, increasingly fearful of offending readers or advertisers, have sublimated the cartoon's potency as a rhetorical weapon that can literally give shape to opinion," he wrote in *Harper's*. "Hard-hitting cartoons have mostly been replaced by topical 'laffs' in gag-cartoon format or by decorative 'Op-Ed'-style illustrations whose meanings are often drowned in ambiguous surrealism."[31]

Yet, it is true that many Muslim communities show a generally lower tolerance towards Islamic heresies than Christians do towards heresies directed at them. Some of that must be attributed to the fact that Christians for the past century or more have lived in highly secularized western societies in which, like it or not, they have learned through experience that their voices are no longer dominant. It is worth noting that there is within Islam a history of debating whether the *Qur'an* is the literal word of God. It is only in relatively recent history that a strongly literalist interpretation of Islam has developed in certain states, and that has been instrumental in getting an oppressed citizenry (such as those who live in Iran, and pre-war Iraq and Afghanistan) to focus on problems elsewhere. At the same time, in an increasingly secularized world, Muslims have developed a sense of being besieged.

As the overwhelming success of the fictional novel *The Da Vinci Code* has shown us, many nominal Christians take it as a God-given right to question the most basic church dogma.[32] It is only unfortunate that outspoken Muslims have not been as vigorous in the defence of Christians against heresy as they have been of their own religion.

Critics of the mainstream media – those that chose not to show the cartoons – framed the debate as a struggle between freedom of expression and capitulation to a hostile and potentially threatening alien culture. This is a laughably juvenile analysis that depends upon a level of cultural paranoia that borders on xenophobia.

Levant, former publisher of the *Western Standard*, went to great pains in a number of columns to position himself as a courageous defender of free expression. Yet, a skeptic could imagine less noble motives for his provocation. The *Western Standard* was a nascent monthly magazine, born out of the ashes of *Report* magazine (once known as *Alberta Report*). Like its predecessor, the *Western Standard* was a niche publication that attempted to appeal to readers in Alberta and across the country who hold fiscally and socially conservative views. Among its key editorial positions, the magazine frequently questioned Canada's multiculturalism and liberal immigration policies – the very policies that encourage immigration of those who hold non–Judeo-Christian faiths. Part of the magazine's appeal was based on an anti-mainstream media philosophy. One would be hard pressed to find an edition of the *Standard* that did not refer to the "liberal" (and Liberal) media, and their alleged biases. Even the Calgary-based dailies – the *Herald* and the *Sun*, both outspoken conservative papers – fall under suspicion because they are owned by large corporations based in Winnipeg and Toronto, respectively. The notion is that if you're not from Alberta, you can't be trusted (a notion that fits neatly with the chronic phenomenon of western Canadian alienation).

In that context, taking a provocative position that pits the small, locally owned *Western Standard* against the big newspapers could be interpreted as a clever marketing strategy that reinforces the relationship between the niche publication and its narrowly focused audience. Thus, Levant's decision to publish and defend publication of the cartoons could be viewed, not as an act of reckless sensationalism, but as a well-considered move to differentiate the product from its competitors. Since it is not a mass-market product, Levant could afford to offend and alienate Muslims because they are not likely to be reading his publication in any event.

I must stress that is only one of several possible explanations. Equally possible is that Levant holds such a deeply rooted suspicion of Muslims that he cannot understand how anyone could hold more moderate views. The slang of the old Wild West somehow seems appropriate: "You're either with us or you're against us." Historically, this view was held by xenophobic Christians of their Jewish neighbours in Europe. The Spanish Inquisition is a historical example when both Jews and Muslims were viewed with such suspicion. Ironically, expelled Jewish residents of Europe found safety among Muslim communities.

With Levant no longer involved with the magazine, I thought it would now be an opportune time to revisit with him the question of motive; his answers surprised me because they were not only at odds with my theories, but also out of sync with what I anticipated he would say. He wrote in an e-mail that neither principle nor profit was the original driver. Instead, he said it was just what a well-trained newsman would do!

> Actually, the decision to publish the cartoons was originally a simple news decision. The publication of the cartoons in 2005 wasn't really news outside of Denmark. But by early 2006, the global riots blamed on those cartoons – that killed 100 people – were indeed international news. Our magazine's motto was 'telling it like it is,' so we could hardly write a story about the cartoons and decline to show the central facts of it. More to the point, there was no reason to do so, except for fear.

Regardless of motive, one tragic consequence of the cartoon initiative is that it acted as a catalyst in the post-9/11 blurring of the distinction between Islam and terrorism. Non-Muslims who see images of Muhammad with a bomb in his turban make an instant connection between the faith and an evil act. This mitigates against a more sophisticated understanding – one that recognizes that extremism exists in all societies (think of misguided U.S. "patriot" Timothy McVeigh and the Oklahoma bombings) and that the tenets of faith are often twisted to establish a false sense of legitimacy for acts most right-thinking followers would consider sinful. Over history, this has happened as often in Christianity and numerous other religions as it has in Islam.

I hardly feel smug about my own decision not to run the cartoons. I must wrestle with the possibility that my decision not to publish had as much to do with the media's general reluctance to offend – as described by Spiegelman – as it did with resistance to the perceived economic imperative.

4. CONCLUSION

While the Danish cartoon controversy may have provided a rare marketing opportunity for some niche media, it posed an unprecedented challenge for the mainstream media and their sincere but untested codes of ethics.

The *Western Standard*'s Levant dismissed mainstream media as a collection of weak-kneed conciliators: "The self-censorship amongst Canada's media was more uniform than had there been a court order banning Canadian media from showing those cartoons.... The self-censorship of 10,000 editors and producers [was] a far more effective attack on the culture of liberty than 9/11 was. That's the soft jihad of censorship and lawfare at work," he wrote to me (personal communication, July 5, 2009).

The simple fact of the matter is the media were unprepared for the complexities of the story that followed the militant Muslim terrorist bombings of September 11, 2001. Although a few news outlets had nibbled around the edges of the story of anti-U.S. antipathy around the world – CBS's *60 Minutes*, for example, interviewed Osama bin Laden in the late 1990s – the threat was apparently dismissed by the U.S. intelligence community as small and manageable, and the media were willing to generally ignore a topic that wasn't in vogue until the country was effectively blindsided by an attack on several architectural symbols of military and economic might. And with the attacks, the greatest reporting challenge in years, they resorted to the familiar: reverting to an almost pornographic emotional indulgence, telling and retelling the stories of the victims, their broken-hearted families, the heroes and all the other clichés that sustain the media's stock-in-trade – catastrophe. I referred earlier to the propensity to exploit the emotional dimensions of crime and automobile mishaps – known in the industry as "ambulance-chasing." For most media, the ensuing coverage of 9/11 became, in effect, ambulance-chasing on a global scale. The complexities and nuances of the story were sacrificed in favour of the provocative and easy-to-digest.

The hard part of this story is understanding why, and it is there that the majority of the media have still not yet met the challenge. Of course, the story is not about Osama bin Laden – as significant a role as he played – it is about understanding the interplay of religion, social consensus, and conflicting international interests. It is about festering resentments and ill-considered and ill-timed foreign aggression. It is about a swaggering, over-confident rich nation flaunting a seemingly godless society to a much poorer world. It is about runaway consumerism, and the imperatives (notably oil supply) such consumption creates. Those stories are being told, but primarily by the alternative media, and primarily on hundreds of web sites and blogs.

The most notable exception to this ineptitude is the June 2006 *Harper's* magazine, which, in publishing all of the cartoons, did so in a highly contextualized manner, delivered with good humour and common sense by Art Spiegelman.[33] Only through his thoughtful analysis did the publication avoid the accusation of provocation such agenda-driven magazines as the *Western Standard* have been unable to refute.

Context is the critical point. If the mainstream media are to learn anything from this experience, it should be the necessity to contextualize in an increasingly complex world. This is not merely a moral responsibility. If newspapers wish to turn around their sagging credibility ratings – which they must, if they are to survive – then they must recognize the economic benefit of delivering a product that more closely aligns with what consumers require – information that provides context. The Danish cartoon controversy is incomprehensible unless a news consumer fully understands the geopolitical forces that have created the circumstances for it to occur. And, once there is a full understanding of the context, an editor who must choose whether to publish the cartoons faces a much simpler ethical decision than it might at first appear.

But editors do not have the luxury of time as news unfolds. They must make almost instantaneous decisions, often in the absence of full information. We – in particular, owners and proprietors of the media, and educators – can help them by bolstering the amount of background they have as stories unfold, and by recognizing that good editors must have a much fuller pallet of skills than just having a way with words. It is, in effect, a compelling argument that the best editors in future will have a sense of history and a grounding in philosophy and will devote every available moment to staying ahead of emerging trends. Doing any less is a disservice to those who rely upon the media to tell them what is going on.

Appendix

NEWS SCHEDULES

The following schedules were taken from the Canadian Press news wire on April 25, 2006. They feature a list of suggested front-page topics provided by Canadian Press along with the selections made by several major Canadian newspapers, and by the CBC, CTV, and Global television networks.

The Canadian Press

Eds: CP suggests the following stories for front-page consideration:

Media Ban on Return of Afghan Dead Draws Fire
OTTAWA – Some Conservative MPs are annoyed at their government's decision to block journalists from covering the arrival of military coffins from Afghanistan. Defence Minister Gordon O'Connor says he banned the media out of concern for grieving families, but critics wonder if it's more about avoiding bad press. 725 words. By Alexander Panetta and Jennifer Ditchburn.

Goth Website Said to Link Teen Girl and Murder Accomplice
MEDICINE HAT, Alta. – An adult male and a 12-year-old girl accused in the slayings of an Alberta couple and their son were to appear in court Tuesday charged with first-degree murder. Friends of the pre-teen girl have said the two accused met on a goth website. 600 words. By Judy Monchuk.

BC-CRIME-Bodies-Found, 1st Writethru. –

10 Arrested in Bomb Attacks on Egyptian Resort
DAHAB, Egypt – Police arrest 10 people in the bombings that ripped apart a crowded Sinai resort town, killing 24 people. Tourists flee the coast as many Arabs react in outrage to an attack that bears the hallmarks of al-Qaida-linked groups, hitting both Egyptians celebrating a national holiday and foreigners on vacation. Some hardline Islamic groups condemn the bombing. 1,000 words. See AP Photos. BC-Egypt-Resort-Blast, 2nd Writethru. Moved.

The Buzz … Troops Approve of Coverage Ban on Casualties
KANDAHAR, Afghanistan – The grief of war widows and families is an intensely private matter that doesn't need to be on display for the whole country to see, some of Canada's fighting troops said Tuesday. Still raw from the events of last weekend, when Taliban militants attacked and killed four Canadian soldiers, the Conservative government's decision to ban the media from covering the arrival ceremonies of war casualties was greeted

with cautious approval among soldiers serving in Afghanistan. 580 words. By Murray Brewster. BC-Afghan-Cda-Soldiers. Moved World (W) and General (G)

Here is what the various news media chose to feature:

Television:

GLOBAL NEWS, APRIL 24, 2006
DAHAB, Egypt – About 20 people are dead after explosions ripped through an Egyptian resort town. COVERED

WASHINGTON – It's not known whether there's a connection between an audio tape released Sunday by Osama bin Laden and the Egypt attacks. COVERED

KANDAHAR, Afghanistan – Soldiers at Kandahar Air Field have bid a final goodbye to four fellow troops killed in a roadside bomb Saturday; the bodies are on their way home to Canada. COVERED

OTTAWA – Debate is raging about whether flags on government buildings should be lowered to half-mast every time a soldier dies in Afghanistan. COVERED

OTTAWA – Farmers, riding in a convoy of tractors, took their fight to the Prime Minister's residence Monday. COVERED

TORONTO – Former Ontario premier Bob Rae and MP Carolyn Bennett have joined the Liberal leadership race.

KASHECHEWAN, Ont. – The First Nations community is being evacuated due to rising flood waters. COVERED

MEDICINE HAT, Alta. – One middle-aged man and a 12-year-old girl have been charged in with a triple homicide murder. COVERED

BANGOR, Maine – Police have traced the movements of a Cape Breton man charged with killing two registered sex offenders using the GPS program on his computer.

SASKATOON – David Milgaard has testified on videotape as part of the inquiry into his wrongful conviction. COVERED

BAGHDAD – An explosion in Baghdad has killed three and injured 15. COVERED

TORONTO – A new study shows milk is beneficial for pregnant women.

KINGSTON, Ont. A family has opened up a restaurant named Schmichael's – a tribute to their dog that rescued them from a fire.

OTTAWA – Federal government bars media from witnessing the return of the remains of four soldiers who were killed in Afghanistan, and flags will not be lowered on Parliament Hill; Defence Minister Gordon O'Connor says the flags will be lowered for any soldiers killed in action Nov. 11; NDP leader Jack Layton says the Conservatives are modelling their approach on that of the United States, which downplays combat deaths by limiting media access. MAJOR ELEMENTS COVERED

KANDAHAR, Afghanistan – Large and emotional ceremony held to send off remains of four soldiers killed on the weekend. COVERED

OTTAWA – CTV News has learned there may finally be a deal in the softwood lumber dispute; details of an agreement have been worked out, including quotas on softwood lumber; the United States will return 78 per cent of the $5 billion collected in unfair duties. COVERED

DAHAB, Egypt – Three bombs rip through the centre of a resort town, killing at least 21 people at the height of the tourist season. COVERED

MEDICINE HAT, Alta. – A 12-year-old girl and a 23-year-old man charged with first-degree murder in the deaths of a married couple and their pre-teen son; police will not reveal the names of the victims. MAIN ELEMENTS COVERED

OTTAWA – Former Ontario premier Bob Rae joins the Liberal leadership race; also on Monday, Liberal MP Carolyn Bennett also joined the race; Rae admits he's made mistakes in office, but says he learned from them; he positions himself in the progressive centre; critics doubt Ontario voters will give him a second chance.

UNDATED – Green party leader Jim Harris announces he will step down; the party will choose a new leader in August. COVERED

OTTAWA – Federal Finance Minister Jim Flaherty will bring down his first budget on May 2.

MONTREAL – New guidelines establish for weight and growth charts for infants based on breast-fed infants rather than those who have been bottle-fed.

UNDATED – Canadian class-action lawsuit alleges GM is at fault for the failure of intake manifolds in some of its vehicles.

CALEDONIA, Ont. – Residents demand an end to a native blockade. COVERED

TORONTO – Businessman and former owner of the Toronto Maple Leafs has died at the age of 78.

OTTAWA – Parents of autistic children go to Parliament Hill to lobby government to pay for the expensive therapy their children require.

CBC NEWS, APRIL 24

KANDAHAR, Afghanistan – Latest Canadian casualties in Afghanistan get a large and emotional send off as their remains are sent home.

OTTAWA – Remains of four Canadian soldiers killed in Afghanistan will return home on Tuesday; the federal government says the flag on the Peace Tower will not be lowered to half-mast, Prime Minister Stephen Harper will not take part in ceremonies when the bodies arrive and media will not be allowed to witness the arrival; Conservatives point to protocol, saying the soldiers are not high-ranking enough to merit the lowering of the Peace Tower flag; critics say the government is modelling its approach on that of the Americans, attempting to downplay the number of casualties by limiting access. COVERED

VANCOUVER – Improvised explosive devices now responsible for two out of every three casualties in Afghanistan; in the attack that killed four Canadian soldiers, the bombers were able to focus their attack on the least armoured vehicle and to detonate at precisely the right moment. MAIN ELEMENTS COVERED

DAHAB, Egypt – Three explosions tear through a town on the Sinai Peninsula at the height of the tourist season, killing at least 20 people; in previous attacks, Egyptian authorities made sweeping arrests of locals, ignoring any connection with terrorist groups such as al-Qaida.

KASHECHEWAN RESERVE, Ont. – Flooding forces nearly half of the reserve's 1,700 residents from the town; more than 40 homes have been flooded and the road leading to the reserve is washed out; a leak in a protective dike has added to the annual spring flooding; residents say help has been slow to arrive. COVERED

CALEDONIA, Ont. – More than 2,000 people show up to protest continuing native blockade; native leaders and government officials are negotiating an end to the blockade.

OTTAWA – Former Ontario premier Bob Rae joins growing list of candidates for the Liberal leadership; Rae alienated both the political left and right during his single term, but says he has learned from his mistakes; he is positioning himself as a progressive centrist, putting fellow candidate Michael Ignatieff to his left. MAIN ELEMENTS COVERED

OTTAWA – Federal Finance Minister Jim Flaherty will bring down his first budget on May 2. COVERED

KATHMANDU, Nepal – King of Nepal agrees to reinstate the parliament in an effort to restore peace.

ROME – Pope Benedict has asked for a study of condom use as a way to prevent the spread of disease. COVERED

MEDICINE HAT, Alta. – Police have laid three first-degree murder charges against two people, a 23-year-old man and a 12-year-old child, in the deaths of a man, a woman and another child; police won't name the victims or say how they were killed.

UNDATED – The Canadian Press reports that Maine police have recovered a chilling computer log that shows a Cape Breton man who killed two sex offenders last week also hunted at least four others the same night.

BATH, Ont. – New facility on the grounds of Millhaven Penitentiary is being called Guantanamo North; its first four prisoners arrived on Monday, all four are being held under security certificates and haven't actually been charged, nor have their lawyers been able to see the evidence against them; Amnesty International worries that the new facility means security certificates are here to stay and that these four will continue to be detained for some time.

Newspapers

VANCOUVER PROVINCE
OTTAWA – Bruce Cheadle – Two weeks ago, Lincoln Dinning wrote to Prime Minister Stephen Harper asking that federal flags be flown at half-mast in the event of future combat deaths – A8.

OTTAWA SUN
MEDICINE HAT, Alta. (Staff, CP) – Girl, 12, charged in triple murder.
MAIN PHOTO: MEDICINE HAT (CP-Ian Sorensen) – Body. Teasers: Florida heat; Double OT Thriller. CP Ottawa.

OTTAWA CITIZEN
Above fold: CAIRO (CP, LA Times) – Bombs rip through Red Sea resort.
UNDATED (Staff) – The continuing terror of Flight 93. (Review, not matching).
OTTAWA (Staff) – Canadians won't see fallen troops come home. (Main elements covered).
Below fold: OTTAWA (Staff) – Harper's 'God bless' signoff just fine with Canadians: Poll.
OTTAWA (Staff) – Military to get 'substantial' boost in budget.

GLOBE AND MAIL
OTTAWA (Staff) – Ottawa fails fallen soldiers, say critics
BELOW FOLD: WASHINGTON (Staff) – Bombs tear apart Sinai resort
WASHINGTON (Staff) – Softwood deal close
MEDICINE HAT, Alta. (Staff) – Man, 23, girl, 12, charged in slayings
TORONTO (Staff) – Rae joins Liberal race

TORONTO STAR
OTTAWA (Staff) – Ban on images of fallen soldiers' return
CAIRO (AP) – Bombs target tourist strip
BELOW FOLD: CALEDONIA, Ont. (Staff) – Angry residents protest blockade
UNDATED (Staff) – Stavro embodied local sporting life

MONTREAL GAZETTE
CAIRO (L. A. Times, AP, CP) – Bombs rip up Egypt resort.
PLATTSBURGH, N.Y. – U.S. group watches borders for "illegals." (Feature, not matching).
BELOW FOLD: OTTAWA (CanWest) – Milk boosts birth weight.
RALEIGH, N.C. (Staff) – Column on Montreal-Carolina series.

Notes

1   Consider, for example, the opening paragraph of this editorial from the Toronto-based *National Post* on September 13, 2001, repeating and supporting accusations that were later proven to be groundless: "It is shocking to think Canada may have had an indirect role in Tuesday's terrorist attack on the United States. But it may be true. Yesterday, it was reported that unnamed U.S. Justice Department officials are saying at least two of the terror suspects entered the United States through Canada. The report, though unconfirmed, is credible: Canada has been a porous staging area and conduit for terrorist conspiracies in the past. The Canadian government should not wait till U.S. authorities complete their investigation. They need to reform our immigration, refugee and visitor entry procedures now."

2   Here's just one example, an excerpt from a February 24, 2003, column by Mark Steyn entitled "Can Muslims be Good Multiculturalists?": "The great issue of our time is whether Islam – the fastest growing religion in Europe and North America – is compatible with the multi-cultural, super-diverse, boundlessly tolerant society of Western liberals."

3   *Quill Magazine*, April 2006, 35.

4   The Pew Research Center for the People and the Press. *Pew Research Center Biennial News Consumption Survey* (Washington, DC: Pew Research Center, June 2004), 106.

5   Andy Kohut (President of the Pew Research Center), Online Newshour: Credibility of the Media. Transcript of April 7, 1997 interview on the National Public Radio program. The full transcript can be viewed at: http://www.pbs.org/newshour/bb/media/jan-june97/credibility_4-7.html (accessed November 1, 2009).

6   *Muslim Free Press*, 1 (April 2006).

7   Art Spiegelman, "Drawing Blood, Outrageous Cartoons and the Art of Outrage," *Harper's*, June 2006.

8   "Nada Raad and Hannah Allam for Knight Ridder Newspapers, Dateline: Beirut, Lebanon" *Calgary Herald* (February 6, 2006), A3.

9   Nelly van Doorn-Harder, "Radical Clerics Stir Muslim Anger," *Christian Science Monitor*, March 2, 2006.

10 "Prophet cartoons come to Calgary: Publishers defend move as free speech," *Calgary Herald* (February 11, 2006), A1.

11 "A Poke in the Eye Invites a Fight," *Calgary Herald* (February 11, 2006), A28.

12 "Violence Blasphemes Islam; Most Unjust Nations in the World Are Those Living Under Strict Sharia Law," *Calgary Sun*, February 12, 2006, 33.

13 Ibid.

14 Ibid.

15 Ibid.

16 "Tasteless Caricature Has No Place Here," *Calgary Sun*, February 15, 2006, 4.

17 *Calgary Herald*, February 11, 2006, A1.

18 Ibid.

19 *Western Standard*, March 13, 2006.

20 It is not insignificant that the *Western Standard* later admitted that it had to cease its print publication because of a loss of advertising and reader support. Levant eventually sold the publication, and it continues in an online-only version. While I was preparing this chapter, I asked former publisher Levant whether there was a link between the magazine's financial woes and the cartoon controversy; he replied: "No. Publishing the cartoons was a financially neutral decision. I think we lost $50,000 worth of ads, but we made slightly more than that in subscription sales. And we received at least a million dollars worth of publicity.... In terms of our readership, we had over 1,000 new subscriptions taken up by people merely wanting to show their support – as opposed to a couple of dozen who cancelled."

21 Superstar columnist Mark Steyn accused the mainstream media of cowardice; Ottawa's David Warren revived the old chestnut of failed British Prime Minister Neville Chamberlain in warning of the danger of appeasement.

22 *Western Standard*, March 13, 2006, 36.

23 *Calgary Herald*, February 11, 2006.

24 Mohaamed Elmasry, "Freedom of Expression and the Offending Cartoons," a speech to the Canadian Association of Journalists, May 15, 2006.

25 Ibid.

26 Personal email communication (with Ezra Levant), July 5, 2009.

27 Ibid.

28 *The Offending Danish Cartoons* (Compas Inc., February 20, 2006).

29 Society of Professional Journalists. *Code of Ethics*. Society of Professional Journalists, http://www.spj.org/ethicscode.asp (accessed March 31, 2007).

30 *Quill Magazine*, April 2006, 35.

31 "Drawing Blood," *Harper's*, June 2006.

32 It is important to note that some fundamentalist Christian sects oppose such thinking as strongly as extremist Islamic sects object to the cartoons. The difference is that they are in relatively small minority of the total Christian population.

33 It was not enough, unfortunately, to avoid a ban from Canada's Chapters/Indigo bookstore chain.

CHAPTER 6

The Terrorist "Other": The Fundamentalist and the Islamist

KARIM-ALY KASSAM
Cornell University

1. TERRORIST AS FUNDAMENTALIST

The characterization of Muslims as the violent "Other" has antecedents in Medieval Christian discourse to facilitate unity among Christendom.[1] In the twentieth century, this "Other" was replaced by the threat of communist evil from the East in order to sustain the Cold War. In the twenty-first century, the characterization of Muslim "Other" has returned. The overarching objective of this collection of essays is to simultaneously understand the tactical use of terror and the metaphorical power of the label "terrorist." To achieve this, historical sensitivity is essential to understand the diverse contexts from which terror arises. An important issue arose in the use of terminology employed by contributors to this volume to describe those who engaged in acts of terror. While the most common term is "terrorist," contributors chose to find more nuanced terms that contextualize a group's objectives. When the label "terrorist" is assigned to an individual or group in the public domain, critical capacity is often suspended. Immediately, the individual or group is considered part of a category of the "other," undertaking an irrational act, and is inherently "evil." When an action is viewed as one-dimensionally evil, questions like: "why has this human being chosen to commit terror?" are not widely asked in the popular media. Contributors tried to choose a vocabulary that was more descriptive of the group's objectives, rather than simply to replicate popular media representations. An editorial task was to establish a conversation on use of terms that were as accurate as possible and sensitive to the diversity of the groups being described. The words "fundamentalist" and "Islamist" are commonly used by ill-informed news media outlets whose aims are to sensationalize in order to maintain high ratings and turn a profit.

For example, the term "fundamentalist," as it is used to describe armed Jewish settlers, Christian evangelists, Hindu nationalists, Sikh separatists, and Muslim militants, suggests that in some essential manner it is the religion, the practice of a faith, that inspires violent action. However, a critical examination reveals that while many religions are a source of identity for various violent as well as peaceful groups, reliance on religion as the sole criterion of identification masks the social, political, and ecological causes that give rise to conflict. If anything, examination of the "fundamentals" of each of these religions reveals that a significant majority of the group members have a tenuous if not limited grasp of the fundamentals, that violence is rarely justified simply on scriptural grounds. While Catholicism is pervasive in the Irish Republican Army (IRA), the acts of terror carried out by this organization are hardly representative of Catholic Christianity. Mother Teresa was inspired by the same Catholicism that members of the IRA claim as theirs. The more meaningful examination would be to ask what are the grievances of the IRA? Similarly, given Gandhi's message of non-violence, one would be hard-pressed to suggest that Hinduism is a faith that inspires violence even though Gandhi was murdered by a man who carried out the killing in the name of that religion. For every verse recited from the various religious scriptures that seem to support violence, there are equal, if not more, that forbid it. The verses that are quoted are chosen out of context. At best, the fundamentalists are literalists who are unable to approach the spirit of a text as a whole. Therefore, the term "fundamentalist" is really not very helpful in understanding the motivations behind terror.

2. Terrorist as Islamist

The term "Islamist" has come increasingly into vogue in the popular media. Like the more general "fundamentalist," it is also vacant in terms of meaning, except in meeting the strategic objective of isolating all Muslims as the "Other." Over 1.4 billion Muslims of diverse cultural origins, a variety of interpretations of Islam, and unique socio-political contexts are homogenously classified as "Islamists." It is as if members of the IRA, David Koresh's Branch Davidians, or the Lord's Resistance Army, renowned for their child soldiers and teenage brides, all neatly fit under the category "Christianists." The term "Islamist" is not only facile, it is also empty of significance when trying to understand an act of terror and its motivations. Yet those who have engaged in acts of terror claim a religious connection to Islam. Various political organizations justify acts of terror by drawing on *a* Muslim identity.[2] Several political organizations that use violence draw inspiration from the Salafiyya movement.[3] While the vast majority who employ a "Salafist" outlook in Islam do not engage in violence to express their grievances, the Salafi movement has had a significant influence in radicalizing some Muslims. Consideration of the social context that gave rise to the Salafiyya movement is therefore necessary to illustrate that categorization without historical context can be problematic.

3. What are the Origins of the Salafiyya?

The concept of "Salaf" is attributed to the Sunni Arab scholar Muhammad `Abduh (1849–1905).[4] His interpretation is particularly important because of his contribution to modern Muslim thought. Muhammad `Abduh was born in Egypt in 1849. He studied at al-Azhar University in Cairo from 1869 to 1877. `Abduh received a classical theological education and was the Grand Mufti of Egypt. In the 1880s he lived in Paris and visited other European capitals such as London. In order to understand the forces that gave the impetus and helped shape `Abduh's view, two factors have to be taken into consideration: the relative decay of Muslim societies in comparison to the militarily and economically strong and essentially Christian Europe; and the great debate of the nineteenth century regarding the relationship between religion and science. The first created a debilitating anxiety caused by the gap between the ideal conception of Islam as the religion which had been perfected for mankind and whose Prophet founded a virtuous society and the actual condition of the followers of the faith who were subservient to European colonial military, economic, and scientific hegemony. The second involved the judgment of science on religion: that religion and the belief in God are tantamount to closing one's mind to enquiry into the mysteries of the universe. Hence, should the theistic ideal be dropped as it was equated to the tyranny of religious superstition and be replaced with scientific positivism? Although these criticisms were aimed at Christianity, they were also levelled at Islam due to the generally poor economic condition of Muslim societies under colonial rule. There was a choice between the overwhelming temptation of wholesale emulation of the socio-cultural and economic trends in Europe or ignoring these developments and suffering the shame of being considered backward, and in reality being subservient, to foreign interests although seeming to maintain religious and moral superiority (however shallow such an assumption might seem in the reality of the nineteenth century). 'Abduh was aware of such a division occurring among the Muslim intellectuals. 'Abduh wanted to avoid the dualistic articulation of 'progress' – namely, a choice between religious fanaticism based on literalist interpretations and anti-religious secularism. He sought to articulate a third way that did not destroy the essential moral and religious fabric for the believer and yet enabled him to participate with all his faculties and benefit from the developments of modernity. In a fragment of his autobiography, the *Tārīkh*, 'Abduh describes one of his major aims as being:

> ... to liberate thought from the shackles of *taqlīd* [blind imitation or traditionalism], and understand religion as it was understood by the elders of the community before dissension appeared; to return, in the acquisition of religious knowledge, to its first sources, and to weigh them in the scales of human reason, which God had created to prevent excess or adulteration in religion, so that God's wisdom may be fulfilled and the order of the human world preserved; and to prove that, seen in this light, religion must be accounted a friend

of science, pushing man to investigate the secrets of existence, sum-
moning him to respect established truths, and to depend on them
in his moral life and conduct. All this I count as one matter, and
in my advocacy of it I ran counter to the opinion of the two great
groups of which the body of the *umma* [Muslim community] is
composed – the students of the sciences of religion, and those who
think like them, and the students of the arts of this age, with those
who are on their side.[5]

In 'Abduh's view, the opposing positions of absolute adherence to the legal
practices (*sharia*), which had become outdated, or a complete imitation of
European culture, were untenable in the context of the future well-being of
Muslim societies. To him the first option was not acceptable because a return
to the past was not possible and the process of change could not be stopped.
The second path was equally undesirable because European ideas and culture
were new to the local culture; acceptance of external ideas without firmly root-
ing them in the existing milieu would only bring about superficial change and
possibly lead to further deterioration and lack of understanding of things foreign. Thus a way had to be found wherein religious scholars would accept the
need for change and simultaneously ground this change in the principles of
the faith. 'Abduh believed that the essential values of the faith would serve the
cause of change and at the same time act as a control over those changes that
might be morally deleterious. He and other Muslim thinkers of this period saw
themselves in a position to contribute to the engagement and reinterpretation
of Islam with modernity. In order to achieve this, 'Abduh studied European
philosophical literature, particularly French thinkers. By the second half of his
life, 'Abduh was fluent in French and was widely read in nineteenth-century
European thought.[6]

For 'Abduh, it was simply historically inaccurate to refer to "Islam" as one
monolithic category to describe a faith that was over a millennium old and had
come into contact with diverse cultures and a variety of intellectual traditions.
In the *al-'Urwa al-Wuthqā* (co-authored with al-Afgānī.),[7] 'Abduh distinguishes between Islam as transcendental idea and Islam as historical phenomenon.
"Islam in the first sense is perfect; Islam in the second sense is open to criticism,

indeed, in its present day state it has become so far removed from the original Islam, that it hardly deserves its name."[8] According to 'Abduh, the golden age of Islam was the first four centuries characterized by a vibrant and virtuous community. He argued that the decay of the community was a result of reliance upon the established practices of Muslims of previous generations, by the acceptance of the beliefs on the authority of their ancestors without question or objection. 'Abduh believed that prophets are social reformers. He believed that the advent of Islam brought humanity two important possessions that had been long denied by religion: freedom of thought and ability to form an opinion based on careful reflection. He maintained that this is what the Protestant Reformation achieved for the Europeans. This is significant because it relates to the intellectual foundations of religious practice, which was of primary concern to 'Abduh. Referring to the 'Ulamā (religious scholars) he said:

> The larger part of the specialists are afflicted with the disease of traditionalism (taqlīd). They believe and then demand proof, but only on condition that the proof shall agree with their belief. If they are confronted with what counters their belief they will have nothing to do with it. Indeed, they oppose it tooth and nail, even if it means jettisoning rationality altogether. The way of most of them is first to dogmatise and then lay claim to proof. Rarely one finds among them any who first prove and then believe.[9]

Thus social regulations relating to a particular time and place were construed to have the same status as the principles of the faith, and the religious leadership demanded obedience to them as if they were the essential precepts of the faith. 'Abduh maintains that Islam at the time of its revelation struggled to shatter the power of taqlīd over men's minds.[10] He argued that Islam liberated reason from the enslavement of taqlīd, allowing it to do its work in judgment and wisdom.[11] Therefore, the practice of ijtihād (reasoned engagement) was no longer reserved for the previous generations but rather should be practised by all Muslims in all ages.

What was the basis of reform of Muslim societies? 'Abduh decided that the political route would be too time-consuming and would yield fewer results.[12]

'Abduh felt that reform must be at a very basic level of Muslim society, at the foundation of their way of life in order to be effective; thus reform had to begin with the religion. He argued: "For to attempt to reform by means of culture or philosophy that is not religious in character, would require the erection of a new structure, for which neither materials nor workmen are available. If the religion of Muslims can work these ends and has their confidence, why seek other means?"[13] Furthermore, "if Muslims improved their characters through religion then they could compete with the Europeans in the acquisition of the [natural] sciences and the obtainment of knowledge and be qualified with them in civilisation and thus it will be easier to cooperate with them."[14]

The Salafiyya movement, as conceived by 'Abduh, simultaneously sought to find an ideal historical form of Islam and to reform Muslim religious practice. How is it that the Salaf, promoted by thinkers like 'Abduh, came to take such an anti-Western stance and is used by political organizations such as al-Qaida? We will return to this irony after we consider another contributor to the notion of Salaf.

Primarily in response to the vast Ottoman Empire whose Sultan claimed to represent Islam as a whole, Muhammad ibn 'Abd al-Wahhab (1703–87) argued that the true Islam existed during the first generation of Muslims guided by pious leaders. He attributed the decline of Muslim economic and military strength to the pluralism prevalent in Islam. 'Abd al-Wahhab was responding to the overwhelming anxiety of being associated with an empire in decay. He objected to the development of mysticism in Islam and its ascetic tendencies; and to the integration of philosophy, arts, and intellectual traditions of the many cultures that comprised Muslim peoples and their neighbours. For al-Wahhab, the Ottoman Sultan had failed to protect "true" Islam.[15] There was an inherent tension between Ottoman rulers controlling lands and representing a Muslim Prophet who was ethnically Arab. The Ottoman rulers were Turkish, descended from the Mongol invaders from the East. Al-Wahhab was linking Ottoman imperial rule, the pluralism that characterized Islam over the centuries, and the military weakness of Muslims to foment an ideology that effectively supported Arab nationalism. He advocated a literalist and stringent application of Muslim law (*shari'a*) that was intolerant of other schools of Muslim thought.

Al-Wahhab joined forces with a dynasty in Central Arabia and provided the ideological justification for the formation of the Kingdom of Saudi Arabia.[16] Even with Wahhabism, the Saudis were relatively insignificant in both the Arab world and the Muslim community as a whole. However, they had two advantages that changed the fortune of Wahhabism: first, the Muslim sacred places (Mecca and Medina) were within Saudi territory; and second, control of the largest reserves of oil known to humanity were also there. Petrodollars could be utilized to finance the hitherto ignored and relatively narrow interpretation of Islam and spread it across Muslim communities.[17]

4. The Construction of the Monolithic "Other"

Classical Arabic, which is the language of the Qur'an, is not widely used by Arabs, except by religious scholars. Furthermore, a majority of Muslims reside outside of the Middle East and are not Arab. In the twentieth century, a growing number of non-Arab Muslim communities needed young trained religious scholars who were knowledgeable in classical Arabic and the Prophetic tradition. Given the economic weakness of newly independent countries of Asia and Africa emerging from the yoke of European colonialism, the use of petrodollars to sponsor the training of religious scholars from poor countries in a narrow and ossifying interpretation like Wahhabism became an effective tool. This particular Wahhabi perspective jealously negated other interpretations of Islam. The ground was prepared for a myopic interpretation of Islam to emerge, fuelled by the legitimate political grievances of these communities. The Wahhabi co-optation of the Salafiyya movement, although still a perspective held by a minority of Muslims, is increasingly gaining a wider audience with the support of petrodollars and poor foreign policy decisions by Western countries. While Wahhabism claims solidarity with all Muslims, it is important to note that it arose out of Arab nationalism in opposition to the Ottoman Empire, which also adhered to Sunni Islam. In other words, European cultures were never the first target of Wahhabi criticism. The first target of Wahhabi criticism has always been other interpretations of Islam – Sunni and Shia alike.

'Abduh applied the idea of Salaf in a different sense than al-Wahhab. He did not conflate the virtues of the first generation of Muslims with a literal interpretation of the traditions of the faith; rather, he sought an intellectual justification for the faith that was commensurate with the increasingly globalized world in which Muslims live. Al-Wahhab's conceptualization of Salaf, while simple, does not take into account the complexities of human societies and the role of the human intellect. While 'Abduh passionately makes a case for reasoned interrogation of tradition and customs, al-Wahhab sees no conflict with his own privileging of certain traditions without concern for their validity in a more modern context. Both Al-Wahhab and 'Abduh seek to reform Muslim societies, but 'Abduh is more sensitive to building bridges with European ideas and cultures. There is a clear contradiction between 'Abduh's desire to seek a historical Muslim ideal and his scathing criticism of traditionalist tendencies among Muslim religious scholars. While al-Wahhab provides the rhetoric that is more easily appropriated by organizations like al-Qaida and disenfranchised and alienated Muslim youth, 'Abduh offers the more demanding path of complexities and paradoxes faced by Muslims as they engage social change and the debilitating effects of imperialism.

'Abduh's intellectual descendants were not able to sustain the complex engagement with their own interpretation of Islam and essentially secular Euro-American industrial cultures. Some chose secular nationalism that surfaced in the formation of Egypt, Iraq, and Syria. Others chose a defensive posture and engaged in a form of literal sclerosis of Islamic law and intellectual thought which resulted in the formation the Jamat-i-Islami in Pakistan and the Muslim Brotherhood in Egypt as reactions to a secular nationalism. Ironically 'Abduh vehemently criticized this ossification of Islamic thought among Muslim scholars. Today Salafists, who constitute a minority of Muslims, are identified with literalism in religious law and interpretation of the Qur'an which 'Abduh rejected. The juxtaposition of 'Abduh and al-Wahhab are informative as they illustrate complexities in the evolution of religious thought and specifically the varying influence they have had on the Salafists. Although al-Wahhab predates 'Abduh, his influence on the idea of Salaf emerged after the Saudi Kingdom became well-established, which was aided by a staunch alliance with the United States. While the Salafiyya movement represents only a single example of many variations in modern Muslim thought, it demonstrates that easy categorization is not possible when dealing with geographically widespread religious communities that are over a billion strong, whose traditions are over a thousand years old, and whose cultures are more diverse than Europe's. There is no single taxonomic classification called "Islamist" just as there is no unitary "Christianist." The term is a misnomer and deceptive. To blame acts of terrorism on religious texts of any faith is both intellectually lazy and politically dishonest.

In pluralistic societies and democracies such as Canada, where there is a recognition in political discourse that European and other immigrant settlement took place in a land where a diversity of indigenous peoples flourished and continue to exist, this position is difficult to maintain because Muslims live side by side with other cultural and religious communities. The demographic and multi-cultural reality of Canadian civil society has the potential of injecting a pluralistic understanding of the "Self" beyond the one-dimensional characterization of "us against them."

Notes

1 See Edward Said, *Orientalism* (London: Penguin Classics, 2003) and Said, *Culture and Imperialism* (New York: Knopf, 1993).

2 The indefinite article "a" emphasizes that there is no historical precedence of a unitary interpretation of Islam as there is no more a single Christianity, Judaism, Hinduism, or Buddhism.

3 A useful reference for a historical examination for developments in Muslim thought is: Marshall Hodgson, *The Venture of Islam* (Chicago: University of Chicago Press, 1974). Useful references on the Salafiyya movement are: John Esposito, *The Islamic Threat: Myth or Reality* (Oxford: Oxford University Press, 1995); Albert Hourani, *Arabic Thought in the Liberal Age 1789–1939* (Cambridge: Cambridge University Press, 1989); and Azim Nanji, *The Muslim Almanac* (New York: Gale Research, 1995).

4 Esposito, *The Islamic Threat*; Hourani, *Arabic Thought in the Liberal Age*; Nanji, *The Muslim Almanac*; and Karim-Aly Kassam, "The Idea of Progress in Modern Muslim Thought: The Views of 'Abduh and Iqbal on Reason and Tradition," *Islamica* 2, no. 4 (1998): 45–49.

5 Muhammad Rashīd Ridā, *Tārīkh al-ustādh al-imām al-shaikh Muhammad 'Abduh* (Cairo, 1908–1931), 11. Volume II was published in 1908, Volume III was published in 1910 and Volume I was published in 1931. This translation appears in Hourani, *Arabic Thought in the Liberal Age*, 140–41.

6 Hourani, *Arabic Thought in the Liberal Age*, 135.

7 Muhammad 'Abduh, and Jamāl al-Dīn al-Afgānī, *Al-'Urwa al-Wuthqā* (Beirut, 1910).

8 Menahem Milson, "The Elusive Jamāl al-Dīn al-Afghānī," *The Muslim World* 58 (1968): 295–307.

9 Muhammad 'Abduh, *Risālat al-tawhīd* (Cairo, 1897), 40. Translated into French by Bernard Michel and Moustapha Abdel Razik (Paris, 1925). Translated into English by Ishaq Musa'ad and Kenneth Cragg (London, 1966), 66.

10 'Abduh, *Risālat al-tawhīd* , 101 (English translation, 126).

11 Ibid., 102 (English translation, 127).

12 See Ridā, *Tārīkh al-ustādh al-imām al-shaikh Muhammad 'Abduh*, 1931: 11–12, where 'Abduh explains why he abandoned the issue of political authority, leaving the matter in the hands of God as the benefits of efforts at political reform could only be reaped over a long period of time.

13 Ridā, *Tārīkh al-ustādh al-imām al-shaikh Muhammad 'Abduh*, 1908: 477, quoted in Charles C. Adams, *Islam and Modernism in Egypt: A Study of the Modern Reform Movement Inaugurated by Muhammad 'Abduh* (London: Oxford University Press, 1933), 110.

14 Ridā, *Tārīkh al-ustādh al-imām al-shaikh Muhammad 'Abduh*, 1908: 480.

15 Hourani, *Arabic Thought in the Liberal Age*.

16 John Habib's study of the Ikhwan of Najd documents the role of a more stringent form of Wahhabism combined with a Bedouin military force that helped effectively to consolidate the Arabian Peninsula. John Habib, *Ibn Saud's Warriors of Islam: The Ikhwan of Najd and Their Role in the Creation of the Sa'udi Kingdom, 1910–1930* (Leiden: E.J. Brill, 1978).

17 Giles Kepel, *Jihad: The Trail of Political Islam* (Cambridge, MA: Harvard University Press, 2002).

CHAPTER 7

Maintaining Environmental Priorities in the Age of Terrorism

JAMES P. LASSOIE
Cornell University

> *Let me assert my firm belief that the only thing we have to fear is fear itself.*
> – President Franklin Delano Roosevelt's First Inaugural Address,
> March 4, 1933

1. INTRODUCTION

I recently needed to find an old family photo of personal importance, one that included me. The choice was easy as it was one that had long stood out from a thousand possibilities. A plump little kid with a "butch" haircut standing in front of a modest two-bedroom ranch, next to a new balloon-tired, one-speed Schwinn with an also new semi-portable radio hanging around his neck. It was June 11, 1958, my thirteenth birthday in Olympia, Washington.

Revisiting this old photograph after so many years I am struck by my expression – it's not one showing the joys of living in middle-class America,[1] but rather one marked by apprehension. For certain, the prominently displayed realtor's "For Sale" sign was unsettling my life greatly. But being a "Baby-Boomer-plus-one,"[2] I also know a much deeper and more pervasive anxiety can be read in my round face, one less directly tangible but potentially much more damaging, one reinforced daily in the news and at home and school – the Cold War with its ominous backdrop of possible annihilation. If you're old enough, you'll remember hunkering under your grade school desk during air raid drills, envying a neighbour's new underground shelter, Khrushchev's promise to "bury us," and being scared to death by *On the Beach*.[3] If you're not, check out *Duck and Cover*,[4] an absurd "educational" film from the early 1950s advising us to do just that when we saw "the flash" from a USSR-delivered nuclear explosion – the speed of light supposedly giving us kids a chance to hide from the "slower" blast front following. Though humorous in retrospect, the idea of covering myself with a newspaper for protection against an impact like those illustrated in ubiquitous documentaries from the Federal Civil Defense Administration[5] left a long-lasting feeling of fear and hopelessness. Of course, I was not alone, as Baby Boomers were also Cold War teenagers.

Armageddon may have come close during the 1962 Cuban Missile Crisis, but it never happened, despite the years of warnings and preparations. Soon Vietnam consumed the attention of most Americans, the military draft forced males to become less concerned with fighting a "cold" war, and "hawks and doves" battled for patriotic supremacy. Fear of the unknowns associated with the Cold War began to wane, vanishing with the collapse of the Berlin Wall and the USSR as we entered the 1990s. But as Cold War anxieties faded into the recesses of personal memories, a new source of fear rose from its ashes, the phoenix of ideological terrorism from abroad, which was abruptly brought home on September 11, 2001.

I was charged to provide a perspective on the impacts of terrorism on the environment. Such an essay could take many directions. Certainly the environmental damages associated with 9/11 could be documented by examining its lingering health effects on first responders and survivors or with the cascading destruction in the Middle East associated with the United States' expanding war on terrorism. An equally obvious direction would be to consider that the many billions of dollars required to fight this "war" here and abroad must come from somewhere, either other government programs, greater national debt, or both, leaving less for protecting and managing the nation's environmental and natural resources. At universities this is most strikingly noted by the increased research funding of "security issues" in sharp contrast to the diminishing support for environmental research, monitoring, and surveillance. These all are certainly worthy issues, but they will not form the basis of this essay. I also will not examine "eco-terrorism" that, since its contemporary beginnings with Edward Abbey's call for "monkey wrenching,"[6] has evolved into damaging and often dangerous acts carried out by radical environmental groups in the name of protecting nature.[7] Nor will I consider "environmental terrorism," the targeting of natural resources directly, which has become a feared tool for ideological terrorists.[8] These are all critical issues that would shape a comprehensive discourse on terrorism and the environment, but I have chosen to address the less obvious.

My essay investigates the thesis that the widespread fear of terrorism, as manipulated by governmental leaders for ideological purposes, has hijacked the decision-making process, thereby deflecting society's ability to adequately address pressing environmental issues. I will argue that, although fear of bodily harm may have motivated environmental activism in the past, today's fears arising from the threat of terrorism, both real and especially perceived, are having just the opposite effect. In fact, such fear may be forcing environmental decisions that could prove far more universally harmful and longer-lasting than most acts of real terrorism. I will use global climate change to illustrate my argument. Although the geopolitical context will be North America, particularly the United States, I believe my comments are relevant to most democracies and their citizens.

2. OUR ENVIRONMENTAL FUTURE ISN'T WHAT IT USED TO BE[9]

As did many Boomers, I became politically and environmentally active during the rebellious decade around Earth Day One (April 22, 1970). I certainly was no fan of those occupying the White House during this period: Lyndon Baines Johnson (1963–69) and Richard Milhous Nixon (1969–74). However, in retrospect I think that our nation's disruptive policies abroad may have biased my feelings. Setting aside the persistent and pervasive pain of Vietnam,[10] a historical perspective would conclude that this same period witnessed some very progressive and unprecedented legislation to protect the rights of women[11] and minorities,[12] and the environment.[13] So, as stated by environmentalists Michael Shellenberger and Ted Nordhaus,[14] we owe this era of leaders and the publics that encouraged and supported them a debt of gratitude for establishing the legal and administrative platform needed for protecting the nation's natural resources, providing clean water and air, and controlling the spread of toxic substances.

So, what's gone wrong? With such a legacy of concern and effectiveness, why do we find contemporary environmental problems so intractable? For example, global climate change may be "An Inconvenient Truth,"[15] but its fictional debunking by novelist Michael Crichton[16] seemed to carry greater credibility in Washington, D.C., adding nonsensical justification for the United States being on a very short list of major countries signing but not intending to ratify the Kyoto Protocol.[17] Not surprisingly, any attempts during the Bush Administration (2000–2008) to promote national legislation to curb global warming failed, forcing some states and cities to take independent actions.[18] Of course, it is very easy to lay blame on a Republican-controlled Congress and White House[19] during this period, as their weak environmental record was widely recognized.[20] However, three controlling "realities" must also be considered within any political context.

The first is that the environmental disasters addressed during the 1960s and 1970s were local, immediate, "end-of-the-pipe" problems directly related to personal health and welfare – contamination of what we drank, ate, and breathed. The solutions were relatively simple engineering fixes (for example, controlling sulphur dioxide emissions[21]) aimed at reducing our habit of using the air, water, and land as garbage cans. The fear of facing poor health and possibly death arising from pollution and contamination was personally relevant and widespread, easily justified economically, and provided the public support needed for enacting innovative environmental legislation and establishing a new federal agency "watchdog," the U.S. Environmental Protection Agency.

What about taking on global climate change in the twenty-first century? It's not that many haven't been trying,[22] and today we know a lot more about Professor Arrhenius's "greenhouse gas theory" of 1896[23] (for example, see Gore, *An Inconvenient Truth*). But, global warming is a very different environmental problem than the pollution problems tackled forty years ago. Its causes are ubiquitous, the processes involved are complex, and the net outcomes are uncertain. It is a problem without a quick engineering solution and is one that demands multilateral co-operation and a consideration of equity across socio-political boundaries and generations. Its solution also would involve potentially significant lifestyle changes in countries that contribute grossly disproportionate per capita levels of greenhouse gas emissions, specifically Australia and the United States – something they so far seem unwilling to do.[24]

The second reality delaying action is that we are trying to address global climate change using the same old legal/legislative "tool kit" proven effective a quarter century ago, but the socio-political context is extremely different today.[25] The United States is now more conservative than when Boomers were "20-something." It's not that the American public is uninterested in protecting the environment, although there are signs that interest has declined over the last decade.[26] Instead, there are higher and more pressing priorities: the economy, jobs, social security, health issues, crime, energy, and, of course, topping the list until the very recent collapse of the global economy was "defending the U.S. from future terrorist attacks."[27] Hence, today's environmental strategies must incorporate such social priorities. This situation likely reflects the "greying" of the Boomer Generation and the prevailing fear of again being targeted by Muslim extremists. This latter point will be revisited in greater detail later in this essay.

Lastly, who's afraid of global climate change?[28] Okay, maybe Al Gore[29] and a bunch of scientists,[30] but not being immediately faced with an agonizing death, financial collapse, or exile, most humans will opt for denial, or at least procrastination. Like the personal aging process, as well as the time-worn adage about bringing frogs to a slow boil, incremental decline is difficult to perceive over the short term and harder to do anything about in the long. So, 75 per cent of Americans may believe in the theory of global warming,[31] but its dangers seem abstract and distant, and will not take precedence over air, water, and soil pollution that can more quickly inflict bodily harm.[32] Will we remain recalcitrant in the face of the warnings of many until *The Day after Tomorrow*[33] when high tides and an overnight ice age come ripping over Manhattan? Let's hope not, but a lot hinges on how society balances and reacts to its real and perceived fears of the unknown – the topic of the next section.

3. Sharks, Airplanes, and Terrorists[34]

My mother was a master of idioms, some more decipherable than others. A popular one was "love nor money" used to emphasize her remote chance of doing something, as in "I wouldn't do that for...." As a kid I certainly understood these motivators of my behaviour, but as mentioned earlier I was more often driven by a third – fear, sometimes rational, sometimes not. As with the individual, these three provide the standards by which modern society functions: love in the form of religious beliefs and ethical norms; money as the basis for an economic system; and fear promulgated through our rules, laws, and regulations.[35] Unfortunately, these can be manipulated to sometimes damaging ends, but a comprehensive review of such is beyond the scope of this essay. I will, however, consider the relative perception of fear and its political use to manipulate public actions, or inactions, for, as I suggested earlier, both are central to my thesis.

Fear may be a great motivator of behaviour and basic to the well-studied "fight-or-flight" response of humans and other animals to pending dangers – but it's lousy at predicting real risks and often defies any semblance of rationality. We fear what we are afraid of, but uncontrolled anxiety and panic can lead to bizarre reactions that hint at possible psychoses.[36] But are we afraid of the "right" dangers?[37] Can we accurately assess all risks equally?[38] The problem is that the statistics of probability bear no relevance in the expression of human emotions, or in predicting related responses. I was reminded recently[39] of having avoided ocean dips for a number of years following a 1975 viewing of *Jaws*[40] – despite the statistical fact that there were many more dangerous elements around.[41] I was not alone in my protracted aversion to salt water, as I remember media reports of declining coastal tourism worldwide during the rest of the 1970s – indicating that the "lingering effects of frightening media"[42] may be especially long-lasting when thoughts of being eaten alive are invoked. I may have sidestepped shark attacks successfully, but one thing is certain, my chance of dying of something is 1 in 1 (100%), just as it is for everyone else, and statistically speaking the various possibilities are predictable for a population.[43]

It's interesting that as humans we are rather fearless when engaging in activities that are potentially quite deadly – driving a car, flying in airplanes, riding a bike, neglecting our health, using vending machines,[44] etc. In fact, we often see our decisions to take on such risks as inherent expressions of our personal freedoms.[45] Granted, the "fear of flying" is fairly common,[46] which is statistically unfounded compared to driving to the airport,[47] but not as irrational as our pervasive fear of large carnivores.[48] I would argue that our fear of flying and of being eaten share common elements – being unfamiliar, out of our direct control, and marked by horrid real-world examples.[49] If we happen to fly, swim, or hike in the "wrong" place at the "wrong" time, our days might be up and there's not much we can do about it! We can, of course, decide to avoid even rare dangers by just staying home – another expression of our freedom of choice.

For the purpose of this essay it is logical to extend the discussion to the "fear of terrorism" that has become so pervasive in the American psyche post-9/11.[50] Brandon Derfler, a student at the University of Washington in 2006, examined the likelihood of being killed by a terrorist with interesting results (see Table 1).[51] It is significant to note that the terrorism figure includes 186 deaths in the 1995 Oklahoma City bombing and 2,953 deaths on 9/11.

If these two events are excluded, the figure drops to 1.6 deaths per year, a bit less than the chance of being killed by a shark. Also important is that the number of terrorist incidences worldwide has *decreased* from the peak in 1988 (~650) to 2004 (~200),[52] but the number of fatalities per incident has increased – a well-known strategy for contemporary terrorist groups.[53] So, like encountering a hungry Great White while surfing, being at the wrong place at the wrong time, no matter how improbable, may prove fatal. Of course, we can always opt to consciously avoid salt water, a personal choice that may not be possible with seemingly random acts of terror.

Cass Sunstein[54] has examined the disjuncture between our fears of terrorism and the probability of a terrorist attack. Building on the work of Paul Slovic,[55] she adds to our examination by introducing the idea of "probability neglect." As with other noted examples, terrorism seems mysterious,

Table 1. Average U.S. Deaths per Year (1990–2001).

Auto accidents	42,000
Homicide	20,000
Weather-related	611
Fall from a ladder	317
Fall/drown in bathtub	312
Terrorism	287

uncontrollable, and certainly terrifying, but the uniquely horrendous events of 9/11 evoked a level of widespread and deep emotion likely not witnessed in the United States since Pearl Harbor.[56] Probability neglect arises in such extreme emotional situations when people ignore the probability of an outcome and focus on a disastrous result, should "by chance" one occur. September 11 provided life-long images of abject horror, and, as discussed by Sunstein, U.S. citizens will be far more concerned with the risk of a repeat event than with the statistically larger risks they commonly confront. Furthermore, she suggests that they will pay and tolerate more to avoid such dangers, and that the government will capitulate to these feelings despite the low probability of their occurrence.[57]

Does this mean we should cast our collective "fate to the wind" and trust the laws of probability when addressing the possible threats from sharks, airplanes, or terrorists? I think not, as only a few would be foolish enough to tempt fate in the face of known life-altering dangers.[58] It is important, however, to remember that there are two kinds of fear and to be able to identify and address each – fear that is rational and empowering, and anxiety that is irrational and debilitating. The Gerard Group International LLC provides a succinct definition of each on their web site.[59]

> 1. Rational Fear is where people recognize that the danger is real and develop proactive resolutions to counter the threat. It is a constructive reaction to a real and present danger. The process of understanding the nature of threat, and taking proactive steps towards definitive

solutions creates an environment in which security can be significantly enhanced and continuity of life and "business as usual" can prevail.

2. Irrational Anxiety is brought about by media hype, false alarms, and other events that result in confusion and denial. This kind of fear is debilitating and counter-productive in every environment. It increases a sense of insecurity and interferes with production and efficiency. Intense anxiety cannot be sustained for extended periods of time. It is soon replaced either by ongoing background stress or by denial and complacency that enable us to ignore the real danger.

A consideration of the benefits of harnessing rational fear to fight terrorism and its effects on the environment would make an interesting essay. Although I will return to this idea in my final comments on supporting environmentalism in the age of terrorism, a complete discussion will need to await another author. In the next section I will consider irrational anxiety and the culture of fear in preparation for returning to the issue of global climate change.

4. "If it Bleeds, it Leads"[60]

The culture and politics of fear in America has a rich literary history that greatly transcends the notion of "media hype" driving irrational anxieties.[61] At issue here is whether the media – newspapers, television, news magazines, movies, and most recently the Internet – can and do influence the public's perception of relative risks. Might the competition for readers and viewers promote an emphasis on dire events statistically disproportional to their actual occurrences? The answer is a categorical "yes" as: "An abundant body of research and theory suggests that the news media contributes to public agendas, official and political rhetoric, and public perceptions of social problems, as well as preferences for certain solutions."[62] Hence, the media's preoccupation with social issues like violence, drugs, disease, and youth at risk has led to widespread belief that crime is increasing (when it's actually decreasing), many kids and moms are becoming psychopaths and deadly (when they aren't), drug use is rampant (when it's declining), and Americans are ultra-susceptible to deadly pandemics (when actually we're able to avoid diseases that plague much of the globe).[63] Also noteworthy has been the media's role in promoting our continuing fear of flying[64] and of being killed by large mammals[65] and fish.[66]

That said, however, it would be overly simplistic and inaccurate to hold commercial journalism solely responsible for inflating the public's perception of risk, as the intentional manipulation of fear for political purposes is certainly also involved. In fact, given the difficult task of unbiased and accurate reporting of the day's events,[67] American journalism has made many positive contributions to society during its 300-year history,[68] and along with non-governmental organizations, serves as the "watchdog" of public, business, and governmental accountability.[69]

As I suggested in the early part of this essay, the threat of foreign terrorism moved into the American psyche as the Cold War faded. The bombing of the World Trade Center on February 26, 1993, established its priority in our hearts and minds as well as its prominence in the news, and both were greatly amplified by the events of 9/11. David Altheide makes a strong case for terrorism being cast by today's media and the recent Bush Administration as being a variant of crime enabling the American people to be defined as victims.[70] This in turn argues for allowing those charged with "Protecting the American People"[71] all but unlicensed authority to carry out their task regardless of the financial costs involved[72] and to promote new laws (e.g., the Homeland Security Act of 2002) and regulations (e.g., airport security procedures) deemed necessary without concerns about infringing on civil liberties or providing details for their simple analyses of complex situations ("Evil people were attacking good people and evil had to be destroyed."[73]).

Many agree that the past administration was very effective at using the "politics of fear" based around 9/11 to amplify the threat of terrorism in order to advance a neo-conservative agenda in the United States.[74] The steady flow of terrorism rhetoric from the Bush White House, Republican Congress, talk shows, and undisclosed sources, matched with constantly changing and meaningless terror alerts and travel advisories, and all working through the news media, was used effectively to focus the public on visions of pending doom and the need to be "protected," regardless of the financial costs and constraints on social and political freedoms involved. Being so preoccupied, critical social and environmental issues faded from the public's attention, allowing progressive, incremental declines in both areas. The "fear card" worked well through the 2004 national election, but the political "regime change" in November 2006, which was reinforced in 2008, suggested that its effectiveness as a political strategy may be waning.

The use of fear to promote political agendas is certainly not new, and even the cause of my teen anguish over the Kremlin's evil military potential was quite overstated.[75] Earlier I suggested that the fear factor related to human health concerns was likely a key backdrop for the promotion of environmental legislation in the 1960s and 1970s. Despite its fictional dramatization in *State of Fear*,[76] I expect that my favourite environmental organizations are not above emphasizing human heath concerns in their conservation messages of today – hopefully accurately and for "good" reasons.[77] However, some suggest that the use of fear cloaked in national security to promote specific ideologies, programs, and business ventures became a pervasive strategy for many groups post-9/11 and a distracting aberration.[78]

These are all interesting ideas worthy of much more discussion. But my purpose now is to consider how the nation's preoccupation with "irrational anxiety" related to the war on terrorism, regardless of its root causes, has led to poor decisions about the environment. To do so, I will examine the ongoing debate over drilling for oil in the Arctic National Wildlife Refuge and how misdirected fear may be clouding the decision-making process with potentially dire long-term consequences.

5. "Oil on Ice"[79]

Debate over opening a portion of the Arctic National Wildlife Refuge (ANWR) for oil extraction dates back to the Jimmy Carter Administration (1977–81), and it remains a hotly contested topic reminiscent of past wrangling over the Trans-Alaska Pipeline System, eventually constructed in the mid-1970s. As will be discussed, however, a notable difference is that today's arguments have been cloaked in political rhetoric aimed at amplifying the public's irrational anxiety over foreign-born terrorism. A cursory review of the ANWR controversy leaves even the informed overwhelmed.[80] Suffice it to say that the "facts" depend heavily on one's socio-political leanings and shade of "green." Ann Coulter has her opinions,[81] along with the U.S. House of Representative's Committee on Resources[82] and the Institute for Energy Research[83]; conservation leaders,[84] the Democratic Party,[85] and various environmental organizations[86] have theirs. Of course, they are diametrically opposed to one another, which comes from interpreting the same data with different perspectives, priorities, and agendas, basically boiling down the classic battle between developing economic prosperity for today and protecting the environment for future generations.

Depending on one's personal perspective, ANWR is either a barren frozen wasteland or a cornucopia of beauty, culture, and biodiversity – and mining oil from a portion of it will feed our thirst for crude for many years, or a matter of a few months; provide a million new jobs, or maybe a few hundred; and enhance economic well-being for local people, or destroy their culture and traditional livelihoods; and make the United States more independent and secure as a nation, or less. I will avoid commenting where I come down in this debate, as it is not relevant to the purpose of this essay. However, I will address how the culture and politics of fear discussed earlier are promoted under the guise of national security, thereby defining the debate for both sides.

As mentioned, arguments for opening the North Slope to promote energy self-sufficiency are not new, the assumed logic being the more oil and gas we produce, the less we need to buy abroad, thereby making us less susceptible to the whims of the Organization of the Petroleum Exporting Countries (OPEC) and rising competitive demands elsewhere (especially China). I guess this is logical *if* couched in a comprehensive national energy policy, which so far has proven to be elusive for successive administrations. Without question, enhancing oil and gas exploration, extraction, and acquisition preoccupied the past Bush Administration,[87] and 9/11 provided the opportunity to wrap this agenda into the war on terrorism,[88] and later, even the war in Iraq.[89] It also helped that administration draw greater attention to ANWR's oil reserves.[90] This transformed the common economics versus environment debate into one more centred on "good" (us) fighting "evil" (terrorists) to protect the American people, thus opening questions of patriotism and loyalty about those opposing development in ANWR.[91] Hence, the debate becomes acrimonious and divisive and the sides more entrenched with both resorting to exaggerations and misinformation to emphasize their positions, obviously consuming limited time, energy, and money that might better be spent doing something else.[92]

Let us assume for my argument that there's a lot of oil that can be extracted from a part of ANWR[93] without disrupting or harming sea and land creatures and local people, and the seven to ten years it will take to bring it online isn't a problem. Given that there are continued uncertainties about how well the war on terrorism is progressing,[94] and that our demand for oil is not likely to lessen,[95] one must wonder if we as a people will feel any better or safer even as millions of barrels of crude are pumped from ANWR's coastal plain. Something makes me think we won't.

6. "The Day After Tomorrow"[96]

The fighting goes on between environmentalists and "oilmen"[97] as the public stays preoccupied sorting their rational fears of terrorism from their irrational anxieties, all the while sidestepping truly fearful situations. It is quite ironic that an implied assumption in the pro-drilling argument over ANWR is the logic of burning more fossil fuel, despite the fact that this will generate more carbon dioxide, further exacerbating climate change. As mentioned, the evidence is mounting that the dangers of global warming are real and will disrupt our economy, health, and welfare as well as damage fragile ecosystems worldwide.[98] Furthermore, the impacts will be greater in developing countries already lacking adequate political-economic infrastructures to maintain social stability, which will add "environmental refugees"[99] to the immigration problems currently facing developed countries worldwide.

The ties between global climate change and national security should appear obvious. Noted environmentalist Peter Gleick, in a testimony before the U.S. Congress Subcommittee on National Security, Emerging Threats, and International Relations was clear in linking climate change to national security.

Global climate change is a real and serious problem. Impacts are already evident and we are worsening rapidly in many parts of the world and the United States. It is vital to identify our greatest vulnerabilities to climatic stresses and the areas where those stresses will most affect national and international security, behaviour, and policy.

Five critical areas stand out as important examples of national vulnerabilities with security implications: agricultural productivity, the availability and quantity of freshwater resources, access to strategic minerals, rising sea level, and the deterioration of political relationships with other countries that result from disagreements about international climate policy.[100]

This seems like something fairly scary and worthy of some attention compared to replacing some of OPEC's oil with a little "home-grown."[101] Maybe we should be focusing on *decreasing* our dependence on gas and oil regardless of their sources. Maybe we'll find that, once the war on terrorism is over, or at least contained, we'll be facing a more intractable opponent, again one of our making. Maybe we are afraid of the wrong dangers, victims of probability neglect. Maybe we'll worry about all that later, tomorrow?

Of course, I am certainly not alone in my call for us to pay more attention to the real dangers posed by climate change and to suggest that our irrational anxieties over terrorism may be clouding our perspectives about its potential impacts. For example, in the two months immediately following 9/11, *Orion* magazine sponsored an online series of twenty-three essays called *Thoughts on America: Writers Respond to Crisis*.[102] Contributor, well-known conservationist, and author David Orr concluded his thoughtful essay with the following insights:

> George Bush, Sr. once told us that "the American way of life is not negotiable." We know now the untruth of that assertion. No way of life based on waste, economic exploitation, military coercion, and a refusal to account costs fully is non-negotiable. The question before us is not whether we can maintain a way of life based on

Middle Eastern oil, imported resources, ecological ruin, exploitation of the poor, and climate change. We cannot. Rather, the question is whether we can summon the wisdom to create a just, secure, and sustainable prosperity that no terrorist can threaten and that threatens no nation or the prospects of our children.[103]

Furthermore, a study by Sandra Hinchman[104] examined the range of impacts on two indigenous groups to the potential opening of ANWR's coastal area to oil and gas exploration. Near the end of her compelling review she noted the following:

> But if the politics of countering terrorism poses the main immediate threat to the ANWR ecosystem, the Porcupine caribou, and the Gwich'in people, there is also the long-term threat of ozone depletion and global warming. In fact, anthropogenic climate change caused by fossil fuel use might threaten the Inupiat, especially those residing in low-lying coastal areas, at least as much as their Athabascan counter-parts.[105]

And then she concluded her paper by stating:

> In the last analysis, the path to both national security and a healthy environment leads away from fossil fuel dependency and toward reliance on energy sources that are renewable, decentralized, and less vulnerable to political and economic vicissitudes or terrorist attack. By contrast, if national security concerns lead Americans to aggravate global warming by despoiling the environment, "the tragedy of September 11" – as one ecologist has argued – "may be amplified many times over."[106]

Lastly, much of Noam Chomsky's work has focused on documenting how U.S. foreign policy over the past twenty years, and especially during the Bush Administration, has incrementally brought the globe closer to seeking nuclear solutions to ideological disagreements. His rational fear of this dangerous trend is strongly stated in his spoken and written words. Even so, he stated in 2006 that: "The only threat remotely comparable to use of nuclear weapons is the serious danger of environmental catastrophe."[107] He went on to chide then President Bush for "staying the course" with respect to his refusal to join multi-national efforts to curb global warming because he "insists we still do not know enough."[108] Professor Chomsky is certainly among many who wonder whether the long-time and close financial relationships between the Bush family and multinational oil interests might have influenced much of the past administration's political agenda involving the Middle East and the environment.[109]

Starting in the days immediately following 9/11 and continuing to the present, the warning calls have been many and consistent in their message: the effects of climate change are upon us and they are being neglected as a real threat to national security and the collective well-being of the globe. However, the past administration ignored this reality and consistently worked to distract public attention from this danger because of its dedication to promoting the self-interests of a favoured subset of American businesses and industries. Bush's often vocalized approach to assuring that national security was linked directly to the war on terrorism was based on a premise that keeping "insurgents" pre-occupied killing Americans and Iraqis in Iraq would give the Department of Homeland Security time to adequately prepare here at home. Until recently, the public seemed to be going along with this tale by remaining quite complacent about climate change and focused on being protected from shadowy terrorist forces looking to disrupt their middle class lives. Might it be possible to worry a bit less about potential terrorists and a lot more about real greenhouse gases? I would like to think so.

7. Lifting the Fog of Fear[110]

In this final section I offer a few ideas about how we might incrementally work ourselves out of our current entrapment where decisions about protecting the environment become clouded by our perceived fear of terrorism. I see two fronts requiring our attention and both are complex, demanding clarity of thought, honesty and consistency, appreciation of socio-economic realities, and diligence. One is reducing our irrational and debilitating anxiety about foreign terrorism; the other is increasing our rational and empowering fear of global climate change.

There are many books and trained professionals to help us deal with our personally debilitating anxieties (a.k.a. "phobias"), but I often wonder how effective they are – I still don't like swimming in the ocean.[111] I do admit that 9/11 and the events following have made me more apprehensive and watchful during my international travels, and I have excluded even considering visits to a few regions, as one would certain inner city streets after dark. Such behaviour seems rational and in my best interest. But the issue is, not how we deal with our individual phobias, but rather society's irrational anxieties over the threat of homeland terrorism that must be addressed collectively through the independent actions of many. I offer three approaches for possibly reducing the nation's anxieties about terrorism – that is, "lifting the fog of fear."

The first challenge is to understand that fear can be and often is orchestrated as a political smokescreen and learn to recognize when it's being used to sponsor a specific ideology. Promoting ideas through policy formulation, of course, isn't always bad, but we must demand accuracy, honesty, and transparency, which require gaining a comprehensive perspective on the complex issue of terrorism. Unfortunately, the basic nature of culture and society and the politics they engender are such that clarity and insight can never come from a single source or two. So, after watching the evening news, whether Fox or MSNBC, we need to turn the television off and do something else.[112] Seek as many perspectives on terrorism and its politics as you can from weekly news magazines, Internet sources, and newspapers, the latter often offering at least a portion of their coverage free online.[113] Visit a bookstore or library and sample the political analyses that are expanding across their bookshelves, as today's socio-political environment is serving up endless fodder for writers from far left to far right. Discuss these topics with others,[114] and consider opposing views with compassion and understanding, as welcoming a diversity of ideas into the debate is an expression of the freedom we fight so hard to promote and preserve.[115]

Yes, this is time-consuming, personally challenging, and at times intellectually and emotionally unsettling, but it is the democratic responsibility of citizens in a diverse and pluralistic society to be able to formulate informed decisions, and then act on those decisions, often in an election polling booth. Like paying public school taxes when you don't have kids, this is a social responsibility, part of the "rent" for living in a democracy.[116]

Second is to recognize that you don't need statistical training to get over probability neglect, just exercise some plain old common sense. Maybe this has become harder in the "information age" when we are inundated every waking moment with facts, figures, and the ideas of others. But at some time we need to step back and rely on our own brain, personal insights, and "gut feelings" when assessing the true dangers posed by having a small segment of the Muslim world radically displeased with us.

I'll call on Noam Chomsky's comments about Nicaragua[117] to illustrate this point. President Ronald Wilson Reagan (1981–89) declared a national emergency on May 1, 1985, because of the security threat posed by the Government of Nicaragua, one of the western hemisphere's poorest countries and a hard, two-day drive from the Mexico-Texas border. The events that followed haven't aged well in the international policy arena, but my point is how ludicrous it was to ever consider Nicaragua a military threat to our national security. Similar logic should have led one to reject the Bush Administration's irrational insistence on connecting Saddam Hussein and Iraq to weapons of mass destruction and terrorism in the United States, and the idea that we were "safer" because of our invasion of Iraq. Let's face it, Operation Iraqi Freedom and pressure to "invade" ANWR have multinational oil interests in common, which respectively exacerbate the growing threats from terrorists and climate change.

My last suggestion is for the citizens of all democracies to accept the responsibility for being the first line of "watchdogs" of those promoting potentially damaging ideologies. Here I mean more than exercising an informed vote at all levels of government. Of course, this is critical and we must neither encourage nor reward politicians who habitually cloud debates in a fog of fear.[118] But shouldn't the same accountability be expected from institutional "watchdogs" – the news media and non-governmental organizations? Of course, here we can easily exert influence through the free market economy by fiscally penalizing those who continually exercise inflated scare tactics. And lastly, we must learn to hold ourselves accountable and avoid playing the "fear card" when fighting for our special interests – even if it's global climate change.

By becoming more informed, using a little common sense, and promoting interlinked accountability, perhaps we can ratchet down our collective irrational anxieties over terrorism. This might provide greater clarity, energy, and resources for designing creative approaches to dealing with major environmental problems like global warming, as well as the many social issues that have been similarly neglected since 9/11.

This leaves us with the paradox of how we can increase our rational fear of global climate change while we lift the fog of fear about terrorism. Of course, my three suggestions for addressing our collective anxieties over terrorism work equally well here, especially the importance of gaining at least a minimal understanding of the issues involved. As discussed earlier, the scientific community understands the intricacies of the climate change debate, but Al Gore's personal crusade on global warming offered some hope for educating a wider audience of the English-speaking world.[119] Contrary to Hollywood's rendition of the instant deadliness of climate change,[120] the movie version of his book[121] is considered scientifically accurate, stating the pending dangers in a rational, understandable manner.[122] Of course, the movie was not without its critics inside Congress;[123] and President Bush likely avoided it like Kyoto.[124] But the book and the movie provide a solid context for promoting open dialogue about global climate change, both the problem and its solution.[125] Time will tell whether enough Americans will rally to Gore's call to do something constructive in the United States, but at least see the movie regardless of your political proclivities and level of scientific prowess, and then join the debate.[126]

Greater appreciation and understanding of the issues involved certainly are major steps toward addressing the threats of global warming in a rational and fact-based manner. However, the environmental community also must adopt new strategies that are well-aligned with the hearts and minds of today's public.[127] Perhaps a healthy fear of global warming might prove empowering by challenging our creativity to design energy policies that promote diversification, conservation, and greater self-sufficiency. For environmentalists, this means building new alliances with businesses and industries by seeing the slowing of global warming as a means for promoting more jobs and economic stability. Moving away from a fossil-fuel-based economy to alternatives opens many avenues for innovation and new businesses bringing greater energy independence, and certainly greater security as a nation.[128] California's legislation requiring businesses to reduce greenhouse gas emissions 25 per cent by 2020[129] is already attracting venture capital and new businesses to the state, greatly supporting the economic viability of such an approach.[130] Perhaps more states should circumvent the political roadblocks in Washington, D.C., by doing the same.[131]

Forging partnerships between businesses and environmental organizations to design a new economic development system that de-emphasizes fossil-fuel consumption will not be easy, but it is necessary. Lester Brown, noted environmentalist, said it this way in 2006:

> We know that sustaining progress depends on restructuring the global economy, shifting from a fossil-fuel-based, automobile-centered, throwaway economy to one based on renewable energy sources, a diverse transportation system, and a comprehensive reuse/recycle materials system. Largely restructuring taxes and subsidies can do this. Sustaining progress also means eradicating poverty, stabilizing population, and restoring the earth's natural systems. Securing the additional public outlays needed to reach these goals depends on reordering fiscal priorities in response to the new threats to our security.

> In this mobilization, the scarcest resource of all is time. The temptation is to reset the clock, but we cannot. Nature is the timekeeper.[132]

In closing I want to re-emphasize that we must individually recognize that our irrational anxieties over terrorism in the recent past have clouded our collective ability to identify and address real dangers like those posed by global warming. I must side with those who believe that climate change may be a greater and more dangerous threat to our health, safety, and welfare than terrorism.[133] Furthermore, I believe that our propensity for probability neglect was manipulated and exploited in the past to promote policies and justify actions, some of which have exacerbated the threats of climate change. Hopefully, this situation is changing within the current socio-political environment in the United States and elsewhere.

I hope that this essay has at a minimum challenged your thinking about the culture and politics of fear as it pertains to maintaining environmental priorities in the age of terrorism. But, I also hope you will commit to making a difference in this debate, a challenge not only for the "young and restless." In fact, this cause could be a Last Hurrah for aging Baby Boomers. As said so well by conservation writer Bill McKibben: "Now is the boomers' chance to reclaim their better, bolder natures and to end their run as it began."[134] I sincerely hope that we can muster the common vision, determination, and means to do so. If successful, perhaps we will be revered again for promoting a new environmentalism in the fit of socio-political unrest, not unlike the society that gave us Earth Day One. To this end, let us all commit.

Acknowledgments

I acknowledge and thank a number of Cornell colleagues, especially Karim-Aly Kassam, Shikui Dong, Charles Geisler, James Gillett, Scott Perez, Jacques Pollini, and Ruth Sherman, for their editorial and content suggestions about various drafts of this essay.

Notes

1   In this essay I use "America" to denote the United States of America and "American" to denote its citizens with full understanding and appreciation that we are a subset of the Americas. More broadly, however, I use these terms as metaphors for democratic societies and their citizens, respectively. This of course includes Canada and Canadians.

2   Baby Boomers are considered the generation born during the period of rising birth rates and economic prosperity following WW II, officially beginning in 1946 and ending in 1964.

3   A 1959 film by Stanley Kramer depicting people in Australia after a global nuclear war dealing with the fact that all life on Earth will be destroyed in a month's time. See: Internet Movie Database, Stanley Kramer [Director] (1959). "On the Beach." [Motion Picture]. http://www.imdb.com/title/tt0497116 (accessed September 20, 2009).

4   See: Internet Movie Database, Archer Productions, Inc. [Producer] (1951). "Duck and Cover." [Motion Picture]. http://www.archive.org/details/DuckandC1951 (accessed September 19, 2009).

5   For a great example, see: Internet Movie Database, University of California Radiation Laboratory [Producer] (1955). "Nuclear operations in 1955 test site for nuclear explosion effects." [Motion Picture]. http://video.google.com/videoplay?docid=8139428890271196390# (accessed September 19, 2009).

6   See: Edward Abby, *The Monkey Wrench Gang* (Philadelphia: Lippincott, 1975).

7   M. Saliba, "The Linkage Between Political and Environmental Activism and Terrorism," *Austrian Scholars Conference* (Auburn, AL: Mises Institute, 2003). http://www.mises.org/asc/2003/asc9saliba.

pdf#search=%22Saliba%20The%20linkage%22 (accessed September 19, 2009).

8   S. O'Lear, "Environmental Terrorism: A Critique," in *September and its Aftermath: The Geopolitics of Terror*, ed. S.D. Brunn (Taylor & Francis, Abingdon, UK, 2005), 127–50.

9   My arguments in this section are influenced by: M. Shellenberger and T. Nordhaus, *The Death of Environmentalism: Global Warming Politics in a Post-Environmental World* (Oakland, CA: The Breakthrough Institute, 2004). www.thebreakthrough.org/images/Death_of_Environmentalism.pdf (acessed September 19, 2009). Also see: M. Shellenberger and T. Nordhaus, *Break Through: From the Death of Environmentalism to the Politics of Possibility* (Geneva, IL: Houghton Mifflin, 2007).

10   Full disclosure: I spent my draft age years quite safe in Seattle, WA, with either a student or family deferment.

11   See: National Women's History Project, "Timeline of Legal History of Women in the United States." 2002. http://www.legacy98.org/timeline.html (accessed September 19, 2009).

12   See: "Milestones in the Modern Civil Rights Movement." http://www.infoplease.com/spot/civilrightstimeline1.html (accessed September 19, 2009).

13   See: "Milestones in Environmental Protection." http://www.factmonster.com/spot/earthdaytimeline.html (accessed September 19, 2009).

14   Michael Shellenberger and T. Nordhaus, *Break Through*.

15   Al Gore, *An Inconvenient Truth: The Planetary Emergency of Global Warming and What We Can Do About It* (New York: Rodale Press, 2006).

16   Michael Crichton, *State of Fear* (London: HarperCollins, 2004).

17 As of February 2009, 183 nations have signed *and* ratified the Kyoto Protocol to the United Nations Framework Convention on Climate Change aimed at curbing global warming. The United States is the only signatory not intending to ratify this treaty. See: http://en.wikipedia.org/wiki/List_of_Kyoto_Protocol_signatories (accessed September 19, 2009).

18 See: B. Reppert, "Global Warming: Congress Still Stalled, States And Cities Act," *BioScience* 56, no.10 (2006): 800.

19 Control of the U.S. Congress, as well as many state legislatures and governorships, reverted abruptly back to the Democratic Party on November 7, 2006, which hopefully will lead to more positive legislation and policies related to energy and the environment. See L. West, "Election 2006: Top 10 potential environmental benefits of the 2006 election." Environment About.com, 2006, http://environment.about.com/od/environmentallawpolicy/a/2006_election.htm (accessed September 19, 2009). Another national election in 2008 further strengthened Democratic control of both the legislative and the executive branches of government, offering revised approaches addressing the economy, health care, education and energy. See: http://www.barackobama.com/issues/ (accessed September 19, 2009).

20 For example, according to the Natural Resources Defence Council, the Bush Administration "has shown again and again that it will cater to industries that put America's health and natural heritage at risk; there is little doubt that more attempts to undermine environmental enforcement and weaken key programs will be made The only threat remotely to the use of nuclear weapons is the serious danger of environmental catastrophe." See: http://www.nrdc.org/bushrecord/ (accessed September 19, 2009).

21 See: U.S. Environmental Protection Agency, "USEPA Module 6: Air Pollutants and Control Techniques- Sulfur Oxides," http://www.epa.gov/apti/bces/module6/sulfur/control/control.htm (accessed September 19, 2009).

22 A Google.com search on July 6, 2009, yielded "about 25,300,000 [*hits*] for global climate change."

23 See: "Svante Arrhenius," http://en.wikipedia.org/wiki/Svante_Arrhenius (accessed March 2, 2007). As an interesting aside, in 1624 Pope Urban VIII informed scientist Galileo Galilei that he could discuss the Copernican theory of a sun-centred universe, so long as he treated it as a hypothesis. He was interrogated before the Papal Inquisition in 1633 and was sentenced to prison for an indefinite term two months later. Galileo died in 1642; the Catholic Church formally admitted that his views on the solar system were correct 350 years later.

24 See note 17.

25 Michael Shellenberger and T. Nordhaus, *Break Through*.

26 Public Agenda, "The Environment: People's Chief Concerns," 2007, http://www.publicagenda.org/issues/pcc_detail.cfm?issue_type=environment&list=3 (accessed March 2, 2007). This link is no longer available.

27 Over 55% of the American public state that "Protecting the Environment" should be a top priority for the U.S. 2006 Congress. See: Public Agenda, "Issue Guides: Environment –. Public View: People's Chief Concerns," 2007, http://www.publicagenda.org/citizen/issue-guides/environment/publicview/people-concerns (accessed September 19, 2009).

28 A 2006 public survey from the Pew Research Center found that only 19% of Americans (and 20% of Chinese) who had heard of global warming worried

about it "a great deal," a position not held in many other developed countries. China and the United States are the greatest producers of greenhouse gases worldwide. See: Pew Research Center, "America's Image Slips, But Allies Share U.S. Concerns Over Iran, Hamas: No Global Warming Alarm in U.S., China," June, 2006, http://pewglobal.org/reports/display.php?ReportID=252 (accessed September 19, 2009).

29 Al Gore, *An Inconvenient Truth*.

30 For example, see: National Academy of Science (http://www.nationalacademies.org/) and Union of Concerned Scientists (http://www.ucsusa.org/). In fairness, a few skeptical scientists can be found, but interestingly some have financial ties to various U.S.-based multinational corporations (see: E. Ellison, "Free Speech vs. Hot Air," *Frontiers in Ecology and the Environment* 4, no. 9 (2006): 504–5).

31 See: Pew Research Center, "Issue Guides: Environment. Public View: People's Chief Concerns," 2007, http://pewglobal.org/reports/display.php?ReportID=252 (accessed September 19, 2009).

32 Ibid.

33 See: Internet Movie Database, Roland Emmerich [Director] (2004). "The Day After Tomorrow," [Motion Picture]. http://www.imdb.com/title/tt0319262/ (accessed September 20, 2009).

34 My thinking here has been greatly influenced by the written and spoken words of Noam Chomsky, see: http://www.chomsky.info/ (accessed September 19, 2009). Thanks to a UN address by Venezuelan President Hugo Chavez in mid-September, 2006, more people have been introduced to his *Hegemony of Survival: America's Quest for Global Dominance* (New York: Henry Holt, 2003). See: http://seattletimes.nwsource.com/html/nation-world/2003270921_wenchomskybook22.html (accessed September 19, 2009). I

also would recommend two more recent volumes: *Imperial Ambitions: Conversations on the Post-9/11 World – Interviews with David Barsamian* (New York: Henry Holt, 2005) and *Failed States: The Abuse of Power and the Assault on Democracy* (New York: Henry Holt, 2006).

35 I acknowledge my Cornell University colleague, Associate Professor Steven A. Wolf for helping me begin to see the prevalence, power, and persistence of these three motivators in social ecology.

36 Many years ago, a colleague accounted a tale of diving headfirst off his bed dead asleep to avoid a dream-world box of snakes he'd spilled.

37 See: B. Glassner, *The Culture of Fear: Why Americans are Afraid of the Wrong Things* (New York: Basic Books, 1999).

38 See: C.R. Sunstein, "Terrorism and Probability Neglect," *Journal of Risk and Uncertainty* 26, nos. 2/3 (2003): 121–36.

39 During a department seminar entitled: *Evaluation of a Wildlife-related Human Behavior Modification Intervention* on April 18, 2006, then PhD student Meredith L. Gore noted that people expressed fear of bear attacks disproportionately to the occurrence of actual attacks.

40 See: Internet Movie Database, Steven Spielberg [Director] (1975). *Jaws* [Motion Picture].

41 The Shark Foundation (see: http://www.shark.ch/Information/Accidents/index.html) reports that: (1) "Between 1959 and 2003 1,857 people were struck and killed by lightening alone in the coastal states of the USA. In the same time frame there were 740 shark accidents, 22 of which were fatal. (2) Alone in the USA and Canada approximately 40 people are killed each year by pigs – six times more than by sharks worldwide. (3) Alone in New York people are bitten 10 times more each year by other people than worldwide by sharks. (4) Around the world, considerably more

people are killed by falling coconuts than are bitten by sharks" (accessed September 19, 2009).

42 J. Cantor, "'I'll Never Have a Clown in My House' – Why Movie Horror Lives On," *Poethics Today* 25, no. 2 (2004): 283–304.

43 The National Safety Council (NSC) keeps track of the odds of dying from something for Americans. See: http://www.nsc.org/research/odds.aspx (accessed September 19, 2009).

44 "According to the U.S. Consumer Product Safety Commission there were 37 known vending machine fatalities between 1978 and 1995, for an average of 2.18 deaths per year," making them more dangerous than sharks. See: D. Emery, "Urban Legend and Folklore." June 29, 2005. http://urbanlegends.about.com/b/a/005445.htm (accessed September 19, 2009).

45 As an example, consider the resistance to the mandatory use of motorcycle helmets. See: "Helmet Law Defense League," 2003, http://usff.com/hldlhome.html (accessed September 19, 2009).

46 A fear common enough to warrant numerous self-help books (A quick search on Amazon.com returned over 1,400 self help books discussing the fear of flying).

47 However, Ben Best, a confessed "life-extensionist," has correctly noted that "On a per-mile basis the risk of dying on a 1,000 mile airline flight are about equivalent to the risks of dying while driving 1,000 miles, because most flying deaths occur on take-off and landing. (Longer flights are safer.)" See: http://www.benbest.com/lifeext/causes.html (accessed September 19, 2009).

48 On average bears, sharks, alligators, and cougars each kill one person or less a year: M. Conover, *Resolving Human-wildlife Conflicts: The Science of Wildlife Damage Management* (Boca Raton, FL: CRC Press, 2002).

49 P. Slovic, *The Perception of Risk* (London: Earthscan, 2000).

50 For example, see: D.L. Altheide, "Notes Towards a Politics of Fear," *Journal for Crime, Conflict and the Media* 1, no. 1 (2003): 37–54; L. Brill, "Terrorism, Crowds and Power, and the Dogs of War," *Anthropological Quarterly* 76, no. 1 (2003): 87–91; and D.S. Paulson, "A Quality Life in the Shadow of Terrorism," *Pastoral Psychology* 51, no. 3 (2003): 241–46.

51 See: B. Derfler, "How Likely Are You to be Killed by a Terrorist?" July 13, 2006. http://students.washington.edu/brandond/terror.html (accessed March 2, 2007). This site is no longer available.

52 This trend certainly must exclude in-country attacks by "insurgents" in the years following the invasion of Iraq (a.k.a., "Operation Iraqi Freedom") initiated on March 20, 2003.

53 B.S. Frey, S. Luechinger, and A. Stutzer, "Calculating Tragedy: Assessing the Cost of Terrorism," CESifo Working Paper No. 1341 (2004). 31p.

54 C.R. Sunstein, "Terrorism and Probability Neglect," *Journal of Risk and Uncertainty* 26, nos. 2/3 (2003): 121–36.

55 P. Slovic, *The Perception of Risk*.

56 I will not discuss the many debates comparing and contrasting 9/11 to Pearl Harbor (both before and after), except to note their similarities with respect to the extreme emotional responses invoked in the U.S. population by both.

57 This suggests that the government responds to the public's inherent fear of terrorism with actions aimed at protection and prevention despite the fact that the probability of an occurrence is very low. In the next section I will consider the reverse: calculated manipulation of the public's fear of terrorism to promote government policies.

58 See: Internet Movie Database, J. Tremaine [Director] (2006). "Jackass Number Two"

[Motion Picture]. See: http://www.imdb.com/title/tt0493430/ (accessed September 19, 2009).

59   See: Gerard Group, "About Terrorism." 2007. http://www.gerardgroup.com/about_terrorism.php (accessed September 19, 2009). As an aside, it is interesting to note this consulting company's timely focus: "GGI's modular Counter-Terrorism Preparedness program provides enterprise-wide security and continuity planning against a terrorist attack or other catastrophic event. GGI's goal is to close potential security gaps, optimize emergency response capability, and significantly lower risk and liability in the event of a catastrophic emergency."

60   This is a common phrase used in journalistic circles to describe the high priority given to covering nasty and deadly events. For example, see: http://www.pbs.org/wnet/insidelocalnews/behind_leads.html (accessed September 19, 2009).

61   In addition to the work of Noam Chomsky mentioned earlier, my thinking for this section has been greatly influenced by Barry Glassner's *The Culture of Fear* and the more recent writings of David L. Altheide: "Notes Towards a Politics of Fear," and *Terrorism and the Politics of Fear* (Walnut Creek, CA: AltaMira Press, 2006). Together they offer a comprehensive review of this topic.

62   D.L. Altheide and R.M. Michalowski, "Fear in the News: A Discourse of Control," *Sociological Quarterly* 40, no. 3 (1999): 475–503.

63   B. Glassner, *The Culture of Fear*.

64   See: Glassner, *The Culture of Fear*, 183–202.

65   A. Medred, "Wildlife Author Killed, Eaten by Bears He Loved," *Anchorage Daily News*, October 8, 2003. http://www.adn.com/front/story/4110831p-4127072c.html (accessed March 2, 2007) This link is no longer available.

66   BBC News, "Shark Attacks: On the Increase?" September 5, 2001; http://news.bbc.co.uk/2/hi/americas/1501063.stm (accessed September 19, 2009) and MSNBC.com (accessed September 5, 2006); "Crocodile Hunter' Steve Irwin Killed by Stingray: Renowned Environmentalist Pulled Barb from Heart Before Death," http://www.msnbc.msn.com/id/14663786/ (accessed September 19, 2009).

67   "The question is what do people need to know, what do they want to know, what do they have the right to know, and if we report this what are the consequences…?" Keith Connors, News Director.

68   For example, see: W.D. Sloan and L.M. Parcell, eds., *American Journalism: History, Principles, Practice* (Jefferson, NC: McFarland, 2002).

69   R. Schmuhl, "Government Accountability and External Watchdogs," *Issues of Democracy* 5, no. 2 (2000): 22–25; http://italy.usembassy.gov/pdf/ej/ijde0800.pdf (accessed September 19, 2009).

70   Altheide, "Notes Towards a Politics of Fear."

71   A popular mantra of President George W. Bush. For example, see: http://www.whitehouse.gov/news/releases/2005/12/20051219–2.html (accessed March 2, 2007; this site is no longer available).

72   C.R. Sunstein, "Terrorism and Probability Neglect," *Journal of Risk and Uncertainty* 26, nos. 2/3 (2003): 121–36.

73   Altheide, "Notes Towards a Politics of Fear" : 37–54.

74   For example, see: F. Furedi, *Politics of Fear* (New York: Continuum International Publishing Group, 2007); and M.G. Gonzales and R. Delgado, *The Politics of Fear: How Republicans Use Money, Race, and the Media to Win* (Boulder, CO: Paradigm, 2006).

75 F. Zakaria, "The Year of Living Fearfully," *Newsweek*, September 11, 2006, 29.

76 Michael Crichton, *State of Fear.*

77 For example: Nature Conservancy, "Mercury Falling: Monitoring Songbirds for Mercury," 2007, http://www.nature. org/wherewework/northamerica/states/ newyork/science/art18734.htm (accessed September 19, 2009); Natural Resource Defense Council, "Limiting Clean Water Act Protection Could Contaminate Drinking Water," 2003, http://www. nrdc.org/media/pressReleases/030611a. asp (accessed September 19, 2009); and Environmental Defense Fund, "Disease Spread as Climate Changes," http:// www.fightglobalwarming.com/page. cfm?tagID=243 (accessed September 19, 2009).

78 "Since 9/11, politicians, business, advocacy organizations and special interest groups have sought to further their selfish agendas by manipulating public anxiety about terror. All seem to take the view that they are more likely to gain a hearing if they pursue their arguments or claims through the prism of security. Businesses have systematically used concern with homeland security to win public subsidies and handouts. And paradoxically, the critics of big business use similar tactics – many environmentalist activists have started linking their traditional alarmist campaigns to the public's fear of terror attacks." See: F. Furedi, "The Politics of Fear: President Bush Isn't the Only One Who Plays This Card," *Spiked,* October 28, 2004. http://www.spiked-online.com/Articles/0000000CA760. htm (accessed September 19, 2009).

79 "Oil on Ice is a vivid, compelling, and comprehensive documentary connecting the fate of the Arctic National Wildlife Refuge to decisions America makes about energy policy, transportation choices, and other seemingly unrelated matters. Caught in the balance are the culture and livelihood of the Gwich'in people and the migratory wildlife in this fragile ecosystem." See: Internet Movie Databasae, Bo Boudart and Dale Djerassi [Directors] (2004). *Oil on Ice* [Motion Picture] http:// www.oilonice.org (accessed September 19, 2009).

80 A Google.com search on October 1, 2006, yielded "… about 1,470,000 [hits] for 'oil and the Arctic National Wildlife Refuge."

81 "Having wearied of opposing the war on terrorism, Democrats are now trying to sabotage the country's energy policy. A better idea, they think, is to continue sending large amounts of money to countries that nurture homicidal Muslims intent on destroying America." Excerpt from: Ann Coulter, "Nine Out of Ten Caribou Support Drilling." April 18, 2002. Townhall http://townhall.com/columnists/AnnCoulter/2002/04/18/nine_ out_of_ten_caribou_support_drilling (accessed September 19, 2009).

82 See: Committee on Natural Resources, "Rahall Statement on DRILL Act," Committee on Natural Resources, 2008, http://resourcescommittee.house.gov/ index.php?option=com_content&task= view&id=401&Itemid=70 (accessed September 19, 2009).

83 See: Institute for Energy Research, "ANWR's 1002 Area," http://www.institute-forenergyresearch.org/anwr/ (accessed September 19, 2009).

84 See: H. Lentfer and C. Servid, eds., *Arctic Refuge, A Circle of Testimony* (Minneapolis, MN: Milkweed Editions, 2001).

85 See: Josh McConaha, "Drilling in ANWR Cut from Budget Bill: Seals, Polar Bears Rejoice," November 10, 2005. Democrats.org, http://www.democrats. org/a/2005/11/drilling_in_anw.php (accessed September 20, 2009).

86 For example, Natural Resources Defense Council, "Arctic National Wildlife Refuge:

Why Trash an American Treasure for a Tiny Percentage of Our Oil Needs?" November 2005, NRDC.com, http://www. nrdc.org/land/wilderness/arctic.asp (accessed September 20, 2009); World Wildlife Fund, "Fight Continues for Arctic Refuge," Panda.org, http://www.panda. org/wwf_news/news/?19192/Fight-continues-for-Arctic-refuge (accessed September 20, 2009); and The Audubon Society, "Arctic National Wildlife Refuge: An Irreplaceable Treasure," http://www. protectthearctic.com (accessed September 20, 2009).

87 J. Efstathiou, Jr., "U.S. Says Plan to Expand Alaska Oil Drilling Should Proceed," Bloomberg.com, http://www. bloomberg.com/apps/news?pid=2060110 3&sid=ansmB0pY7Gvo&refer=news (accessed September 20, 2009).

88 See: T.A. LeBeau, "Energy Security and Increasing American Oil and Gas Production," *Natural Resources and Environment* (2002): 193–99.

89 See: Press Release of Senator Inhofe (R-OK.), "National Security Dependent on Domestic Oil/ANWR," Office of Senator Inhofe, March 19, 2003, http://inhofe.senate.gov/pressapp/record.cfm?id=191540 (accessed September 20, 2009).

90 For a scholarly consideration of this topic, see: K.L. Scholosser, "U.S. National Security Discourse and the Political Construction of the Arctic National Wildlife Refuge," *Society and Natural Resources* 19, no. 1 (2006): 3–18.

91 For a "red-green" consideration of this topic, see: A. Austin and L. Phoenix, "The Neoconservative Assault on the Earth: The Environmental Imperialism of the Bush Administration," *Capitalism, Nature, Socialism* 16, no. 2 (2005): 25–43.

92 See S.D. Watch and Epp Law Report, "Idiots in ANWR," March 29, 2005, http://www.thunewatch.squarespace. com/display/ShowJournal?moduleId=10

1945&categoryId=10331 (accessed September 20, 2009).

93 ANWR is 19 million acres in size with the coastal area under consideration (the 1002 area) being 1.5 million acres. See: USGS, "Arctic National Wildlife Refuge, 1002 Area, Petroleum Assessment, 1998, Including Economic Analysis," http:// pubs.usgs.gov/fs/fs-0028-01/ (accessed September 20, 2009).

94 For some diverse and interesting reading, search "are we winning the war on terrorism?" on Google.com.

95 See: US Energy Information Administration, "Annual Energy Outlook: *Potential Oil Production from the Coastal Plain of ANWAR – US Oil Consumption*," 2001, http://www.energy.senate.gov/ legislation/energybill/charts/chart8. pdf#search=%22oil%20consumption%20in%20the%20us%22 (accessed September 20, 2009).

96 See: Emmerich, *The Day After Tomorrow.*

97 Although President Bush never changed his "stay-the-course" stand against Kyoto, the 2006 mid-term and 2008 national elections bode well for the nation's environmental agenda, including reducing the threat of oil exploration in ANWR.

98 See: Al Gore, *An Inconvenient Truth*; Environmental Defense Fund, "The Dangers of Global Warming," http:// www.fightglobalwarming.com/dangers.cfm (accessed September 20, 2009); and N. Stern, *The Economics of Climate Change: The Stern Review* (Cambridge: Cambridge University Press, 2007). See: http://siteresources. worldbank.org/INTINDONESIA/Resources/226271-1170911056314/3428109-1174614780539/SternReviewEng.pdf (accessed October 21, 2009).

99 N. Myers, N. and J. Kent, *Environmental Exodus: An Emergent Crisis in the Global Arena* (Washington, D.C.: Climate

Institute, 1995). http://www.climate.org/ PDF/Environmental%20Exodus.pdf (accessed September 20, 2009).

100 P. Glick, "The Implications of Global Climatic Change for International Security," Pacific Institute, May 16, 2006, http://www.pacinst.org/publications/ testimony/gleick_testimony_congress_5-16-06.pdf - search="congress site%3Apacinst.org" (accessed September 20, 2009).

101 Slang from the 1960s–70s, now meant to imply produced locally.

102 "More than just a nation, America is an idea, a cultural concept – an entirely novel and a historical proposition. Throughout American history, pen and sword have crossed in times of crisis, often resulting in positive cathartic developmental leaps." Excerpt taken from OrionSociety.org, introducing a section on the responses of regular contributors to the tragic events of September 11, 2001. http://www.orionsociety.org/pages/oo/ sidebars/America/index_America.html (accessed March 2, 2007) This link is no longer available.

103 D.W. Orr, "A Perspective from the Periphery," Orion, September 27, 2001. OrionSociety.org. www.davidworr.com/ files/Perspective_Periphery.pdf (accessed September 20, 2009). For a more complete discussion, see: D.W. Orr, The Last Refuge: Patriotism, Politics, and the Environment in an Age of Terror (Washington, DC: Island Press, 2004).

104 S. Hinchman, "Native Resistance to Industrializing the Arctic," in Science and Stewardship to Protect and Sustain Wilderness Values. Seventh World Wilderness Congress Symposium; 2001 November 2–8. Port Elizabeth, South Africa. Proc. RMRS-P-27. A. Watson and J. Sprougll, comps. (Ogden, UT: USDA, Forest Service, Rocky Mountain Research Station, 2003), 77–84.

105 The potential severe impacts of global warming on peoples of the Arctic have been extensively documented, including significant work by the editor of this volume. For example, see: Karim-Aly Kassam, Biocultural Diversity and Indigenous Ways of Knowing: Human Ecology in the Arctic (Calgary: University of Calgary Press, 2009).

106 Interview by Jonathon Ahl (October 4, 2001) for North Country Public Radio. Will September 11th Hurt Environmentalist Cause? The quote was by Dr. B. Thomas Lowe, Associate Provost and Dean of University College, Ball State University (now retired). He also expressed concern about new pressures to open ANWR for oil exploration. http:// www.northcountrypublicradio.org/ news/story/1560/will-september-11-hurt-environmentalist-cause (accessed September 20, 2009).

107 Noam Chomsky, Failed States: The Abuse of Power and the Assault on Democracy (New York: Henry Holt & Co, 2006), 16.

108 Ibid., 17.

109 The literature here is very rich; two comprehensive texts are: A.F. Ide and J.R. Auliff, Jihad, Mujahideen, Taliban, Osama bin Laden, George W. Bush & Oil: A Study in the Evolution of Terrorism & Islam (Dallas, TX: Tangelwuld Press, 2002) and C. Unger, House of Bush, House of Saud: The Secret Relationship Between the World's Two Most Powerful Dynasties (New York: Scribner, 2004).

110 I crafted this title from Errol Morris' compelling 2003 documentary film, The Fog of War, where Robert S. McNamara recounts his years as U.S. Secretary of Defense (1961–68) (Errol Morris [Director] (2003). The Fog of War [Motion Picture].) See also: http://www.sonyclassics. com/fogofwar/indexFlash.html (accessed September 20, 2009). The term is used to imply the confusion and uncertainty

James P. Lassoie 193

surrounding the heat of battle, which can cloud the decision-making process. Since the movie first appeared, it has been associated with the culture of fear in the 'blogosphere'; for example, see: "Words Matter: The Fog of Fear and its Effectiveness as an Agent of Control," Aug. 13, 2006, http://findingwords.blogspot.com/2006/08/fog-of-fear-and-its-effectiveness-as.html (accessed September 20, 2009); "Drowning in a Fog of Fear," October 19, 2004, http://lists.ibiblio.org/pipermail/homestead/2004-October/001665.html (accessed September 20, 2009); and elsewhere (for example, D. Broe and L. Spence, "The Media and the New Cold War," *Cinema Journal* 43, no. 4 [2004]: 96–97).

111 Full disclosure: I never really liked to swim, my phobia being deep water with or without sharks, whose presence or absence I can deal with statistically.

112 See: "Kill Your Television" at http://www.turnoffyourtv.com/ (accessed September 20, 2009). For some gruesome facts and self-help ideas for beating TV addiction.

113 For example, see *US News & World Report* at http://www.usnews.com/ (accessed September 20, 2009); the *Christian Science Monitor* at http://www.csmonitor.com/ (accessed September 20, 2009); and the *New York Times* at http://nytimes.com (accessed September 20, 2009).

114 This is relatively easy for those spending their lives in academic institutions, albeit the perspective is often rather liberal, but many other formal and informal opportunities are available for others.

115 Here I acknowledge long-time department colleague, Professor Richard A. Baer, now retired, whose ideas on social order and politics I seldom embraced personally, but I always appreciated the debate.

116 This was a favourite saying of my father's who spent forty-two years as a public school administrator. My wife, Dr. Ruth E. Sherman, and I have no children.

117 Noam Chomsky, *Imperial Ambitions: Conversations on the Post-9/11 World – Interviews with David Barsamian* (New York: Henry Holt, 2005), 32–33.

118 Perhaps the political collapse of the Republican Party in the United States, beginning with mid-term elections in 2004 and punctuated by the 2008 national election with the loss of both Congress and the White House, might be viewed optimistically from such a perspective.

119 Gore's book, *An Inconvenient Truth*, was ranked 91st in book sales at Amazon.com on October 6, 2006; Crichton's mass paperback edition of *State of Fear* ranked 10,663rd.

120 For example, see Emmerich, *The Day After Tomorrow*.

121 See: Internet Movie Database, David Guggenheim [Director] (2006). "An Inconvenient Truth" [Motion Picture]. http://imdb.com/title/tt0497116/ (accessed September 20, 2009).

122 S. Borenstein, "Scientists OK Gore's Movie for Accuracy," *Associated Post,* June 27, 2006, http://www.washingtonpost.com/wp-dyn/content/article/2006/06/27/AR2006062700780.html (accessed September 20, 2009).

123 U.S. Senate Committee on Environment and Public Works. Majority Press Release. "AP Incorrectly Claims Scientists Praise Gore's Movie," June 27, 2006, http://epw.senate.gov/pressitem.cfm?id=257909&party=rep (accessed September 20, 2009). The Majority here is, of course, Republican, reflecting the make-up of the 109th Senate; the Committee Chair is James M. Inhofe (R-OK).

124 Associated Press, "Bush Gives Thumbs Down to Gore's New Movie: President Says He's Unlikely to Watch Documentary on Global Warming." *Associated Press,* May 24, 2006, http://www.msnbc.

msn.com/id/12930351 (accessed September 20, 2009).

125 See: "The Climate Crisis: Share Your Solutions at http://www.theclimate-project.org/ and Take Part: Climate Change," http://www.takepart.com/issues/climate-change/3 (accessed September 20, 2009).

126 It is interesting to note that people who watched *The Day After Tomorrow* were more aware and understood climate change more that those who didn't (A.A. Leiserowitz, "Before and after The Day After Tomorrow: A U.S. study of climate change risk," *Environment* 46, No. 9 [2004]: 22–37). Hence, it seems that even Hollywood's fictional rendition of the dangers can effectively raise the public's awareness of the climate change problem.

127 Here I return to the ideas and recommendations of M. Shellenberger and T. Nordhaus, *The Death of Environmentalism*; www.thebreakthrough.org/images/Death_of_Environmentalism.pdf (accessed September 19, 2009). Also see: M. Shellenberger, and T. Nordhaus, *Break Through*.

128 For example, see: B. Hendricks and G. Goldstein, "A Strategy for Green Recovery," 2008, http://otrans.3cdn.net/0457703aa3edbf137d_vzm6bos7j.pdf (accessed September 20, 2009) and "Global Warming Solutions," 2009, http://www.ucsusa.org/global_warming/solutions/(accessed September 20, 2009).

129 See: California, Office of the Governor, Press Release, "Gov. Schwarzenegger Signs Landmark Legislation to Reduce Greenhouse Gas Emissions," September 27, 2006, http://gov.ca.gov/press-release/4111/ (accessed September 20, 2009).

130 See: K. Breslau, "Go Green, Get Green," *Newsweek*, October 9, 2006: 9.

131 The Obama Administration's informed and rational approach to forging a new energy policy that addresses climate change has reset the national agenda for addressing this issue, thereby offering some promise for the future. For example see: "New Energy for America" at http://www.barackobama.com/issues/newenergy/index.php (accessed September 20, 2009) and "Barack Obama on Climate Change" at http://www.unep.org/Documents.Multilingual/Default.asp?DocumentID=556&ArticleID=6044&l=en&t=long (accessed September 20, 2009).

132 L.B. Brown, *Plan B 2.0: Rescuing a Planet Under Stress and a Civilization in Trouble* (New York: W. W. Norton, 2006).

133 BBC News. "Global Warming 'Biggest Threat': Climate Change is a Far Greater Threat to the World than International Terrorism, the UK Government's Chief Scientific Adviser Has Said," BBC News, January 9, 2004, http://news.bbc.co.uk/1/hi/sci/tech/3381425.stm (accessed September 20, 2009).

134 Bill McKibben, "A Last Best Chance for Baby Boomers: Calling on Gray-Hairs to Ramp Up the Outrage," *Orion* 25, no. 6 (2006): 14–15.

CHAPTER 8

Responding to the Terror of Genocide: Learning from the Rwandan Genocide of 1994

BRENT BEARDSLEY
Royal Military College

> *We wish to inform you that tomorrow we will be killed with our families.*
>
> – Tutsi parishioners to their spiritual leader in Rwanda,
> April 12, 1994.

> *Your problem has already found a solution. You must die.... You must be eliminated. God no longer wants you.*
>
> – Alleged response from Pastor Elizaphan Ntakirutimana,
> their Pastor[1]

1. INTRODUCTION

The premise of this chapter is that the crime of genocide is the ultimate form of terror, which continues to plague humanity in the early twenty-first century. With encouragement, patience, and support from the editor, I have attempted to combine my personal experience in Rwanda in 1994 with a broader analysis to support the thesis of this paper. I am not an academic or scholar, a journalist or an expert, or even a particularly gifted writer. Therefore, I will break with convention and present this paper more in the form of a highly personal narrative in the first person. I will conclude with my insights regarding the allies of genocide: these may seem simplistic but I ask the reader to remember I have witnessed the horror of genocide while diplomats and politicians engaged in rhetoric that was tantamount to indifference.

I am a Canadian soldier, who in 1993 and 1994 had both the privilege and horror of serving as the personal staff officer to then Major-General Romeo Dallaire, the Canadian Force Commander of the United Nations Assistance Mission for Rwanda (UNAMIR), before and during the genocide in that country. When I was posted to that position in 1993, my career manager had informed me that I was going on a boring and easy peacekeeping mission to a place called Rwanda. I was naive enough to believe him. I knew nothing about Africa, Rwanda, Rwandans, or the conflict and more importantly the background to the conflict in that country. However, neither did General Dallaire or any of the other soldiers, policemen, diplomats, or bureaucrats who would be deployed on this mission. The ill-informed entered the Byzantine labyrinth of Rwanda in 1993 with their eyes wide open, over-confident, and unaware.

We were deployed to Rwanda in the fall of 1993 with a traditional chapter 6 peacekeeping force which grew to approximately 2,500 troops from over twenty countries by early 1994.[2] By "traditional," I mean in the Pearsonian tradition of a lightly armed, modestly equipped military force with a strict mandate, restricted rules of engagement that permitted the use of force only in self-defence, limited financial and logistics resources, and most importantly the near-total absence of a combat or fighting capability. We were on a peace mission at the invitation and full transparent support of the parties to the conflict.[3]

The civil war from 1990 to 1993 had killed thousands of Rwandans, displaced hundreds of thousands more, generated gross human rights violations, led to crimes against humanity mostly against the Tutsi minority, and had seriously damaged the physical and social infrastructure in Rwanda.[4] However, we were in Rwanda at the invitation of both of the parties and we expected the mutual consent of the belligerents and freedom of movement for action within our mandate. In turn, we would be impartial in assisting the parties with post-conflict reconstruction and reconciliation.[5]

Our specific mission was to assist the parties, the Rwandan Government, and the Rwandan Patriotic Front (RPF) with implementing the Arusha Peace Agreement (commonly referred to as Arusha), which had been negotiated and agreed to by the parties with assistance from the international community. The parties had called upon the United Nations to provide a peacekeeping force with the primary task of establishing a climate of security essential for the establishment and subsequent successful operation of a Broad Based Transitional Government, which would implement the mandated requirements and timetable of Arusha and bring peace, democracy, human rights, reconciliation, and reconstruction to Rwanda.[6]

From the moment of our arrival in Rwanda, things began to go seriously wrong. It rapidly became apparent that there were in fact three parties in play in Rwanda. The first party consisted of the moderates, both Tutsis and members of the majority Hutu community in the Rwandan Government, who genuinely wanted peace, democracy, human rights, and group reconciliation. They had no armed group to support them and therefore were totally dependant on the international community, represented by UNAMIR, to protect them and the peace process they were labouring so hard to bring to their country. Despite our repeated cautioning that we were there only to assist in implementing the peace process, they interpreted our deployment and presence in Rwanda as a guarantee by the international community for protection and human security. Emboldened by our presence, they emerged, albeit divided into many factions, to openly challenge the ruling elite, who had dominated and exploited Rwanda for decades. They were to pay the most terrible price for their misplaced trust and confidence in the international community.[7]

The second group, the RPF, was Tutsi-dominated, but largely made up of refugees and offspring of refugees from the diaspora in neighbouring countries. They had fled Rwanda around independence in 1959–63 and had lived a miserable life and existence as stateless and abused refugees. They had formed a political (RPF) movement and an armed wing (Rwandan Patriotic Army or RPA) to secure a return to the land of their forefathers and to obtain full equality and rights in a nation many of them had never seen. They initially attempted to negotiate a right of return and political change in Rwanda. However, in frustration, they turned to the use of force to achieve their political objectives by invading Rwanda in 1990 and conducting a three-year civil war. The RPF were suspicious of the sincerity of the Rwandan Government and, while they fully complied with all the Arusha requirements that they had agreed to in the peace agreement, they also prepared their forces for a resumption of hostilities should the peace process fail.[8]

The third group, which came more and more to the forefront in Rwanda, was made up of extremists. A vast network of Hutu extremists had been built over the years to serve a small elite. It became rapidly apparent that this elite focused solely on maintaining exclusive control of the government and the economy. Greed and corruption permitted them to enrich themselves and the organs of their regime, which kept them in power. They had almost exclusive control of the national army and police. They never had any intention of implementing the Arusha peace process and sharing power with the moderates or the RPF. In fact, they were planning a "final solution" to consolidate their power and wealth.[9]

From our arrival in Rwanda in the fall of 1993 until April 1994, the security situation began to unravel and seriously deteriorate. Riots, grenade attacks, assassinations, arms distribution to militia groups, hate-filled propaganda in the media, a stalemate in the political process, the Machiavellian manipulations of the president and his cronies, the engineered disintegration of the moderates into ever-more disputing camps, and the frustration of the RPF with a failing process combined to form a powder keg, which only required a spark to ignite Rwanda.[10]

UNAMIR never achieved even a minimum operational effectiveness. The UN was burdened by debt and increasingly its patrons were frustrated with the rising costs of peacekeeping. In addition, these patrons were increasingly becoming frustrated with the frequent failures of traditional peacekeeping in Croatia, Bosnia, Somalia, and now Rwanda. While troops arrived from many countries, most of the contingents came without vehicles, communications equipment, and all manner of general and technical supplies. There were no reserves of water, food, ammunition, or fuel, the lifeblood of any military force. The few medical supplies had rapidly been exhausted and nothing could be replaced or provided because UNAMIR never had a budget. When some funds were finally allocated, they were totally inadequate to satisfy the essential operational requirements and demands of the force.[11]

More significant than the lack of capability on the ground was the apparent lack of political will in the international community. They expected the mission to be easy, cheap, bloodless, and successful. It became rapidly apparent to UNAMIR that without the will of the international community, the means would never be found to conduct the mission nor would UNAMIR be able to respond effectively if the peace process failed and hostilities resumed. Despite repeated warnings of preparations for war and of the potential for a campaign of murder against civilians, the UN Security Council paid little if any attention to Rwanda. Instead, the Security Council issued threats that if the process failed or if hostilities resumed, the continued presence of UNAMIR in Rwanda would have to be reviewed. This was an indication that the UN could withdraw and abandon the country to a fate of continued civil war and potentially much worse. To the extremists, this was an invitation to derail the peace process and resume hostilities because the international community would withdraw and give them a clear field of fire in Rwanda.[12]

In letters to my wife until April 1994, I frequently explained that Rwanda would explode into an orgy of violence. On the evening of April 6, 1994, the airplane carrying President Habyarimana to Kigali was shot down on its approach to the airport by persons unknown. Within hours, Rwanda exploded, not only into a resumption of hostilities between the military forces of the Rwandan Government and the RPA, but also into something far worse and obscene. From April to July 1994, a period of a hundred days, approximately 800,000 men, women, and children were murdered in one of the fastest and deadliest genocides of the twentieth century.[13]

2. Genocide Defined

Genocide is a relatively new term for a very old crime. Genocides have been conducted from antiquity to the present, but the word was only coined in 1943 by Raphael Lemkin. Lemkin was a Polish Jewish jurist, who combined the Greek word *genos*, meaning a people or tribe, with the Latin word *cide*, meaning killing or murder.[14] He created the word to describe what he knew was taking place in Nazi Europe in what came to be known as the Holocaust. By 1945 the Holocaust would claim the lives of 6 million Jews and 5 million other human beings in a deliberate and intentional, premeditated murder campaign against entire groups of people.

The moral shock and outrage generated by the Holocaust, directly contributed to the newly created United Nations focusing much effort and attention on drafting a *Convention on the Prevention and Punishment of the Crime of Genocide*, which was unanimously passed by the General Assembly on December 9, 1948, and came into force ninety days after its ratification by the twentieth member state of the UN on January 12, 1951.[15] Since 1951, approximately 142 states have ratified the convention and another forty-two states are signatories to the convention.[16]

Since it was so enthusiastically created, the Convention has unfortunately obtained a failing grade in actually preventing, suppressing, and punishing the crime of genocide. Attempts to upgrade or amend it have failed. Throughout the Cold War, it was largely ignored as genocides occurred, for instance, in Bangladesh, Burundi, Iraq, and Cambodia. In the early post–Cold War period in Croatia, Bosnia, and Rwanda, it also failed to deter genocides in those countries in conflict.[17] However, it was largely due to these genocides and the sustained activism by scholars, human rights advocates, journalists, and some political leaders that momentum was gained to use the Convention to prevent or stop genocides and in other cases to punish those who committed the crime. Military force was used in Kosovo and Timor to prevent and stop acts of genocide, and International Criminal Tribunals in The Hague and Arusha have convicted and punished perpetrators of the crime of genocide.

Nevertheless, given the ongoing genocide in Darfur and the impunity with which the Government of Sudan has acted to date, much still needs to be done if the Genocide Convention is to ever achieve its stated intention of preventing and punishing this crime. It is yet to become a deterrent to a leader or group using genocide to achieve their aims.[18]

Why is genocide the ultimate act of terror? According to the Convention, "genocide means any of the following acts committed with intent to destroy in whole or in part, a national, ethnic, racial or religious group as such":

a. Killing members of the group;
b. Causing serious bodily or mental harm to members of the group;
c. Deliberately inflicting on the group conditions of life calculated to bring about its physical destruction in whole or in part;
d. Imposing measures intended to prevent births within the group;
e. Forcibly transferring children of the group to another group.[19]

Genocide is considered the ultimate crime because it denies the right to exist; namely, the right to live for members of an entire group. These human beings are marked for death by whatever political, ideological, religious, or any other reason that distinguishes them. The victims in the case of genocide are not necessarily soldiers or subversives. They are civilian men, women, and children whose lives are targeted in the ultimate act of terror.

3. GENOCIDE DESCRIBED

The morning of April 9, 1994, in Kigali, Rwanda, started out much the same as the previous two mornings since President Habyarimana's airplane had been shot down at Kigali Airport on the evening of April 6. The city appeared empty of people. Firing of all types of weapons was sporadic around the city. Chaos reigned at the headquarters of the United Nations Assistance Mission for Rwanda (UNAMIR) as we tried to make sense of the anarchy, which appeared to be spreading throughout Rwanda. We knew most of the moderate politicians we had been working with for the past six months to achieve our mission of implementing the Arusha Peace Agreement were either dead or in hiding. We had taken casualties when ten of our Belgian soldiers had been brutally murdered on April 7. We had little water, gasoline, and ammunition, and no food or medical supplies. We had accounted for most of our military personnel, but we were still attempting to locate some civilian staff. The expatriate community was preparing to leave Rwanda with the assistance of elite military forces from France, Belgium, Italy, the United States, and other western nations. The Rwandan Government army and gendarmerie controlled most of the city, except for those areas where the forces of the Rwandan Patriotic Army (RPA) were expanding their area of control in and around the capital. The RPA elements in the capital were attempting to link up with a major RPA offensive advancing from the north towards Kigali. Since April 8, open hostilities had resumed. Rwanda had returned to a state of civil war and our mission, for all intents and purposes, given the warnings of the Security Council, was over. Or was it?[20]

Our Headquarters in New York appeared to be in a state of panic, as were the national capitals in Europe and North America. The same phones and faxes, which had not returned very many of our calls and the bureaucrats who had not shown much, if any, interest in our mission for the past six months, suddenly came alive, but the words were not encouraging. No one was talking about reinforcing the mission to try and control the situation in Rwanda and protect Rwandans from the murder and mayhem we had witnessed in the capital over the last forty-eight hours. Instead, subtle hints were being made that perhaps UNAMIR, like the diplomatic community and the expatriates in Rwanda, should just pack up and leave and let Rwandans sort out their own country.

April 9 was a special day for me. It was my wedding anniversary. Thoughts that day often drifted to my wife and three children (4, 2, and 3 months) in Canada and how thankful I was that they were safe and spared the hell into which Rwanda was descending. My thoughts also drifted to my Rwandan acquaintances and friends, some of whom I knew had already been murdered and others who had disappeared. How would they survive this carnage and how were we, the UN, Canada, the International Community, humanity, going to rescue them?

April 9 also offered me the first opportunity I had in almost forty-eight hours to get out of the Headquarters and into the streets of Kigali. It permitted me the chance to get away from the two telephones that had rung at a rate of a hundred calls an hour, as people, some of whom I knew and most of whom I did not, called begging for help and rescue. Too often, I had heard the sound of terror in their voices as I tried in several languages to find out where they were in a city that had few street names. Too often their pleas were interrupted by the shouts of the killers, the screams of the victims, and the shots of gunfire, which ended in silence. That deafening roar of silence brought with it the realization that yet another Rwandan had died because we had failed to rescue them.

We tried to mount rescue missions, but except in a few rare cases, we always seemed to be blocked by mobs or militia roadblocks that delayed our progress and inevitably we arrived too late to rescue the victims. Usually we found bodies or empty homes. We were often too late to save the people who had come to believe that we were in Rwanda to protect them. We were a toothless tiger, a façade of action from an indifferent international community. We had failed in our mission of peace and now we were failing to save the lives of many Rwandans.

The chance to get away from that exhausting horror was welcome even if it meant jumping into the war zone that Kigali had become. This day would be different. I would get away from the phones and actually get out on the street and rescue some people. I teamed with two Polish Military Observers, borrowed some weapons (I had a pistol with 9 bullets, my two companions had an AK-47 with 30 rounds and an SKS assault rifle with 5 rounds) and we travelled in a Bangladeshi Armoured Personnel Carrier with a crew of five armed soldiers. Off we went to protect as many Rwandans as we could, before we had to return at dusk.

We came under fire from one party and then the other as we passed through the RPA area of control, through the no man's land and then into the area of government control. As we progressed we increasingly ran into what seemed like an endless net of roadblocks. First army, then gendarme, and finally, endless roadblocks with civilians, some armed and in para-military uniforms, whom we knew to be the Interahamwe militia. The Interahamwe had supposedly been the youth wing of the extremist party but in fact had evolved into an armed fanatical militia, made up mostly of young angry men, drawn from the ranks of the poor and unemployed, who had been brainwashed with hate, lies, false promises, and the opportunity for sanctioned rape and looting. They were trained to kill Tutsis and *any Hutu who did not believe that Tutsis were snakes.*[21] Spurred on by their leaders and local officials, inspired by the hate-filled music and rhetoric of Radio-Télévision Le Milles Collines (RTLM), they had appeared early in the morning of April 7 and seemed to be growing in numbers and becoming more violent. They would become the primary killers in this genocide.[22]

As we progressed through our mission, we were shocked to see increasing number of bodies in the streets, in the alleys, or just lying in fields. Up until this day, we in UNAMIR had been convinced that what we were witnessing in Rwanda was a *coup d'état* and a resumption of the civil war. The extremists, most of whom were well known to us, had formed an Interim Government on April 8. Absent in that government were all of the moderate ministers who were dead or in hiding. The president had been killed. The army had rapidly gained control of the city. The Presidential Guard had been murdering first moderate political leaders, and then others who in many cases we knew opposed them and their plans. Hostilities had been initiated with the RPF. Informants for months had told us that such a bloody event would occur and that Tutsis would die. While their warnings were coming true and Tutsis were obviously being murdered, we still held onto the hope that this was just another coup. It would just be a matter of days until the extremists had firmly seized power after eliminating their major opponents and spreading fear into moderate Hutus and Tutsis. Could this really be the beginning of the campaign of murder to destroy an entire people that informants had warned us about for months? Of course not! This was the post–Cold War new world order. This was the dawn of the twenty-first century. The United Nations, the International Community, the world's sole remaining superpower, laws of the UN Charter, the UN Declaration of Human Rights, the Hague, the Geneva Conventions, and the Genocide Convention would all act in concert not to permit something that horrendous or criminal to occur in the 1990s. No, this was a coup and a civil war.

After conducting several missions where we rescued several diplomats, aid workers, and UN employees, we received a faint call on the radio around noon from two unarmed Polish military observers whom we knew resided with Polish priests at Gikondo Parish Church. The battery strength of their radio was dying, but their message was clear. Something had happened and they needed help. We proceeded as rapidly as we could to their location through or around the maze of roadblocks that had been erected in Kigali.

When we arrived at the church, it was too quiet. The entire area appeared deserted, except for an alley full of bodies across the street. We dismounted and, while the gunner in the APC covered us, we split into two teams. My team went into the church. The other team went to search the residence. My mate entered as I covered him and maintained visual contact with the APC. Inside the church was a scene that the overwhelming majority of Canadians will hopefully never see. The church, a sanctuary, which was well known to us and where on occasion we had worshipped, was covered in bodies. There was some movement, some sighs of pain. The pews and the floor were covered with the bodies of dozens of men, women, and children.

The bodies bore the wounds of mutilation with what were clearly machete cuts. The Polish priests were performing first aid on a few survivors who had suffered such brutal wounds that it was surprising to find them alive. We helped the living with water and first aid, but, on further examination of the corpses, this nightmare just got worse. Girls from age 6 to women of age 60 had been dragged to the corners and had been raped, most likely repeatedly, before having their sexual organs mutilated and their lives taken by machete blows. Children, including babies, had been murdered, obviously in the arms or in the near vicinity of their powerless mothers and fathers. Every face, even in death, bore an expression of anguish and horror, suffering and even disbelief. One of the few survivors was a baby, crying as it tried to suckle its dead mother's breast. Parents had obviously watched their children being murdered and the children had watched their parents being murdered. The killings, we were told by the priests and our comrades, had taken all night, hours and hours of the most painful suffering imaginable. Terror defies a universally accepted definition, but in many cases it is like pornography. You know it when you see it, and what we witnessed at Gikondo Parish Church on April 9, 1994, was terror laid bare.

These victims were not politicians, subversives, activists, soldiers, terrorists, guerrillas, freedom fighters, protesters, or radicals and did not pose any threat to the Rwandan government. These were innocent men, women, and children who had been trapped by the army, rounded up and registered by the police, murdered by the militia and their names erased from government records by bureaucrats, all under the orders of a very well-educated and sophisticated political elite. These victims were literally erased from humanity. In too many cases, no record exists that they ever lived, loved, dreamed, or hoped, or even where, when, and how they died. They were simply and brutally erased.

This was not a normal coup or a civil war. It foreshadowed what was still to occur in the subsequent days, weeks, and months in Rwanda. This was a very well-planned, organized, and thoroughly executed genocide that would claim the lives of over 800,000 Rwandans, mostly Tutsis, in just one hundred days. This would be the ultimate act of terror in Rwanda.

What happened at Gikondo Parish Church on April 9, 1994, was just one small instance of what happened across Rwanda on a much larger scale. It is what happened to the Herrero at the turn of the century, to the Armenians before and after the First World War, the Ukrainians in Stalin's Soviet Union, to Jews, gypsies, and many others during the Holocaust and at other times and other places in every decade during the twentieth century. Some scholars have labelled the twentieth century "the age of genocide."[23] In this century, which witnessed the worst conflicts in history, more civilians were murdered in genocides than soldiers were killed in war.

The ultimate act of terror was committed in Rwanda from April 7 until July 18, 1994, a period of about a hundred days in which approximately 800,000 men, women, and children died. The saddest and most shocking aspect of the Rwandan genocide is that we will never know exactly who and how many died. Humanity had failed to stop the most rapid genocide in history. Such a failure in the final decades of the twentieth century raises the question: In the face of such genocidal terror, what should the response of humanity be?

From 1939 until 1945, my father, my grandfather, and many other relatives in my family gave up a significant part of their youth to fight and defeat the Nazi regime in Europe. Some died, others were severely injured, and all of them carried the scars of that war. Some witnessed both the First and the Second World Wars in their lifetime. When it ended, humanity, with virtually one voice said *never again*.[24] In response, the United Nations was created to prevent war and guarantee international peace and security. The Universal Declaration of Human Rights guaranteed every man, woman, and child on this planet the same basic human rights.

However, before the ink was dry, nations reneged on their commitments. The period from the late 1940s to the present is filled with crimes against humanity and gross human rights violations.[25] Why have we failed so starkly to stop the crime of genocide?

4. Three Allies of Genocide

I firmly believe, based on my experience in Rwanda, that genocide is the ultimate form of terror and therefore demands an effective response from humanity as a whole. Organs of the international community have a major role in preventing, stopping, and punishing this crime. From the case of Rwanda, each of us must acknowledge that if we continue to look to government, to politicians, to the United Nations, or to other organizations for the response to genocide, we will continue to see humanity suffer. The responsibility for confronting and defeating genocide rests with each and every one of us. My experience of genocide in Rwanda tells me that, in order to rise to this challenge, each of us must defeat the three primary allies of genocide, first in ourselves and then in the wider human community. These allies are indifference, greed, and hypocrisy.

Since the Rwandan genocide, far too many have tried to find a scapegoat for humanity's failure. The Hutus, the Tutsis, the United Nations, the United States, the major powers, the developed world are all culpable. Why do we blame others? It is easier to blame than confront our own individual failings. Every organization, state, military, bureaucracy, and most adult citizens in the western world knew exactly what was going on in Rwanda in 1994. They individually and collectively chose to ignore the genocide. Why expect our leaders, our institutions, or anyone else to act when each of us is indifferent to human suffering on the scale that was witnessed in Rwanda in 1994? What have we done to end the terror in Darfur, which is now into its third year and has claimed the lives of at least 400,000 black Muslims and has the potential to claim at least two million more?

It is never too late. Philippe Gaillard, the head of the International Committee of the Red Cross (ICRC) in Rwanda, illustrates commitment in the face of indifference. When the civil war broke out in Rwanda, Gaillard could have removed the ICRC mission, like the overwhelming majority of humanitarian aid workers, diplomats, journalists, and expatriates who washed their hands of Rwanda and fled to safety. Gaillard chose to stay and remained in Rwanda throughout the genocide, exposing himself and his staff to all of the dangers of a war zone and ultimately saving the lives of tens of thousands of Rwandans.[26] Others from around the world also contributed their time, their efforts, their money, or their influence to ensure he had the tools he needed to respond to the terror of genocide in Rwanda. Similarly, across Canada today, hundreds of ordinary students, teachers, human rights activists, and citizens have decided to act and give of themselves, their time, their energy and their resources to raise public and political awareness in this country to act in stopping the genocide in Darfur. We can choose to act, each in his own way, or we can choose to ignore and ally ourselves with genocide's greatest ally, indifference.

Greed is also an ally of genocide. We who live in the northern, developed world are blessed with peace, freedom, and prosperity. We spend more on ice cream, cosmetics, and pet food than we contribute to water, food, sanitation, health care, and education in the developing world. Yet we still we expect more. We expect our lives to get better each year. We expect a raise, more savings, less debt, less taxes, increase possessions, and we want our children to have even more than we have while over half of humanity tries to survive on less than US$2.00 a day. We demand more but we ignore how we obtain it. The impulse of greed exists in each and every one of us. The cost of our reluctance in sharing wealth is the failure to prevent genocide. Dr James Orbinski, who later went on to lead Doctors Without Borders, chose to leave the peace, comfort, and relative wealth of a medical practice in Canada to go to Rwanda and apply his skills to saving lives. Operating in a war zone, exposed to constant danger, working with insufficient staff, facilities and resources, overloaded with the sick, wounded, injured, and dying, he and many like him saved the lives of thousands of Rwandans. Again, supporting him were thousands of others around the world who gave of themselves and their personal resources to respond to the genocide.[27] Greed was put aside by some individuals who realized that "to whom much is given, much is expected." Greed must take a back seat to humanity if humanity is ever to prevent genocide.

Finally, the last ally of the terror of genocide is hypocrisy. We say we care and most of us truly believe we care, but when the time comes to utilize our resources or put our lives on the line, we always have reasons not to act. We say one thing, but consistently do another. And the result is that millions of human beings have been murdered in campaigns of terror. Most cases were preventable if only we had done what we say we believed to be right. The classic example of defeating hypocrisy was provided by General Romeo Dallaire during the genocide in Rwanda in 1994. When provided with the opportunity to withdraw UNAMIR and return to the safety of his home, he demanded to stay in Rwanda and do the best he could with what he had to stop the genocide.[28] Along with him were 450 other soldiers, drawn from twenty countries, who also chose to stay in Rwanda and try to confront genocide. While many will regard their actions as a failure to prevent genocide, they at least acted while politicians in the international community shamefully retreated. These soldiers will be judged by their actions under the resource-starved conditions they were placed in.

5. CONCLUSION

A friend of mine went to Darfur with a commission of inquiry to interview victims of the terror that continues to plague this region. It was a dangerous task for her, but not as risky as the potential consequences for the Darfurians she interviewed. If government spies, soldiers, police, or militia were able to identify an individual who had given information to a foreign investigator, that individual would no doubt be killed.

She interviewed a girl 14 years of age who had described in graphic detail how the Sudanese Air Force had bombed her village and how the police and army had cordoned off the village to prevent anyone from escaping. She went on to describe how the Janjaweed militia entered the village and murdered her father and brothers in front of her family, how her mother and young siblings were herded like cattle into the desert without water, food, or any possessions that could sustain life. She also described how her home and village had been looted and burned, and then how she had been taken and tied to a stake the way an animal is leashed. She had then been repeatedly raped over a number of days as she fell in and out of consciousness, and finally, when she was bloodied and almost dead from dehydration, starvation, and injury, she had been cut loose and sent into the desert to die. Luckily, she was picked up by a humanitarian aid agency and she survived.

When she was informed of the risks of her testimony and was cautioned to be careful after the interview, she responded that it did not matter, as she was already dead. Her body might be alive and her future could be bright, but in her mind and her heart she was dead. At 14, she had essentially given up on life and could imagine no future worth living. When asked more pointedly why she had volunteered to tell her story that was obviously so painful and humiliating, she responded that she wanted her story told to the world and specifically to us in the northern, wealthy, developed, rich, white world, because she was convinced that if we only knew what was going on in Darfur, we would immediately stop the terror and help her and the other victims of this latest genocide. We would have to care, we would have to act, and we could not ignore such suffering amongst our fellow human beings.

I have reflected upon this case at length and considered the question: how do you look into the eyes of this young girl and so many other victims of genocide and say no it is not true? They don't care, they won't help, and they won't make the effort to stop this horror. How do you look into the eyes of a victim and tell them that in the big picture of our world, they individually and collectively have just ceased to matter or do not seem to merit our action in rescuing them from the horror. Indifference, greed, and hypocrisy are the allies of the terror of genocide and against human life. As a soldier, I believe we must first defeat indifference, greed, and hypocrisy in our families, our communities, our country, our world and ourselves, if we will ever rise to the challenge of ending the terror of genocide. Then and only then will we ever be able to give some real meaning to the cry *Never Again*.

Notes

1. Philip Gourevitch, *We wish to inform you that tomorrow we will be killed with our families* (New York: Picador, 1988), 28. Gourevitch was one of the first journalists to enter Rwanda after the genocide and did extensive research from the macro- to the micro-level of the genocide in Rwanda. His award-winning book remains one of the best narratives of the genocide in Rwanda. Ntakirutimana was subsequently arrested in the United States and extradited to the International Criminal Tribunal for Rwanda (ICTR) in Arusha, Tanzania, where he was tried and convicted of genocide. See the ICTR web site (http://www.ictr.org/) for details on his indictment, trial, findings, and judgment.

2. Romeo Dallaire with Major Brent Beardsley, *Shake Hands with the Devil: The Failure of Humanity in Rwanda* (Toronto: Random House, 2003). Chapters 3–9 provide an inside account of the development of the mission and the serious deficiencies of UNAMIR before the genocide. United Nations; *The United Nations and Rwanda 1993–1996* (New York: United Nations Press, 1996). Commonly referred to as the Blue Book, it provides the major primary sources of UN involvement in Rwanda, including the various mandates, reports, and letters related to the UNAMIR experience.

3. Michael Barnett, *Eyewitness to a Genocide: The United Nations In Rwanda* (Ithaca: Cornell University Press, 2002). Barnett provides one of the best works on the evolution of peacekeeping in the early post–Cold War world and the challenges faced by the United Nations in adapting classical peacekeeping to the major conflict during this period. Barnett combines the wisdom of a scholar with the practical experience of a desk officer in the Mission of the United States to the United Nations

during the period before and during the Rwandan genocide.

4. Gerard Prunier, *The Rwandan Crisis: History of a Genocide* (New York: Colombia University Press, 1995), 93–186. Prunier provided one of the first and still one of the best works on the Rwandan Genocide. A regional scholar, Prunier in chapters 3, 4, and 5 provides an excellent examination of the civil war and its impact on Rwanda before the genocide.

5. United Nations, *United Nations and Rwanda*, 221–33. Documents 23 and 24 provide the Secretary-General's request to the Security Council of September 24, 1993, to establish UNAMIR and the UN Security Council Resolution 872 of October 5, 1993, which provided the mandate of UNAMIR.

6. Ibid., 165–67. Document 16 of the Blue Book provides the joint request by the Government of Rwanda and the RPF concerning the stationing of a neutral international force in Rwanda.

7. Dallaire, *Shake Hands with the Devil*, 98–220. Chapters 6, 7, 8, and 9 provide the perspective of UNAMIR on the events before the genocide, including the interaction with the moderates.

8. Colin Waugh, *Paul Kagame and Rwanda: Power, Genocide and the Rwandan Patriotic Front* (Jefferson: McFarland, 2004). In this work, Waugh traces the history of the Tutsi diaspora, the development and growth of the RPF, and the central role of Paul Kagame in the events before, during, and after the genocide.

9. Human Rights Watch, *Leave None to Tell the Story: Genocide in Rwanda* (New York: Human Rights Watch, 1999). In this report, Allison DesForges provides a major examination of the Rwandan Genocide and describes, in detail, the organization of the genocide machine

in Rwanda from the national to the local level.

10 Report of the International Panel of Eminent Personalities to Investigate the 1994 Genocide in Rwanda, *Rwanda: The Preventable Genocide* (Addis: Organization of African Unity Press, 2001). Chapters 9–13 describe in substantiated detail the deterioration in the security situation in Rwanda before the genocide and provide the evidence that what was taking place was widely known in decision-making circles throughout the international community. In the opinion of the author, this report is the most comprehensive single source document on the Rwandan Genocide.

11 Report of the Independent Inquiry into the Actions of the United Nations during the 1994 Genocide in Rwanda (New York: United Nations, 1999), 39–41. The official UN commission of inquiry in conclusion 6 describes in detail the inadequate resources and logistics provided to UNAMIR as a major deficiency that directly contributed to the failure of the mission.

12 Dallaire, *Shake Hands with the Devil*, 219–20. The impact of Security Council Resolution 909 dated April 5, 1994 (contained in the Blue Book as Document 36) and the impact which its message had on UNAMIR and Rwanda are presented by General Dallaire in his memoir.

13 Prunier, *The Rwandan Crisis*, 261–65. was the first scholar to investigate the genocide, and he estimated the number of victims as between 800,000 and 850,000. Des Forges, conducted a later investigation and estimated the victims at no fewer than 500,000. The current Rwandan government frequently cites the number at 1.1 million. The reality is that we will never exactly how many victims died in the genocide due to the destruction of documents and bodies. 800,000 has become the most commonly cited number of victims.

14 Raphael Lemkin, *Axis Rule in Occupied Europe* (Washington: Carnegie Endowment for International Peace, 1944), 79–80. Lemkin is honoured and widely acknowledged as the one who coined the term "genocide." He worked tirelessly to bring the crime of genocide under international law.

15 William Schabas, *Genocide in International Law* (Cambridge: Cambridge University Press, 2000), 553–58. Schabas dedicated the first two chapters of his book to the efforts to develop the Genocide Convention and in the pages noted above provide the first two drafts of the convention and the final version, which was adopted into international law. Samantha Power, *A Problem from Hell: America and the Age of Genocide* (New York: Basic Books, 2002), 17–170. Power provides three chapters on the struggle to develop the genocide convention and then the struggle to get it ratified by nations like the United States.

16 Eric Weitz, *A Century of Genocide: Utopia of Race and Nations* (Princeton: Princeton University Press, 2003), 9. This was the confirmation in 2000.

17 Frank Chalk and Kurt Jonassohn, *The History and Sociology of Genocide: Analyses and Case Studies* (New Haven, CT: Yale University Press, 1990), 65–377. This seminal work on genocide provides within those page limits case studies of fourteen genocides from the Melos of Ancient Greece to the Holocaust and a further six until 1990.

18 As in Rwanda, the debate over whether or not the current situation in Darfur is genocide is ongoing. A U.S. State Department Inquiry concluded genocide was taking place in Darfur but a UN Inquiry concluded that it was not. The debate has divided scholars, politicians and

journalist. The decision to label the situation in Darfur as genocide rests with the author, who believes the situation meets the threshold of the genocide convention and therefore must be considered to be genocide.

19 Schabas, *Genocide in International Law*, 553–58.

20 Dallaire, *Shake Hands with the Devil*, 221–327. The events of the first days of the genocide from the perspective of UN-AMIR personnel is contained in chapters 10 and 11 of Dallaire's memoir.

21 Jean Hatzfeld, *Machete Season: The Killers in Rwanda Speak* (Vancouver: Douglas & McIntyre, 2005). Hatzfeld provides a unique insight into the Interahamwe militia. Hatzfeld tracked down and extensively interviewed several genocidiaries, including hardcore interahamwe, the volunteers who joined them, and some who were coerced. Their testimony is chilling. The words in italics refer to a popular song that was frequently played on RTLM during the genocide which stated "I hate Hutus, I hate Hutus, I hate Hutus who don't believe Tutsis are snakes."

22 Dina Temple-Raston, *Justice on the Grass: Three Rwandan Journalists, Their Trial for War Crimes, and a Nation's Quest for Redemption* (New York: Simon & Schuster, 2005). Temple-Raston provides a detailed account of the role played by extremist journalists in the media during the Rwandan Genocide.

23 Weitz labelled his work *A Century of Genocide*, and Power subtitled her book *The Age of Genocide*.

24 "Never again" was taken from the Bible, where in the aftermath of the flood, God promised Noah that never again would he destroy mankind. "Never again" became and remains the rallying cry of anti-genocide activism.

25 Any of the references contained in this paper provide a discussion on the lessons learned or not learned from the Rwandan Genocide. The author wrote a paper entitled "Lessons Learned or Not Learned from the Rwandan Genocide of 1994?" and presented the paper at the 7th Annual Graduate Student Symposium held at the Royal Military College of Canada on October 29/30, 2004. It is available on the internet at: www.cdfai.org.

26 Dallaire, *Shake Hands with the Devil*, 297, 319, 493.

27 Ibid., 297, 413, 440, 454.

28 Ibid., 293–96, 312–13, 319–20.

CHAPTER 9

Psycho-Dynamics of Terror: A Perspective on the Evolution of Western Civilization

Ronald Glasberg
University of Calgary

1. Introduction

Context is everything when seeking to understand a problem. While terror is usually considered from the perspective of some conflict with respect to the fundamental cultural assumptions within a given civilization, in this case that of the West, I would like to consider terror from a more intrinsic than extrinsic perspective. As one might well suspect, the two forms are probably related; and should that prove to be the case, the problem of the more familiar extrinsic form, associated with such atrocities as 9/11, is apt to find a solution if the intrinsic form is better understood.

No doubt the foregoing remarks must appear odd. How can there be such a thing as intrinsic terror with respect to a civilization, the very purpose of which is to protect the individuals living within its capacious ambit from external forces deemed to be a threat? How can a civilization itself be the source of some kind of terror for those living within it? This is the paradox that the present discussion will attempt to explore by examining some of the classic "terror texts" of the West. By classic terror texts, I mean those works that elaborate both the fundamental assumptions of Western civilization and how those assumptions articulate the latent fears infusing everyday life. I thus hope to paint an unusual portrait of Western civilization by outlining the changing nature of this fear – a fear of which we are not always conscious and one which has not diminished as the trajectory of the West has unfolded under the heroic banners of scientific rationality. Indeed, using intrinsic terror as a frame of reference, our current crisis with extrinsic terror can be seen in a new and perhaps useful light.

Obviously, given the scope of my project, I must paint in broad strokes. The set of exemplary texts to be subjected to a "hermeneutic of terror" must be well chosen in terms of its ability to represent the main features of the evolution of Western civilization. But before I can plunge into the temporal context of terror, a conceptual context needs to be elaborated. By "conceptual" I mean an understanding of terror as an emotion situated within a field of complementary emotions designed to shed light on each other.

2. What Is Terror?

At its most simple level, terror is an emotion characterized by an abject fear that someone (i.e., the "terrorist") seeks to inflict for a variety of complex reasons. That the infliction of such fear might be endemic to a culture seems at first to be highly problematic. Could there be social mechanisms that somehow terrorize individuals living within society? Of course, legal and religious institutions could terrorize the wayward for the purposes of maintaining a sufficient measure of social control. Up until the eighteenth and nineteenth centuries, before prison reform took hold, terrorizing certain classes of prisoner was not unusual.[1] However, such banal observations do not take us into the heart of the phenomenon. If we are to understand how terror might infuse the life of those who are not religiously or judiciously beyond the pale, we must consider the emotion in relation to its opposite and articulate thereby a more fertile framework for understanding.

What then is a feeling most opposite to the one associated with terror? If terror can be associated with abject fear, then is it not reasonable to suppose that its opposite is a state of burgeoning or flourishing confidence? This is more than the mere absence of fear, for absence does not yet parallel an emotional intensity that mirrors the extreme nature of terror. Thus, if fear and its more extreme cousin, terror, entail a shrinking back in on oneself in a hyper-defensive posture, then the flourishing confidence must be associated with an extension of oneself out into the world with a passion of total openness that must have some affinities with love – love of others, love of the world, love of life, love of God. In place of extreme defensiveness, a courageous vulnerability characterizes the individual. Moreover, if we ask how such a courageous vulnerability is possible, it can only arise from a place of secure connection with some larger whole of which the courageous individual is an intrinsic part. By "intrinsic" I mean to make an important contrast with the "extrinsic" – for an extrinsic connection can be removed by the flow of circumstance whereas an intrinsic one cannot. To put it another way, courageous vulnerability that flows into the world with love cannot be dependent on some external foundation (e.g., material wealth or military power), which is as "sand" compared to the "rock" of one's inner and hence unremovable connection with some greater whole. "Rock" and "sand"? If these words seem to suggest Jesus' famous "Sermon on the Mount,"[2] that is no coincidence. This perhaps foundational text of Christianity is in certain ways addressed to the question of fear and the possibility of living without it, should an individual be able to trust in the love of the heavenly Father.

By way of the foregoing conceptual contextualization, then, the feeling of terror can be elaborated as being based on a sense of intrinsic disconnection with a larger whole inasmuch as its opposite – courageous vulnerability – appears to make sense as being based on a contrary sense of intrinsic connection with a larger whole.[3] At this point more light can be shed on the endemic roots of terrorism by examining certain representative terror texts with a view to considering three interrelated themes: (1) the whole from which one is disconnected; (2) how the disconnection occurred; and (3) the nature of the cultural strategies designed as a kind of response to the disconnection.

3. Ancient Terrors – The Case of Sophocles' Oedipus[4]

That terror plays a role in Sophocles' famous play is undeniable. The fear of the protagonist, Oedipus, becomes infused with horror as he feels himself pursued by a relentless fate that pushes him to commit unspeakable acts: parricide with respect to his father and incest with respect to his mother. Oedipus is haunted by a fear that he is foredoomed to commit these acts; and the horror underlying the play comes from the fact that his very response, which is to leave the place where his supposed parents are living, propels him into a situation where he does precisely that which he fears most. In short, there is a fear of fate, but the fear becomes elevated to the level of terror when two conditions co-exist: (1) the fate is horrible in terms of what it asserts will befall the doomed individual; and (2) there is no possibility of escape.

How can sense be made of this situation in terms of the following categories of analysis: the nature of the reality from which the individual is disconnected, how the disconnection occurred, and the possibilities of some kind of culturally sanctioned response? First, it would seem that Oedipus is disconnected from nothing. Indeed, it seems to be the case that he is closely connected to some mysterious force called "fate." Yet, if one looks more closely, the sense of terror that stalks Oedipus as well as the viewer of the play can be traced back to a radical disconnection – a disconnection that complements the intense embrace of an evil fate. The disconnection is nothing less than a disconnection from that to which one would hope to be close – namely, oneself. It is the ignorance of oneself, of one's true motives, of one's true identity, of one's true connection with the host of other identities that define a person's role in society – such is the disconnective ignorance that flashes through the play like a blood-red thread; and if a valid knowledge of these connections gives one a confidence-inspiring security, then disconnection in this area can only be terror-inspiring. Moreover, it is no accident that Socratic questioning of the self is a potential remedy in this context, and perhaps it is also no accident that Socrates was put to death for embodying a method of inquiry – i.e., ongoing questioning of taken-for-granted assumptions – that threatened to bring people face to face with the fatal disconnection.

All this leads to the second point, namely, how the disconnection from the self occurred. To answer this question, one must consider what the self is, at least with respect to the figure of Oedipus. Since he is held accountable for his crimes despite his unwitting commission of them, the self that is responsible is not something inessential to the person of Oedipus. In other words, the true self of the protagonist is internal to the person and not something external to him. (If the inner self were somehow external to Oedipus, the attribution of responsibility would make no sense.) Freud picked up on this issue in his exploration of that inner dimension called "the unconscious" – a dimension that is often repressed but nonetheless contains our most forbidden desires. Thus, the "Oedipus complex" is the male child's desire for the mother and concomitant hostility to the father. Whatever the differences between the respective cultural contexts of Freud and Sophocles, is it then reasonable to suppose that disconnection from the internal is rooted in a repression that serves the ends of containing dangerous human tendencies? Furthermore, does the repression serve to paradoxically increase the power of these tendencies and make them more ferocious and hence terrifying?

Unfortunately, the play does not answer these questions, at least not directly. We appear to be left with a disconnection from the internal realm, here understood to be a self of which one is ignorant. Yet that inner dimension is not in a void. It is deeply entangled in a pattern of external events known as fate, and with respect to that pattern one is deeply and inescapably connected. The assumption here being articulated is that of imbalance, where one's internal disconnection is matched by an external connection, albeit one that is dangerously engulfing. Again, the reason for the imbalance is not given. Nonetheless, the structure of the play itself suggests an answer to what is now a dual question: why the disconnection from the internal and the threatening connection with the external? As one might suspect, each question sheds light on the other to the point that one would be hard-pressed to answer either without considering its complementary partner.

The key structural element that opens the way to probing the problem of disconnection is the role of power. Oedipus is the king of Thebes, albeit a king who earned his position via the death of the previous king (whom Oedipus killed unknowingly and who also happened to be Oedipus's true father) and a certain prowess demonstrated by Oedipus in freeing the city from a terrifying monster (the Sphinx). As a ruler wielding power, Oedipus must naturally orient his life, his choices, his priorities toward the external world. Consequently, the inner world – the locus of the self – is downplayed. Could that denigration be the cause of lack of self-knowledge, which we have associated with a disconnection from the inner world? Let us recall that the whole point of analyzing disconnection from the internal is that it must be generative of some kind of overwhelming fear. The emphasis on power over externals is significant, not only because it pulled Oedipus away from the internal, but also because that tendency has been magnified in our own science-oriented culture that has increased power over externals to such an extent that the very notion of the internal has become suspect – suspect to the point that many prominent philosophers deny its very existence.[5] There is only the external world and that world is best understood by way of an objective rationality oriented toward ever-increasing degrees of external control. The internal world is but an illusion generated by a brain that is also to be understood in externalist terms which neuroscience is pursuing. The key to the inner self is a scientific elaboration of brain processes.

Obviously we can go no further in understanding the world of internal connection if the theme of power – political in the time of Sophocles and techno-scientific in our own day – renders the whole notion of internality problematic. If we are to make any headway in understanding both disconnection from the internal and the cause thereof, the idea of the internal must now be expanded beyond the sphere of self-knowledge. We have already mentioned that the internal was something that could not be taken away, whereas the external was, by virtue of its being outside of us, subject to removal. Yet there must be more than security of possession to render the internal a sphere of fearlessness. Here we must note that the internal and external entail each other. It is impossible to think of one without the other. Moreover, there must be some kind of boundary between them – some kind of "wall" that separates the internal from the external. Obviously there can be walls that separate two external spaces from each other (e.g., the boundary between two countries), but there are also boundaries that separate an internal from an external sphere. What is outside can often be understood as that which is alien, fragmented, resistant to us, albeit to differing degrees, while what is internal to us seems to be characterized by a greater measure of flow, contiguity, oneness, spontaneity, and the capacity for creation. Of course, one can also create in the external realm, but that often involves opposition, struggle, and an overcoming of some kind of resistance. While that can be true of the internal, the creative imagination allows one to envisage alien worlds, "impossible" creatures, etc., without much effort.

Now taking this internal realm to be real and experiencing one's connection to it as a foundational part of one's life, the self may be understood in terms of an infinite network of intimate relations associated with the contiguity and unity that characterizes consciousness. Moreover, the relative lack of resistance that characterizes the internal world suggests freedom that, in the external realm, is only conditional upon the holding of some kind of power over others or over the physical environment. Internal freedom is not so conditional; and if the self is rooted or dependent on a whole of which it feels itself an intrinsic part, then such freedom is totally resistant to loss. Contrariwise, alienation from such a realm of oneness, contiguity, and freedom can only engender anxiety and, if the alienation is great enough, ultimate fear, which is, of course, pure terror.

In this context, Oedipus's ignorance of self, as a function of his role as an externally oriented holder of power, will draw him away from the internal realm. But what is the evidence of terror? Here we must return to the nature of his crimes and what they really signify. Patricide and incest are closely linked to the theme of power, but power as an absolute. Killing the father suggests rejecting a dependence on the past, on traditions, on one's roots. As a power holder, one has maximized one's range of action if one is independent of all constraints, and respect for the traditions of the past, of one's temporal connection with a greater whole, is a very powerful constraint on the use of power. Then, to take the place of the father and procreate with one's own mother is a kind of inappropriate intimacy where one clings in an excessive manner to one's immediate foundation – a kind of spatial counterpart to the temporal one associated with the father killing. To let go is to be open to finding or creating a new foundation – a process of establishing mutual interdependencies within the world. One gains self-knowledge by growing, and one grows by developing relations with others. One remains stagnant if one rejects the possibility of interdependency, and in that context self-knowledge is futile because there is little of a self to know. The opposite of such interdependency is then extreme self-dependency, which is symbolized by patricide and incest.

These are terrifying crimes, not just because they violate others as well as the crucial possibility of growing as an interdependent self, but also because they reflect a stance of extreme fear of anything that stands in the way of perfecting power. To put it another way, the "mother" in a relationship of inappropriate intimacy represents our fear of going out and finding new relationships. Killing the father represents fear of anything that might restrain our wish to dominate the external world. Thus, incest and patricide are indicative of a power-based fear of the external as well as a response to that fear characterized by setting up a regime of total domination. While a weak relation to the internal might cause one to direct one's attention to the external, that kind of emphasis can only serve to weaken the internalist foundation even more and subsequently increase the external foundation in a never-ending cycle of fear. To sum up, then, Oedipus's fear-inspiring disconnection from the internal is more than ignorance of the self (i.e., a locus of internality to be sure). His ignorance of the self is itself rooted in an inappropriate focus on the external based on the dynamics of power. Appropriate internalist links are possible, not only via mystical oneness with some spiritual foundation, but also by respecting traditions (i.e., not killing the father) and adopting a stance of openness and even vulnerability with respect to the wider world (i.e., not moving in a kind of incestuous self-dependency situation). Such an internalist stance might not be as powerful as one characterized by a mystic oneness with a higher spiritual being; but if a lesser level of internality entails sharing, a sense of mutuality, and an egalitarian respect for others, it is nonetheless a valuable antidote to an externalist position of one-sided domination over others.

The dynamics of power call for maximal self-dependence; but because self-dependence entails an equally extreme alienation from an internal space of contiguity, unity, and oneness with something other than the self, a feeling of terror must ensue – a terror so great that one is inexorably pushed to become a self-dependent fortress, dependent on no one else but one's fearful self. Just how great is this fear? So great that we cannot admit it without giving up the power orientation that inspired it; so great that it must remain in the unconscious; so great that it drives us to perfect our external control by finding different ways of murdering the father and possessing the mother. What, after all, is our current ecological crisis but a mad attempt to possess Mother Earth? What is our techno-culture but an ongoing destruction of our relationship to God the Father as well as our potential for more internal forms of growth?

The issue of power as the cause of the dissociation from the internal also clarifies the nature of the fear – a patricidal and incestuous movement toward self-dependence that, to the extent that it is successful, only exacerbates the original fear, which then calls for more intense forms of repression or greater levels of unconsciousness. How the orientation to power began is, of course, an interesting question in its own right. Suffice it to say that it seems linked to the rise of a post-tribal urban culture in the context of certain environmental calamities.[6] Yet, whatever the reason for the focus on external power in Western civilization, the picture would not be complete without examining how the culture responds to this endemic source of terror.

The response, I would argue, is not one of increased awareness. Instead, the creation of an underworld of repressed consciousness seems to characterize Western civilization; but just as repressions drive us to act in certain ways and infuse our sense of right and wrong, this cultural unconscious pushes the West to increase its strategy of external control. This emphasis on making the external world the object of domination is not just a phenomenon to be associated with the rise of modern technology. It can be seen in one of the fundamental texts of Roman culture – Virgil's *Aeneid* (Book VI).[7] There, the underworld is mapped out by Virgil to illustrate the repression of internalist tendencies; and, while the rise of Christianity began as a rebellion against this externalist orientation, one could argue that this spiritual tradition could be and ultimately was used to gain a more effective control over the internalist dimension. The ultimate gamble of the West is the one that is based on the possibility of controlling fear without becoming too conscious of it, lest consciousness entail the breakdown and reconstruction of the very foundations of the West. The next two sections of this essay will examine how the spiritual tradition of Christianity attempted to strike a viable balance with the sphere of externality only to succumb to the more radical externalism of the modern West.

4. Medieval Terrors – The Case of Dante's Inferno

The Middle Ages (approximately AD 500 to 1350) were the culmination of the Christian critique of terror, as enunciated by the figure of Jesus. The goal of living without fear was discussed in the famous "Sermon on the Mount," wherein trust in a loving heavenly Father, clearly understood in an internalist sense, was the basis of a fear-free existence. Jesus strongly downplayed externality as a foundation for life, realizing that such an orientation was bound to lead to insecurity. Clearly this philosophy struck a deep-seated chord in the hearts of many; and the chord reverberated freely as long as Christianity, as an organized religion, remained outside the mainstream of power politics. But that separation from power was undermined by the very success of Christianity as an ever-greater portion of society was drawn to its internalist philosophy. The fearlessness of martyrs before the terrors of death in the Coliseum could only strengthen its ultimate appeal.

Yet if power must be directed to external concerns and since society remained structured according to various protocols of power (e.g., aristocratic hierarchy), some kind of compromise had to be worked out with respect to the Christian emphasis on internality. Power, after all, works on the principle of obedience to external authority; and if an internally oriented individual ignores the directives of power, society cannot function in an externalist vein. The history of the necessary compromise is nothing less than the history of the entire medieval period and is obviously beyond the scope of a short discussion. However, Dante's vision of the *Inferno*,[8] as a place of terror within the structure of a "Christian" society, is illustrative of the basic principles.

To begin, the *Inferno* is only a part of Dante's great distillation of medieval thought as worked out in his poetic masterpiece, *The Commedia* – often called *The Divine Comedy* because, like all comedic works, it suggests the possibility of ultimate reconciliation with God. Tragedies, like that of *Oedipus The King*, point to a failure to achieve reconciliation. Oedipus has seen things so horrible that he must blind himself, and one might interpret what he saw as the terror-inspiring depths of alienation from an underlying internalist foundation – the very foundation that Jesus espouses in the form of a loving and trusting relationship with a heavenly Father. Dante also experiences things so horrible that he, as a figure in the poem, swoons before what the *Inferno* has to offer.

The basic theme of the *Commedia* is the experience of disconnection from the internal (in *The Inferno*) before purgation of sin (in *The Purgatorio*) and reconciliation with God in a concluding heavenly vision (in *The Paradiso*). The goal is to map out a way in which alienated individuals could overcome externalist tendencies in such a manner that they could nonetheless function within secular society and reduce the occasions for evil behaviour. In other words, the strategy was to reduce the worst aspects of an externalist orientation without fundamentally challenging the externalist tendencies of a society still wedded to the dynamics of power. If these tendencies were sufficiently muted by a strong internalist position, social actors would be better people because their sinful propensities would be reduced. Thus, society would be characterized by a higher level of morality because the terror associated with disconnection from the internal would be overcome to a significant degree.

Dante's vision of disconnection in the *Inferno* certainly evokes feelings of terror that are normally suppressed because they are so horrific. His goal appears to be to make readers face the terrors of disconnection from God (i.e., an internalist foundation) so that a serious commitment to the tenets of institutionalized Christianity might be encouraged. In the world of Sophocles, Oedipus seems terrified of being the plaything of an external force called "fate," and the question is raised as to whether a lack of internal foundation, based on extremes of self-dependency, places externally oriented individuals in a position where the external realm that they seek to control has horrific power over them. In Dante, the feelings of disconnection are explored as pure pain – a good reason why they are relegated to an underworld, which is an obvious symbol of the unconscious as a field of repression. The terror comes from having to face the pain of stagnation, which is a kind of failure to grow as a human being. In Dante's hell, wretched sinners are doomed to repeat or somehow re-experience their commitment to a purely external form of life as if to imply that growth or true evolution of soul is possible only at an internal level.

In order to come to grips with this incredibly complex text, it is wise to focus on a few elements and relate them to the place of terror in Western civilization. One crucial element is the functioning of hell or what might be called the "psycho-dynamics of fear." Closely related to these psycho-dynamics is the matter of how people fall into that fear in the first place – the fear that causes them to commit those acts that ultimately cause a level of pain, the fearful nature of which is rigorously kept outside the range of conscious awareness.

Although the *Commedia* has a strongly Christian emphasis, the pain of disconnection from the internal has a universal significance in terms of its psycho-dynamics. In this regard Dante's hell is understood as a place of repetitive retribution. That is, what sinners have done to others is now visited upon them and that visitation is effectively without end. To put it another way, the people of hell are stuck, and being stuck is indicative of a failure to grow. The psycho-dynamics of this situation are not difficult to understand, for hell embodies a fear of growth that is written into Dante's very architecture of the *Inferno*. Hell is organized in the form of levels, where these levels are concentric circles that emphasize the repetitive quality of hell. Someone who does not grow simply goes around in circles.

Why the retribution? There is more at play here than the actions of a vindictive "God." Retribution in the *Inferno* suggests a kind of identification with the victim because the victimizer is now experiencing his or her sinful act from the perspective of the victim. What we have here is the pain associated with identification with an "other" – an other whom one has hurt during the course of one's life. Moreover, this identification seems to be inescapable, in the manner of a Greco-Roman fate. The reason for this can be connected to the very nature of the internalist dimension of existence, which we have described as the sphere of continuity, contiguity, oneness, and the like. If we are not rooted in this foundation, we feel fear, but in the absence of such rootedness, we direct our attention to what lies beyond the boundary of the internal, namely the external. In death, however, the external, in the form of physicality, is lost and whatever internalist relationship we have cultivated is all that is left to us. If the only internalist relationship is that in which we have caused pain to other individuals, then that pain must ultimately redound upon us. How can it not? After physical life comes to an end, there is no longer any externality in which to hide from one's disconnection from the internal. Because our souls are, in their basic nature, fundamentally internalistic, they are centres of unity; but if the tenor of personal development of that unity was away from a more foundational level of internality and instead toward the inflicting of pain on others, then the soul is doomed to have nothing else but that pain. Thus, while the erstwhile inflictor of pain does have an inner dimension, that dimension is oriented away from the broader and deeper levels of unified consciousness known as God. The only sphere of consciousness available to this truncated soul is that of the victim whose pain fills the void created by the victimizer having rejected a more divine fulfillment.

Fear is relegated to the underworld of the unconscious as long as we have externalist diversions to distract us. Since the repression is fear-based, what Dante has presented us with is a fear of becoming aware of a hidden level of fear – that being the fear of an upcoming retribution of which the soul has some precognitive understanding. Dante seeks to bring this deeper fear to the surface so that the appropriate steps can be taken while a person's individualized consciousness has the opportunity to deepen its connection to an internalist foundation. Christianity clearly takes internality seriously.

The second element in this fear complex is the motivation to commit the hurtful act in the first place. There is an aspect of repressed terror in facing up to the consequences of the sinful act in the context of an impending loss of externality and a confrontation with an inescapable internality. The internalist remnant is nothing less than a soul that had a tenuous relationship with a much greater internalist foundation known as God from a Christian perspective. Here we have the scene for a significant moral choice – the choice between good and evil. To choose good is the way of salvation and a viable relationship with the internalist foundation. To choose evil is the way of sin and a rejection of that internalist foundation in favour of a more externalist security. To choose the former is to overcome one's fear of the threats of the external world. To choose the latter is to succumb to that fear by seeing it as so terrifying that the only response can be a counter-terror. For evil here may be understood as a counter-terror based on a fear of the external world in all its potential horror, its overwhelming capacity to inflict pain and suffering in a manner that Hobbes outlines in his *Leviathan*.[9] Any fear of retribution is countered by repression or banishing to the underworld of the unconscious the sense of empathy for one's victim. The other and more modern strategy is to rely on the principles of an externalist science that denies the very existence of any kind of internalist dimension. Thus, when the physical life of a sinner comes to an end, there can be no fearful identification of one soul (one's personal internality) with the suffering of that soul's victim or victims.

Dante's work in the *Inferno* is a rich anatomization of the phenomenon of sin, and examining human fear of the external world (based on a failure to choose the way of internality) can enhance our understanding of this way of living and hurting. In general there are three types of sin: sins of incontinence, of wrath, and of deceit, and these are well symbolized by the three beasts that the poet encounters (Canto I) before his journey into hell. It is they who block the way to God or internality, and it is only by facing up to the pain that they cause the sinner when externalist distractions are put in abeyance that an individual may be empowered to make the choice of seeking to develop his or her relationship with a much greater internalist foundation.

The first beast to block the way to Christian salvation is the Leopard of deceit. The gaudy pelt represents all the distractions that can lead us into error, but at a deeper level the deceit can be understood as the network of lies and falsehoods that take us to a position where we are no longer in touch with reality. In our more scientifically based society, we normally call such out-of-touchness "insanity" and ascribe to some electro-chemical dysfunction of the brain the cause. That, originally, was the position of M. Scott Peck, until he could no longer hold to this secularist interpretation and took up the more religious idea of evil to explain certain abnormal behaviours.[10] From the point of view of this discussion, however, Peck's view of evil is of particular interest since he associates it with lying in some morally culpable sense. One lies to gain advantage over others, but lying here also reflects a dissociation from the real, especially if the liar has chosen that dissociation. Now for the liar to be effective, the dissociation cannot be from the external world since that is where the fraud must take place if it is to have any effect on a set of victims. The only place where the dissociation can be occurring, then, is with respect to the internal world – the place of oneness, continuity, etc.; and the only reason the lying stance has been adopted is because a lack of trust in that internal dimension as well as a certain level of fear in the external both come together in the form of an immoral choice.

The other two beasts follow directly from the first: the Lion of wrath and the She-Wolf of incontinence (or avaricious craving). The first represents violence in at least two senses. There is the violence done to oneself by way of the dissociation from the internal, and then there is the violence done to those who are the victims of the sinner's lies. Should the lie be discovered, the sinner must resort to brute force, the most obvious manifestation of violence, in order to maintain the fear-based dissociation from the internal. Since violence begets a counter-violence, the sinner must fall into a fear of those who have been wronged and increase his or her level of violence. And so begins a never-ending cycle that is the tragic way of the world. The second beast (i.e., of incontinence) is perpetually hungry and reminds one of the addict who can never be fulfilled by what is used to temporarily fill the void. Again, this situation follows from the primary dissociation from the internal foundation because it is natural to seek substitutes for what has been lost. If what has been lost is the internal, then one will turn to the external to fill the emptiness. However, since the external can never give what the internal represents, it can only function as an addictive substitute. In other words, like the She-Wolf, we can only aspire to devour the external, but (as is the case with this beast) we remain gaunt and starved since the external can never give us what the internal can, that is, a grounded security founded on being part of a greater whole. Such an immoderate relationship to the external causes a fear-based conflict not only with other addicts but also with those who are deprived of a more moderate share of what the external world has to offer. Moreover, those possessed by the She-Wolf must be seized by a more intrinsic fear – namely, that of their own void-like emptiness, of which they are mercilessly reminded whenever their savage hunger possesses them and which they can only deny by sinking to a lesser level of consciousness. The life of the addict is in that sense one of repetition, and, of course, repetition characterizes the stagnation of hell.

At the very bottom of hell (Canto XXXIV), the great traitors exist in eternal torment. They are the betrayers of secular and spiritual unity. Brutus and Cassius, who betrayed Caesar as the symbol of secular unity, are being savagely chewed in the mouth of Satan, who sought to betray God. Also in Satan's mouth is Judas, the betrayer of Christ. Satan, himself, is frozen into the immobility of an ice-pack, which he ironically generates by the futile beating of his wings. Betrayal of the possibilities for unity suggests betrayal of the internalist aspect of existence as well as of our own souls, which are internalist in their very nature. Dante thus ends his tour of the *Inferno* with a sense of the stakes involved in making the dissociative choice that rejects the internal. Whatever fear might have prompted us to cleave to the external, that fear is nothing compared to the levels of fear that ensue from making such a misconceived choice. By showing the reader the deplorable results of that choice and by indicating how our world could have enjoyed a fear-reducing unity if fear-based treachery were not the way of the world, Dante opens the way toward embracing traditional Catholic strategies for establishing viable relationships with the internalist foundation known as God. Yet that path was not taken. The vast sphere of internality that was opened by Christianity succumbed to a new externalist strategy – a very "reasonable" one indeed.

5. Contemporary Terror: The Case of Kafka

Kafka's name is perhaps synonymous with a sinister and subtle terror that is as all-pervasive as it is hidden. The text to be analyzed here is *The Trial*[11] because it embodies with great clarity the terror that infuses everyday life. Like most of Kafka's work, there is an atmosphere of nameless dread that pervades the seemingly banal world of bureaucratic futility. In the story a bank employee, by the name of Joseph K., is informed that he has been placed under arrest by a mysterious court. Court officials appear at his rooming house but can give him no indication of the nature of the charges brought against him, and the protagonist spends the rest of the story seeking to understand the nature of these charges and to prepare some kind of defence. The climax occurs in a cathedral (Chapter 9), to which Joseph K. was summoned on the pretext of meeting a client of the bank and showing him around. Instead, he meets the prison chaplain – an individual attached to the court and sent to warn Joseph K. that his case is going badly. In the course of their discussion, the chaplain seeks to disabuse the protagonist of the idea that he (i.e., the chaplain) can be trusted, and he attempts to explain this situation by way of a short parable called "The Man Before The Law." The parable appears in the "writings which preface the

. Law"; and as the parable is told to Joseph K. and explained, Kafka may be articulating the principles of the society that seems to generate a sense of terror.

In the parable, a man from the country comes seeking the "Law," which in itself is a kind of complex symbol of order, justice, meaning, rectitude, etc. However, at the entrance-way to the law stands a doorkeeper who says he cannot admit the man just yet. Years pass with the man making endless importunities and the doorkeeper refusing to admit the man, although, as with Joseph K., there is never a clear reason given as to what the rationale might be for this situation. Indeed, the idea of systemic complexity is introduced as a key theme. As the man finally reaches the end of his life, he asks the doorkeeper why no one else ever sought admittance to the law; and the doorkeeper bends down to the dying man and says that the door was meant only for him and that now he is going to shut it. Joseph K. and the chaplain discuss the implications of the parable; and as they do, Kafka appears to be constructing a complex metaphor for the functioning of Western civilization during our time.

From the perspective of terror, the man seems to fear the doorkeeper and disempowers himself with respect to what is only a functionary of a complex system – and the lowest of functionaries at that since the doorkeeper claims that beyond the door are other doorkeepers who are so terrifying that he (the doorkeeper) can hardly stand to look at them. While it is not clear whether the primary doorkeeper has ever really seen these other more terrifying doorkeepers, it seems that these doorkeepers are part of a complex system that mediates the ultimate principle of the "Law" with respect to those who would seek it. The doorkeepers are somehow empowered to the extent that they are part of the system, although they might not themselves understand what it is that they are a part of. The man before the law does not appear to be terrified of the doorkeeper, but the reader of the story might well be shaken by the stance of vulnerability that the man has adopted. In short, the man, who is a kind of "everyman" in the context of contemporary Western civilization, has rendered himself superfluous with respect to the priorities of a complex system, which is nothing less than the principles of civilization that are meant to sustain his life. Kafka is thus bringing us face to face with the horrifying contradictions of modern society – a society that negates the very individuals it is meant to sustain because of the sheer complexity of its system-based protocols. At the core of the culture is some principle, a "Law" which is meant to contain us and thus define a sphere of internality. Yet because life has become so complex as modern society has had to organize and co-ordinate the lives of multitudes, we are effectively excluded by a variety of rules, regulations, etc., which are the doorkeepers. This may or may not be an exclusion from internality defined as God, for the Law may be any kind of all-encompassing space, but the results of the exclusion are all the more horrifying for being based on some inescapable complexity.

What is more terrifying than a mysterious fate inscribed in the moral order of the universe? It is a fate that we have created for ourselves in order to escape such mysteries. Here I am referring to the techno-system that arose in the wake of the scientific revolution and the ensuing bureaucratization of modern society. Life must be subject to rational organization if we are to put the powers of mass production at our service; and if that means, as Jacques Ellul suggested in *The Technological System*,[12] organizing mass consumption via advertising, then that becomes the key in which the theme of modernity must be played. We created this system to serve us, but like the man before the Law we end up being subservient to its protocols. We gain power, if at all, by becoming part of the system and functioning as doorkeepers to those who seek some deeper purpose or meaning that the system was originally intended to embody. Moreover, this situation entails a crucial choice – not that between good and evil as defined by Dante's Christian vision, but between becoming part of an externalist mechanism that oppresses others and being outside some common sphere of meaning because one has chosen not to serve the system. It is the latter position that is terrifying and indeed epitomizes the terror endemic in contemporary Western civilization.

Not only are we totally vulnerable to the utter indifference of the system with respect to the aspirations of the individual, but we are banished to a realm of pure externality in two senses. On the one hand, we are outside that for which the system is supposed to exist – i.e., the Law or the rationale for the current social order. On the other hand, having accepted the legitimacy of the system (as the man before the Law blindly accepts the legitimacy of the doorkeeper and accords him an unjustified degree of power), we also accept the externality that animates the system. That is, the system, by virtue of its instrumental rationality, has to deny internalist realities such as individual feeling, spirituality, and ultimately morality itself. In short, the individual is left in a state of extreme dissociation from the internal because the external is the sole source of legitimacy. With no internalist foundation and no clear grasp of that lack, a sense of nameless and hidden terror infuses the lives of all those who have not become appendages (i.e., doorkeepers) of the system. It is the terror of absolute rootlessness, where one is even alienated from an understanding of the internalist foundation that would offer some security. Such is the culture we have created for ourselves – a culture the worst implications of which are illustrated in such dystopic films as the recent "Matrix" trilogy, where individuals have been unknowingly reduced to being parts of a computer network that totally controls them.

Another name for this systemic structure is "military-industrial complex," to which we may add other key elements such as "communication," "education," and "entertainment." In his farewell address, President Eisenhower warned Americans (and perhaps the world) of the danger of this new Leviathan. How ironic that he used the term "complex," given its linkage to Oedipal repressions of consciousness in Freud. For the military-industrial complex also involves the repression of consciousness – namely, consciousness of the internal realm, which is perhaps the essence of consciousness itself. In other words, to give the Freudian unconscious a twist, we have lost touch with our own consciousness and, in addition to repressing forbidden urges, we have also repressed our capacity to link up with any kind of internalist foundation at all and, in consequence, have had to repress the terror associated with that dissociation. No wonder Kafka's sense of nameless dread is the hallmark of contemporary Western civilization.

It not surprising that the events of September 11, 2001, inspire such terror. The twin towers reaching toward heaven are a metaphor of the system. Their destruction was a direct and undeniable challenge to the system. Reminiscent of the tower of Babel, the need to deal with the internal creates confusion and opens up diverse ways of coming to terms with one's humanity. While horrifying, sadly it is not the 2,500 lives lost that generates fear, because regularly many more lives are lost in equally if not in more grotesque and meaningless ways. Consider Rwanda. Yet human civilization looks the other way. Rather, with 9/11 the foundations of the architectural structure of the system have been challenged, raising a question that forces us to look inward: Why do they hate us so much? This type of self-engagement is terrifying.

6. Conclusion – Awakening from the Nightmare

What can be concluded from this brief sketch? Western civilization has gone through at least three stages of endemic terror as articulated by some of its most foundational texts. Dante, with his Christian emphasis, was in a position to face the internal dimension, which was repressed by the dynamics of external political power in the Ancient World and by the dynamics of external techno-systemic power in the Modern West. Dante may thus be considered the internal medieval filling of a sandwich, bounded on one side by a Sophoclean "slice" and on the other by Kafka's cutting vision of human superfluity with respect to the system. Christianity was the West's lost opportunity to deal with the roots of fear, but given the involvement of the Catholic Church with the dynamics of power, it fell into the Oedipal trap of seeking the self-dependency that ultimately alienates one from the internal. The incestuous relationship of the Catholic hierarchy was less with Mary than with itself, as Holy "Mother" Church, and the murdered "Father" was often nothing less than Christ or God, since the spirit of loving compassion associated with Jesus' message was more often betrayed than honoured. What is worse, endless attempts at reform both within and outside the Church ultimately foundered on the reefs of power politics. The breakthroughs associated with scientific rationality pushed the civilization in the direction of an even more intense externality. Political power, with its externalist orientation, was supplemented by technological power, where the latter, unlike the former, was in a position not only to deny internality in a philosophical sense, but also to eliminate it in some absolute manner by turning human beings into "soul-less" servants of the military-industrial-communications-education-entertainment complex.

Can we be de-souled? De-souling is a kind of perverted cultural strategy that seeks to deal with the unconscious terror attendant upon dissociation from the internal by destroying or undermining our very capacity to relate to the internal. It is a foolish strategy because that capacity is nothing less than our humanity, which is our ability to act and react to each other in loving and compassionate ways. But to move in a more internalist direction it is necessary to face our fear, to make the journey to hell. The solutions might not be exclusively Christian, but they do need to take into account the reality of an internal dimension and somehow define a viable relation between that dimension and its external complement.

Unfortunately, too many focus on external terrors rather than the internal ones. The two most prominent sources of external terror in the present day are, of course, political terrorism as epitomized by the events of 9/11 and impending ecological catastrophe as epitomized by global warming (not to mention the ever-approaching exhaustion of our fossil fuel reserves). As I have been suggesting, these external threats may be linked to the West's cultural disconnection from the internal. If the West could establish an authentic and viable relationship in this sphere, the need to dominate other civilizations as well as the natural environment might be attenuated and the external threats associated therewith accordingly reduced.

One promising possibility of the West overcoming its strongly externalist bias can be seen in the much-quoted work of Fritjof Capra, *The Tao of Physics: An Exploration of the Parallels between Modern Physics and Eastern Mysticism*.[13] Here the strongly dichotomous aspect of Western civilization is traced back to ancient Greece; and while that dichotomy is not directly correlated with the internal–external split that is central to this argument, Capra does contrast Western attitudes to nature to certain non-Western ones (i.e., India and China). Because the latter approaches are, to use our terms, not purely external, a crucial source of alienation and fear is mitigated. While domination of nature is present in all cultures to some extent, there is a big difference if that which is to be dominated is taken to be totally alien or other, as appears to be the case in the West. The good news is that as the post-classical physics of quantum mechanics advances, the Western emphasis on the otherness of nature becomes (according to Capra) ever more untenable. The bad news is that the insights of contemporary physics have yet to make serious inroads in the large number who are either scientifically illiterate or still enmeshed in mechanistic modes of thinking rooted in the eighteenth and nineteenth centuries.

No doubt we have a long way to go, and many fears have to be faced – not the least of which is that of our civilization having taken a wrong turn and falling into a state of what might be termed "compromised consciousness." As many have already surmised, we are asleep; and if reason cannot expand to be more open to the internalist dimension, it will be plagued with nightmares. Goya's famous etching of a sleeping "*philosophe*" having a nightmare of monstrous owls (perverted wisdom?) sums up the situation all too well. His famous caption reads: "The sleep of reason produces monsters." Let not the terror from without blind us to the terror from within.

Notes

1   On this point, see M. Foucault, *Discipline and Punish: The Birth of the Prison*, trans. Alan Sheridan (New York: Vintage, 1979), 3–31.

2   *The Gospel according to Matthew: The Holy Bible Revised Standard Version* (New York: Collins, 1973), chaps. 5–7.

3   Obviously the figure of Jesus elaborated on the disconnection theme in so powerful a manner that the trajectory of Western civilization was significantly altered. But not all texts pertaining to the subject of terror raise the issue to such a high level of consciousness. Indeed, I suspect that a more typical response to the problem of endemic terror entails a diminution of awareness, if not a fall into or creation of a realm of unconsciousness. If one is not aware of the existence of the disconnection or somehow denies its power, then the terror can itself be denied with respect to its place at the heart of the civilization supposedly designed to vanquish fears. What is worse – perhaps terrifying – is a response to terror of such limited consciousness that one becomes a terrorist, that is, an individual or group dedicated to terrorizing others so that one can engineer an ultimately ineffective escape from terrors so great that they are not allowed to approach the boundaries of consciousness. What I am suggesting is that the more familiar form of terrorism, the one associated with an assault from external enemies, might be based on a psychological strategy of drowning out one's own fears by generating greater fears in some set of victims. The "cause" motivating the terrorists is ultimately irrelevant; and one suspects that if all enemies were "terrorized" out of existence, new ones would have to be found so that the terrorist could continue to find temporary relief in the screams of new victims.

4   Sophocles, *Three Theban Plays: Antigone, Oedipus The King, Oedipus At Colonus*, trans. Theodore Howard Banks (New York: Oxford University Press, 1956).

5   See Daniel C. Dennett, *Consciousness Explained* (Boston: Little, Brown, 1991), 454–55.

6   See Steve Taylor, *The Fall: The Evidence for a Golden Age, 6,000 years of insanity, and the dawning of a new era* (Winchester, UK: O Books, 2005), 50–68.

7   Virgil, *The Aeneid*, trans. C. Day Lewis (New York: Doubleday Anchor, 1952).

8   Dante Alighieri, *The Divine Comedy*, trans. John Ciardi (New York: New American Library, 2003).

9   T. Hobbes, *The Leviathan Or The Matter, Forme And Power Of A Commonwealth Ecclesiastical And Civil*, ed. Michael Oakeshott (New York: Collier, 1962), chap. 13.

10   See M. Scott Peck, *People of the Lie: The Hope for Healing Human Evil* (New York: Touchstone, 1983), chap. 2.

11   Franz Kafka, *The Trial*, trans. by Willa and Edwin Muir (New York: Schocken, 1968).

12   Jacques Ellul, *The Technological System*, trans. Joachim Neugroschel (New York: Continuum, 1980), 310–25.

13   Fritjof Capra, *The Tao of Physics: An Exploration of the Parallels between Modern Physics and Eastern Mysticism* (Boston: Shamabala, 2000), 21–24.

Conclusion: "The Global War on Terror" Overdetermined as a Clash of Civilizations

KARIM-ALY KASSAM
Cornell University

1. TERROR AS TACTICAL AND METAPHORICAL POWER

An important feature of this collection of essays is that in order to understand terror one must recognize the tactical qualities as well as metaphorical power of the label "terrorist." The objective of this collection has been to engender discourse by bringing together diverse and informed perspectives on the notion of terror. Contributors have shed light on various groups who have used terror, their motivations, and how terror has been perceived. Some of the findings from this collection indicate that not only do marginalized groups utilize terror as a tactic to draw attention to their grievances but state elites also use terror to achieve their own aims. State and non-state actors benefit from acts of terror as governments seek to promote their own agendas and private companies capitalize on economic benefits. In essence, terrorism generates political as well as economic currency. As the downing of Air India has shown, in many, if not all, instances, lip-service is given to the victims of terror and their families.

The rhetoric of "the global war on terror" shows that terrorism is not only a tactical measure to express grievances but an idea pregnant with metaphorical power to express moral judgment. Pack journalism has resulted in reporting that favours spectacle and is vacant of critical analysis. "The global war on

241

terror" is really a war for public opinion. The heroic "Self" is engaged in a struggle, a *jihad* if you will, against the barbaric "Other." Often, the barbaric "Other" is determined to be Muslim. Due to the populist nature of "the global war on terror," there are clear dangers to Muslim minorities in Canada and other Western countries. For instance a Pew survey of attitudes conducted in 2005 illustrates that when members of western countries were asked "which religion is most violent," the majority of the respondents identified Islam.[1] Yet hardly any of the respondents had basic knowledge of the tenets of Islam or historical information on Muslim societies. Their views were formed primarily by media images.

2. OVERDETERMINATION OF A CLASH

"The global war on terror" is overdetermined[2] as a clash of civilizations. The causal argument arises from the work of Samuel Huntington's *Clash of Civilizations and the Remaking of the World Order* and has gained pre-eminence in policy circles as a justification for "the global war on terror."[3] The collapse of the Soviet Union has given way to another superstructure, which is being represented by a self-fulfilling clash of civilizations. Civilizations are the new paradigm, it is argued, by which to understand global conflict and cohesion. This perspective establishes a taxonomy of civilizations with the "democratic" Euro-American West at the top and the "assertive" Sinic (Chinese) and "bloody" Islamic near the bottom. On the basis of this simplistic construct, the clash of civilizations hypothesis explains the nature of future conflicts. The objective of the clash of civilizations argument is to provide institutional structures with the ideological basis from which to control, marginalize, and disempower the Muslim "Other." The "Other" is imagined to be what the "Self" is not. A key proposition of this argument is that another Cold War, this time with Muslims, will serve to strengthen Euro-American identity. Such a view presents civilizations as culturally monolithic, rather than diverse, and static, rather than dynamic historical processes.

This overdetermined explanation of conflict attempts to predict the behaviour of civilizations. The clash of civilizations perspective concludes that

"Muslims have problems living peaceably with their neighbours.... The evidence is overwhelming."[4] Racism and prejudice are similarly overdetermined explanations. For example, characterization of African-Americans as strong but not intelligent is widely held in American sports media and has its roots in the justification of slavery.[5] Early depiction of First Nations as savage and heathen was used to rationalize acquisition of their lands and perpetrate cultural genocide.[6] Similarly, portrayal of the Irish as dirty and violent facilitated the occupation of Northern Ireland.[7] The *Clash of Civilizations* is imbued with the type of determinism one finds in books like *The Bell Curve*.[8] Unlike *The Bell Curve*, which engages in biological determinism predicting behaviour through intelligence capacities of races, *The Clash of Civilizations* applies this type of thinking on the religious front. This desire to rank groups by some intrinsic worth is not new and goes back to ancient Greece. More recently, it has been used to justify the mass extermination of Jews and gypsies in the Second World War and the brutal killings of Tutsis and moderate Hutus in Rwanda. Entire social structures are developed to sustain these cultural assumptions; apartheid in South Africa, segregation in the United States, residential schools for Native children in Canada, and now "the global war on terror" internationalizes prejudice against Muslims. The clash of civilizations hypothesis is an illustration of causal overdetermination.

The squinted view of history promoted by the clash of civilizations is not a trivial accident. Effectively, the language of "the global war on terror" promotes the indispensability of a power elite in protecting the public. The continuous and constant threat of terror promoted by state and media actors controls public discourse and makes "the global war on terror" perpetual and self-justifying. A monopoly of "experts," reinforcing similar points of view, leaves little room for alternate perspectives and limits examination of the motivations behind terror. Shallow analysis citing religion, at the expense of socio-economic concerns, has become the primary explanation. The state benefits from these perceived threats. The danger of an imminent attack justifies the existence of military bases around the world and ever-increasing weaponization. It keeps military budgets fat and plump and subsidizes a corporate industrial base, albeit, inefficiently. A new McCarthy-style "pinko" or "red" has to be found to counter the subversion of Western civilization. It is as if the myopic interpretation of Islam held by al-Qaida and the promoters of a clash of civilizations perspective are "objective allies." Each gives the "Other" a reason for existence. In a baptism of superficiality and spectacle, the Euro-American "Self" purifies himself using the Muslim "Other."

The Danish cartoons are literally an illustration of overdetermination of the Muslim as terrorist. Yet this collection of essays indicates that terror emerges from multiple causes producing the same effect, fear. Religion has not played a significant role. For example, the suicide bomb, a tactic initially utilized by the Tamil Tigers (who were Hindu), is conveniently associated with "extremist" Islam. The circumstances that led to this action are not interrogated in the context of the socio-cultural milieu that produced the bomber. Media treatment of suicide bombers has aided the perception of this action as bizarre and incomprehensible. It is as if the terrorist behaves unfairly when dealing with the presence of occupational forces that have the might of the air force, tanks, and the latest weaponry. For their part, the suicide bombers have appropriated this image of the barbarian and have given it meaning by instrumentalizing their bodies against the technologies of domination. They have been effective in being noticed and recognized, albeit not heard through the onslaught of media representations. The fantasies of savagery projected onto Muslims have been appropriated, literalized, and enacted by the suicide bombers reproducing the savagery they encounter at the hands of the state. Unlike the detached weaponry of an air strike, land mines, or cluster bombs, the suicide bomber requires deep personal involvement, a process that is both psychologically and physically painful. It forces the acknowledgment of one's existence in this world, obliging the purified "Self" to recognize the "Other." In this sense, the act of terror taps into a new domain of meaning where the symbolic and material weapon are not just important but a social symptom that must be understood in a historical perspective.

3. Fragmentation as Identity

According to the premise of a clash, civilizational identities will be the basis from which cohesion, disintegration, and conflict will take place. As a result of the end of the Cold War, people are asking: "who are we?"[9] "We know who we are only when we know who we are not and often only when we know whom we are against."[10] In other words, "people define their identity by what they are not."[11] The clash of civilizations hypothesis maintains that at a time of crisis "people rally to those of similar ancestry, religion, language, values, and institutions."[12] It is not possible to have a clash of civilizations between Muslims and the essentially Christian West because they draw their roots from the same Abrahamic tradition; they are part of the same family of civilizations of the Mediterranean and near East. Their fundamental values, such as belief in the Creator, the presence of divine guidance to humanity, rational questioning of worn traditions, emphasis on just behaviour, and concern for the needy, are largely shared. Perhaps these disputes seem so emotional because they involve members of the same historical family. The very fact that Muslims refer to Jews and Christians as "people of the book" speaks to this common heritage.[13] Despite media representations of Muslims as terrorists, the Pew Global Attitudes Project indicated that, in countries like Great Britain, France, Canada, and the United States, where there is a significant presence of a multicultural civil society, respondents viewed Muslim populations in their midst favourably.[14]

Canada has had its own experience with terror during the FLQ crisis. As a response, it developed legitimate democratic means for such groups to express their concerns. The grievances between the largely Catholic Quebec and an overwhelmingly Protestant Canada were not framed on religious grounds. Since October 1970, civil society in Quebec has repeatedly used institutional means to effect change without recourse to the violence associated with the FLQ. This historical and policy trajectory has enabled Canada to retain a political distance from the United States in its global war on terror.

The clash of civilizations explanation produces a problem of group think, where the terrorist "Other" is separate from the superior "Self." In the twenty-first century, this position is not tenable because the grievances that the terrorist are responding to are not external to the West but intimately connected in an ever-shrinking world with massive movements of populations. Much like the literal sclerosis I noted (in Chapter 6) with respect to some Salafist religious scholars, the clash of civilizations engages in a similar myopia where terror is seen on religious grounds rather than within the context of human rights,

poverty reduction, economic development, ecological crisis, and access to resources. "The global war on terror" is itself inappropriately framed because it
ignores all these factors.

The clash of civilizations is instrumental inasmuch as it facilitates polarization and justification of a growing military-industrial complex. This perspective generates paranoia and hostility: paranoia, because it arouses fear and
suspicion through the "us against them" mentality; and hostility, because these
feelings of insecurity manifest themselves in expressions of anger. In this sense
the terror within, as explained by one of the contributors, becomes the impetus
for the manifestation of the terror without. It makes statements like "you are
either with us or against us" possible in international discourse.[15]

4. PLURALISTIC CO-EXISTENCE AS IDENTITY

Canadians do not define themselves according to who they are not. Canadian
domestic policy of multiculturalism[16] and Canadian foreign policy[17] indicate
that Canada welcomes civilizational pluralism and cultural diversity. In 1955,
over forty years before Samuel Huntington articulated his clash of civilizations
hypothesis, Lester B. Pearson had the foresight and described the potential
of civilizations replacing nation states as the main actors in the international
system. Recognizing that the renaissance in the cultures of Muslim, Indian,
and Sinic civilizations will bring the possibility of conflict, he welcomed the
diversity, vitality, and vision of these cultures. Instead of Huntington's clash,
Pearson saw the opportunity for peaceful co-existence and mutual enrichment
of civilizations.[18] He explained: "We are now emerging into an age when different civilizations will have to learn to live side by side in peaceful interchange,
learning from each other, studying each other's history and ideas and art and
culture, mutually enriching each other's lives. The alternative, in this over-
crowded little world, is misunderstanding, tension, clash, and catastrophe."[19]

The Canadian articulation of civilizational diversity is one of hope rather
than fear, welcoming rather than suspicion, mutual co-existence rather than
clash. As this collection of essays illustrates, the response to the grievances of
Quebeckers, the decision by two leading Calgary papers not to republish the

Danish cartoons, the presence of Canadian peacekeepers in Rwanda, all stem from a vision of hope rather than fear. Fear in societies, driven by a besieged mentality, results in paralysis and debilitating anxiety. Defining identities of pluralistic societies on the basis of the negative, what we are not, leads to fragmentation of societies. It weakens their social fabric rather than reinforcing cultural identities. At the dawn of the twenty-first century, the World Bank undertook a study entitled "Voices of the Poor." All the reports that emerged from this study indicated that insecurity led to social fragmentation.[20] Despite the diversity of 60,000 participants from fifty countries, men and women consistently pointed to peace and good relations between communities as the basis of well-being.[21] The case of Rwanda is compelling because it confirms that social fraying, fragmentation of the "Self" fuelled by fear and hostility led to mass murder. Fear, insecurity, and worry lead to a deep sense of powerlessness, frustration, and anger. The clash of civilizations hypothesis is self-fulfilling because, once accepted, it breeds fear, anger, and hostility. Evidence from the marginalized indicates that people yearn for relationships, a complex connectivity with their surroundings. While accepting diversity, they prefer peaceful co-existence, which acknowledges interconnectedness between different societies.

This collection of essays interrogates "the global war on terror" from a distinctly Canadian perspective. Collectively, the essays question the fear of the imminent terrorist attack and reject the acceptance of the facile conclusion that "you are either with us or against us." These essays articulate diverse perspectives in order to transcend trite characterizations of the "Self" and the "Other." It is not possible to make a conclusive statement on terror because the contexts are so diverse. Understanding terror requires questioning that is intellectually and personally challenging. The best outcome resulting from interrogation of terror is discussion. While not conclusive, this collection reveals certain important insights. Acts of terror are undertaken to express grievances. Both state and non-state actors use terror to advance their strategic interests. Concern for victims and their families has been slow and limited. Terror is both a military tactic and a powerful metaphor. As with the electron, which is both wave and particle, understanding terror requires sophisticated consideration and does not lend itself to trite conclusions. This dual characteristic of terror lends itself to moral judgment. This judgment is presently manifested in "the global war on terror" and has hijacked more pressing issues such as climate change and survival of entire ecosystems. The discussion of a clash of civilizations is empty of meaning when the very prospect of biodiversity of life is in question. The metaphor of terror utilizes the Muslim "Other" as a foil for the Euro-American "Self." In order to understand terror without, a searching self-examination is required. The fear within is linked to the terror without. Canadians are Aboriginal, Euro-American, Asian, African, etc. – in short, Canada is a pluralistic society. It is not possible to make simplistic conclusions about the "Other" without implicating the "Self."

Notes

1 The Pew Global Attitudes Project, "17-Nations Pew Global Attitudes Survey," (2005). http://pewglobal.org/reports/pdf/247.pdf (accessed June 14, 2007).

2 The notion of "over-determination" was first presented by Sigmund Freud in psychoanalysis of dream content. See Sigmund Freud, *The Interpretation of Dreams*, 1911. http://www.psychwww.com/books/interp/toc.htm (accessed June 27, 2007).

3 Samuel Huntington, *The Clash of Civilizations and the Remaking of World Order* (New York: Simon & Schuster, 1996).

4 Ibid., 212.

5 Richard C. King and Charles Springwood Fruehling, "Body and Soul: Physicality, Disciplinarity, and the Overdertmination of Blackness." In *Channelling Blackness: Studies on Television and Race in America*, ed. D.M. Hunt (New York: Oxford University Press, 2005).

6 Marie Garroute, *Real Indians: Identity and the Survival of Native America* (Berkeley: University of California Press, 2003); Ronald Wright, *Stolen Continents: The "New world" through Indian Eyes* (Toronto: Penguin, 1993).

7 Begona Aretxaga, "Dirty Protest: Symbolic Overdetermination and Gender in Northern Ireland Ethnic Violence," *Ethos* 23, no. 2 (1995): 123–48.

8 Richard Herrnstein and Charles Murray, *The Bell Curve* (New York: Simon & Schuster, 1994).

9 Huntington, *The Clash of Civilizations* 1996, 21.

10 Ibid.

11 Ibid., 67.

12 Ibid., 126.

13 Karen Armstrong, *A History of God: The 4000-Year Quest of Judaism, Christianity and Islam* (New York: Alfred Knopf, 1993); Bruce Feiler, *Abraham: A Journey to the Heart of Three Faiths* (New York: HarperCollins, 2002).

14 Pew Global Attitudes Project.

15 Huntington, *The Clash of Civilizations,*, 125–30.

16 Janice Gross Stein et al., *Uneasy Partner: Multiculturalism and Rights in Canada* (Waterloo: Wilfrid Laurier University Press, 2007).

17 Lester B. Pearson, *Democracy in World Politic* (Toronto: S. J. Reginald Saunders, 1955). It is noteworthy that at the time of publication of his book, Pearson was the Canadian Secretary of State for External Affairs and two years later received the Nobel Peace Prize as Canada's prime minister.

18 Michael Keren, "A Canadian Alternative to the 'Clash of Civilizations,'" *International Journal of Canadian Studies* 37 (2008): 41–56. I am indebted to Dr. Keren, who first directed me to Pearson in our discussions.

19 Pearson, 1955, 83–84.

20 Deepa Narayan et al., *Can Anyone Hear Us?* (Washington: World Bank Poverty Group, 1999). http://www.worldbank.org/prem/poverty/voices/reports/canany/vol1.pdf (accessed June 14, 2007).

21 World Bank, *Crying Out for Change* (Oxford: Oxford University Press, 2000). http://www.worldbank.org/prem/poverty/voices/reports/crying/cry.pdf (accessed June 14, 2007).

INDEX

coined to describe Holocaust, 201
    prevention, 202
Genocide Convention. *See Convention on*
    the Prevention and Punishment of
    the Crime of Genocide
Gerard Group International LLC, 172
Gerges, Fawaz, 68
Gikondo Parish Church, 206–7
    instance of Rwandan genocide, 208
Glasberg, Ronald, xiii, 2, 10
Gleick, Peter, 177
global climate change. *See* climate change
"global war on terror." *See* "war on terror"
global warming. *See under* climate change
Globe and Mail, 52, 59, 89, 136
Gore, Al, 169, 183
    An Inconvenient Truth, 168
Gouzenko spy scandal, 49
    arrests and convictions, 39
    government control of story, 40
    'made in Canada' look, 38
    political policing, 41
    Soviet role downplayed, 40–41
Goya, Francisco, 238
    The Disasters of War, 16
greed (ally of genocide), 209–10, 212. *See*
    also incontinence
greenhouse gas theory, 168. *See also* climate
    change
Guantanamo, 57
Guardians of the Islamic Revolution, 73, 79
guerrilla revolutionaries, 23–24, 27
    Marxist ideology, 19
guerrilla war, 19
    decolonization model, 17–18, 21
    lacking strategy for final victory, 16
    Mao Tse-tung's success, 16–17
    moral questions, 15
    Napoleonic wars, 16
    sponsoring of, 13
    success only in a specific environment,
        15, 22
    terrorism as category of, 4, 13, 15–23
    urban (*See* urban guerrilla warfare)
Guevara, Ernesto ("Che"), 23

H

habeas corpus, 39, 44
Haberman, Jürgen, *The Structural*
    Transformation of the Public
    Sphere, 108
Habyarimana, Juvénal, 201, 203
Hague, 202
Halpern, Nelson, 134
Hamas, 30, 112, 114
Harper, Stephen, 49, 60
Harper Conservative government, 59
    Abousfian Andulrakik case, 58
    increased military presence in
        Afghanistan, 48
    Omar Khadr case, 57–58
Harper's magazine, 140, 144
Harris, Arthur, 14
Henighan, Stephen, 102–3
Herman, Edward, 107
Hersh, Seymour, 77
hijacking, 24, 29, 34, 68, 74, 81, 109, 167, 248.
    see also aerial mass murder
Hinchman, Sandra, 179
Hiroshima, 14
Ho Chi Minh, 17
Hobbes, Thomas, *Leviathan*, 229
Holocaust, 202
Homeland Security, Department of, 60
Homeland Security Act, 174
House Committee on Un-American
    Activities, 41
Huffman, Richard, 26
Huntington, Samuel, *Clash of Civilizations*,
    242
Hussein, Saddam, 69, 182
hypocrisy (ally of genocide), 209, 211–12

I

IEDs. *See* improvised explosive devices
    (I.E.D.s)
Ignatieff, Michael, 111, 118
    belief in "war of civilizations," 111
    The Lesser Evil, 110
Immigration and Refugee Protection Act, 55

improvised explosive devices (I.E.D.s), 68, 70, 73, 80, 82

In Retrospect (McNamara), 18–19

incontinence, 230–31. *See also* greed (ally of genocide)

An Inconvenient Truth (Gore), 168

Indian Government
alert to Canada, 87–88
indirectly responsible for bombings (suggestion), 89
infiltration of Canada's Sikh community, 89

Indian High Commission, 85, 87–88

indifference (ally of genocide), 209–10, 212

Inferno (Dante), 226–32
anatomization of phenomenon of sin, 230
betrayers of secular and spiritual unity in, 231
sins blocking way to Christian salvation, 230

Integrated National Security Enforcement Teams (INSETs), 60

internal (or intrinsic) terror, 10

International Civil Aviation Organization (ICAO), 76–78

International Committee of the Red Cross (ICRC), 209

international community. *See also* UN
lack of political will to help Rwandans, 201
misplaced trust in, 199
peacekeeping failures, 200
US defiance of, 57, 200

intrinsic terror, 217–18

IRA. *See* Irish Republican Army

Iran Air disaster, 5, 69, 79
compensation to families, 79
shot down by U.S. Navy, 72
victims, 93

Iraq war, 33–34, 69, 112, 176
demarcation between Canada and the US, 48–49
genocide, 202
weapons of mass destruction claim, 182

Irish National Army, 4

Irish Republican Army (IRA), 27, 154
abandoned violence (1997), 27
Libyan support for, 13

Irish war of independence (1919-20), 18

irrational anxiety, 173, 178, 181. *See also* rational fear
political rhetoric aimed at amplifying, 175

Islam, 114. *See also* Danish cartoon controversy; Salafist movement; Wahhabism
"bloody" Islamic civilization, 242
engagement with modernity, 157
freedom of thought under, 158
golden age of, 158
as historical phenomenon, 157
over-determination, 11
suspicion in North America, 126
as transcendental idea, 157

"Islamist," 8, 18
isolating all Muslims as the "Other," 155
misnomer and deceptive, 162
terrorist as, 155

Israel, 69, 114
invasion of Gaza, 102, 110
pre-emptive strikes against terrorism, 114–15

Italy
urban guerrillas (1970s and 1980s), 26

J

Japanese Red Army, 27

Jesus' "Sermon on the Mount," 219, 226

Jewish Free Press, 7, 131–32, 134

jihad, 111, 242
as "metaphysical," 116

"Jihadism," 114–15
mass media and, 117

Johnson, L.B., 167

Johnson, R.W., 78

Josephson (Justice), 91

Jyllands-Posten, 133

K

L

M

terrorism, 32, 35. *See also* genocide; terror
  apocalyptic overtones, 112
  as category of guerrilla war, 13, 15–23
  complex issue of, 181
  defining, 102–6, 112
  demagogic atmosphere, 109
  designer, 4, 25–28
  Devji's use of term, 117
  "forbidden zone" of unquestioned
      legitimacy, 105
  foreign-born terrorism, 176–77
  generic term of vilification, 113
  impacts on the environment, 166–67
  inherent hollowness of term, 114
  lack of consensus (1980s), 69
  meanings in Western countries, 105
  media use of term, 103–4, 106, 120, 174
  metaphorical power, 6–7, 153, 241, 247
  metaphysical quality of life and death
      struggle, 112
  need to stop using as term, 118–21
  new source of fear, 166–67
  politically motivated term, 110
  popular resistance movements and, 112
  "Protecting the American People" and,
      169, 174
  state control of terminology and use, 102
  United Nations' failure to define, 106
  urban, 24–25
  us versus them model, 6, 115
  used as propaganda, 107–8
"Terrorism and Art" (Wilcox), 113
terrorist movements with "Trotskyist"
    ideologies, 25
"terrorist states"
  contradictory phrase, 113
terrorist thought
  ethical dimension, 118
Thoughts on America, 178
train bombings in Madrid, 48
Trans-Alaska Pipeline System, 175
The Trial (Kafka), 10, 232–35
  systemic complexity idea, 233
  terror in everyday life, 232
"Trotskyist" ideologies, 25
Trudeau, Pierre, 46
Trudeau government

less than truthful about October Crisis,
    45
Tupamaros of Uruguay, 24
Tutsi minority, 198, 206
Twin Towers as metaphor of system, 235

U

UN
  formation of, 202, 208
  lack of support (burdened by debt), 200
UN Assistance Mission for Rwanda
    (UNAMIR), 198–99, 203–4, 206,
    211
  lacking operational effectiveness, 200
  lacking political support, 201
UN Security Council
  little attention to Rwanda, 201
unconscious, 221, 224, 227, 229, 235
United Nations. *See* UN
United States. *See* UN
Universal Declaration of Human Rights, 208
urban guerrilla warfare
  media attention, 24
  la politique du pire, 24–25
urban guerrillas (1970s and 80s), 27
  naiveté and narcissism, 26
urban terrorism, 24–25
US, 14, 161
  America First imperatives, 49–50, 62
  conquest of Afghanistan, 33, 112
  conservatism, 169
  defiance of international conventions
      (torture), 57
  ethnic profiling, 59
  Iran Air disaster and, 72, 79
  in Iraq (*See* Iraq war)
  Korean Airlines disaster and, 5, 78, 92
  Kyoto Protocol and, 168
  nuclear solutions and, 179
  perception of Canadian security, 52
  pre-emptive strikes in self-defence
      against terrorism, 115
  'security trumps economy' approach, 51
  treatment of 'enemy combatants'
      (Muslims and Arabs), 56
  urban guerrillas (1970s and 80s), 26